DNW
RCL
LG/HB
8/13/08

Designing Instruction for Technology-Enhanced Learning

Patricia L. Rogers
Bemidji State University
Minnesota State Colleges and Universities, USA

 Idea Group
Publishing

 Information Science
Publishing

Hershey • London • Melbourne • Singapore • Beijing

Acquisition Editor: Mehdi Khosrowpour
Managing Editor: Jan Travers
Development Editor: Michele Rossi
Copy Editor: Jennifer Swenson
Typesetter: LeAnn Whitcomb
Cover Design: Tedi Wingard
Printed at: Integrated Book Technology

Published in the United States of America by
        Idea Group Publishing
        1331 E. Chocolate Avenue
        Hershey PA 17033-1117
        Tel: 717-533-8845
        Fax: 717-533-8661
        E-mail: cust@idea-group.com
        Web site: http://www.idea-group.com

and in the United Kingdom by
        Idea Group Publishing
        3 Henrietta Street
        Covent Garden
        London WC2E 8LU
        Tel: 44 20 7240 0856
        Fax: 44 20 7379 3313
        Web site: http://www.eurospan.co.uk

Library of Congress Cataloging-in-Publication Data

Designing instruction for technology-enhanced learning / [edited by] Patricia L. Rogers.
        p. cm.
    Includes bibliographical references and index.
    ISBN 1-930708-28-9 (cloth)
      1. Instructional systems--Design. 2. Educational technology. I. Rogers, Patricia L.,
1956-

    LB1028.38 .D49 2001
    371.33--dc21   2001039615

British Cataloguing in Publication Data
A Cataloguing in Publication record for this book is available from the British Library.

NEW from Idea Group Publishing

- **Data Mining: A Heuristic Approach**
  Hussein Aly Abbass, Ruhul Amin Sarker and Charles S. Newton/1-930708-25-4
- **Managing Information Technology in Small Business: Challenges and Solutions**
  Stephen Burgess/ 1-930708-35-1
- **Managing Web Usage in the Workplace: A Social, Ethical and Legal Perspective**
  Murugan Anandarajan and Claire Simmers/1-930708-18-1
- **Challenges of Information Technology Education in the 21st Century**
  Eli Cohen/1-930708-34-3
- **Social Responsibility in the Information Age: Issues and Controversies**
  Gurpreet Dhillon/1-930708-11-4
- **Database Integrity: Challenges and Solutions**
  Jorge H. Doorn and Laura Rivero/ 1-930708-38-6
- **Managing Virtual Web Organizations in the 21st Century: Issues and Challenges**
  Ulrich Franke/1-930708-24-6
- **Managing Business with Electronic Commerce: Issues and Trends**
  Aryya Gangopadhyay/ 1-930708-12-2
- **Electronic Government: Design, Applications and Management**
  Åke Grönlund/1-930708-19-X
- **Knowledge Media in Health Care: Opportunities and Challenges**
  Rolf Grutter/ 1-930708-13-0
- **Internet Management Issues: A Global Perspective**
  John D. Haynes/1-930708-21-1
- **Enterprise Resource Planning: Global Opportunities and Challenges**
  Liaquat Hossain, Jon David Patrick and MA Rashid/1-930708-36-X
- **The Design and Management of Effective Distance Learning Programs**
  Richard Discenza, Caroline Howard, and Karen Schenk/1-930708-20-3
- **Multirate Systems: Design and Applications**
  Gordana Jovanovic-Dolecek/1-930708-30-0
- **Managing IT/Community Partnerships in the 21st Century**
  Jonathan Lazar/1-930708-33-5
- **Multimedia Networking: Technology, Management and Applications**
  Syed Mahbubur Rahman/ 1-930708-14-9
- **Cases on Worldwide E-Commerce: Theory in Action**
  Mahesh Raisinghani/ 1-930708-27-0
- **Designing Instruction for Technology-Enhanced Learning**
  Patricia L. Rogers/ 1-930708-28-9
- **Heuristic and Optimization for Knowledge Discovery**
  Ruhul Amin Sarker, Hussein Aly Abbass and Charles Newton/1-930708-26-2
- **Distributed Multimedia Databases: Techniques and Applications**
  Timothy K. Shih/1-930708-29-7
- **Neural Networks in Business: Techniques and Applications**
  Kate Smith and Jatinder Gupta/ 1-930708-31-9
- **Information Technology and Collective Obligations: Topics and Debate**
  Robert Skovira/ 1-930708-37-8
- **Managing the Human Side of Information Technology: Challenges and Solutions**
  Edward Szewczak and Coral Snodgrass/1-930708-32-7
- **Cases on Global IT Applications and Management: Successes and Pitfalls**
  Felix B. Tan/1-930708-16-5
- **Enterprise Networking: Multilayer Switching and Applications**
  Vasilis Theoharakis and Dimitrios Serpanos/1-930708-17-3
- **Measuring the Value of Information Technology**
  Han T.M. van der Zee/ 1-930708-08-4
- **Business to Business Electronic Commerce: Challenges and Solutions**
  Merrill Warkentin/ 1-930708-09-2

Excellent additions to your library!

**Receive the Idea Group Publishing catalog with descriptions of these books by calling, toll free 1/800-345-4332
or visit the IGP Online Bookstore at: http://www.idea-group.com!**

Designing Instruction for Technology-Enhanced Learning

Table of Contents

Preface

The majority of educators in pre-K-12 and higher education have access to some form of newer technology. We can make PowerPoint presentations, use email, design Web sites, or even author our own software. But many educators are unsure exactly how and why these newer technologies have any real impact on teaching and learning. The question is constantly raised: how do I connect my new skills to teaching? Is there a connection between technology and learning? Will my teaching change when new technology is introduced? How will I make the most of the technology in my school?

Most often, when forced to use new technologies in teaching, teachers will default to a technology-enhanced lecture method, rather than take advantage of the variety of media characteristics that expand the teaching and learning experience. For example, instead of presenting a static lecture on the laws of physics, we could design an interactive module that would allow students to experiment with physics without a large expenditure for elaborate equipment. For a small investment, science teachers can add various electronic probes to computers to read temperature, movement, heart rates and other measures critical to understanding physical and earth sciences, rather than have students read about such measures in books. How do teachers learn to take advantage of the expanded learning possibilities of technology in the classroom?

This book addresses the connection between technology skills and application of those skills in teaching and learning. Using sound instructional design principles, authors in this book guide the reader from focusing on the technology to focusing on the educational environment. Technology is presented as a tool, as a learning partner, and as an integral part of the classroom that supports and facilitates the teaching and learning experience.

The intended goal of this book is to pool the expertise of many practitioners and instructional designers and to present that information in such a way that teachers will have useful and relevant references and guidance for using technology to *enhance* teaching and learning, rather than simply adding technology to prepared lectures. The chapters, taken together, make the connection between intended learning outcomes, teaching strategies, and instructional media. This book is meant to be a resource for "teacher-designers" at beginning and intermediate levels of designing instruction that is enhanced by newer technologies.

In **Section I: Instructional Design: An Overview of the Field**, I introduce the concept of "teacher-designer" and discuss how instructional design is applied in real classrooms. I include a practical working model adapted for teachers and provide a brief overview of the field.

Section II: Foundations of Instructional Design. The chapter, written by J. Ana Donaldson and Nancy Nelson Knupfer, provides excellent documentation of the history of instructional design, its origins in educational psychology, developmental theory, and the field's current orientation grounded in constructivist theory. Several excellent Web sites are provided as resources for teachers.

Section III: Designing for Learners in Primary and Secondary Education. This section is dedicated to designing instruction for elementary students, but as with all of the chapters in this book, there are many practical and useful strategies and suggestions for designing for students at all levels. Sara Dexter begins the section with eTIPS, a set of educational technology integration principles appropriate for integrating technology in classrooms. Next, Gay Fawcett and Margarete Juliana discuss designing for middle school students and describe the success of their university's Ameritech classroom and provide brief case studies of how teachers using the classroom have changed their teaching strategies and how their students have gained new knowledge. Finally, Diane Judd offers guidance on designing for elementary classrooms and provides plans and activities for several tested projects for using computers in the classroom. Diane has also built a Web site for resources for the projects included in this book (see her article for specific URLs).

Section IV: Designing for Learners in Higher Education. The higher education section begins with Lin Muilenburg and Zane L. Berge's article on designing for discussion in the online classroom. Many of us have had difficulty with students having meaningful discussions in e-learning courses, and this article offers sound advice for overcoming such problems. Next, Tracy Chao and Bruce Stovel describe an undergraduate English course that focused on blues lyrics as lyric poetry. Far more than a listening/writing course, the case study described in this article is an excellent model of the vast possibilities of online learning. Completing the chapter on higher education is Som Naidu's article on designing and evaluating e-learning. Since many institutions are concerned about the quality and effectiveness of their online programs, this timely article from an expert in evaluation should become a part of every administrator's reference list.

Section V: Designing for Learning Environments. This section includes articles that address training and learning environments rather than designing for just one course. This collection of articles should be required reading for anyone planning to infuse technology in their curriculum. First,

Lorna Uden takes on the large and complex world of designing for hypermedia. Lorna's article makes a strong connection between models of learning theories and how best to apply them in hypermedia design. Similarly, Anne-Marie Armstrong describes instructional design from the adult learning theory perspective in her article on training. Though she is focused on the very active field of workforce training, Anne-Marie's insight and application of constructivist models in learning are appropriate for any level. Anne-Marie has also provided easy-to-read and practical methods of writing objectives, matching media to methods, and useful checklists for teacher-designers. Next, Barbara Rogers Bridges, Mary C. Baily, Michael Hiatt, Deborah Timmerman, and Sally Gibson describe a "paradigm shift" in a teacher education program. In the article, they document exactly what it takes to change a traditional campus-based program into a program for distributed learning. Brief narratives from key faculty and administrators are included.

Expanding the story of changing a university's approach to teacher education, Sólveig Jakobsdóttir documents the journey from campus-based to distance education at the Iceland University of Education. This university is now graduating students from its successful program and is in the midst of an extensive internal and external evaluation. We know this model program is doing something right when we consider that their retention rate in distance education courses is consistently between 80 and 95 percent.

Finally, Cynthia Krey, Christopher Stormer, and Janet Winsand describe what to do with a C.O.W. in the classroom. Computers on carts (wheels) is not a new event in higher education, but the wireless, adaptable application of the C.O.W. described in this article will give school media specialists many great ideas.

I am very excited about this book and believe it will be of tremendous use to teachers and administrators alike. I agreed to this project for one reason: I wished for a solid, practical textbook for helping pre-service and in-service teachers and university teachers to understand how instructional design is used when creating effective instruction for e-learning. I wanted teachers at all levels to recognize their role as teacher-designers and to provide a resource for demystifying the instructional design field in such a way that a practical and relevant application of instructional design would be possible in the "real world" classroom. I believe my wish was granted. Thank you, everyone!

Patricia L. Rogers, Ph.D.
Bemidji State University, Minnesota State Colleges and Universities (MnSCU)
and Kennaraháskóli Islands
April 2001

ACKNOWLEDGMENTS

Completing a project like this one is a very big job and certainly more than I could handle alone. I am a typical American. When faced with trying to thank everyone involved in a project of this size, my tendency is to be a bit effusive and perhaps overwhelming in my praise. For the sake of our international group of authors and readers, I will be brief and straight to the point, though most Americans will understand the difficulty I have in doing so.

I would first like to acknowledge the considerable time and effort the authors have invested in this book. Because I had a vision of creating a book that would be very practical and accessible in scope and language, I had to be almost brutal in my editorial comments and guidance. These are very intelligent and seasoned authors whose patience, good humor, excellent dialogue, insights, and comments shaped that vision into reality. Thank you for being so gracious under fire.

Thanks also to the very small team who provided reviews and comments to the first drafts of the articles. Their careful attention to details made my job much easier and I thank them. I hope you enjoyed the chocolate.

Special thanks must go to the Idea Group Publishing team, and in particular Jan Travers and Michele Rossi, who had to put up with my unique long distance situation. Much of this book was written, reviewed, assembled, and finalized while I was completing a Fulbright project in distance learning in Iceland. Even with their busy schedule, the team devised a unique way for me to complete all of the tasks and stay on deadline. Jan and Michele deserve nomination to publishing sainthood. And a big thank you to Mehdi Khosrowpour for encouraging me to stop grumbling about wanting a practical instructional design book...and just build it!

Finally, I must thank my Icelandic hosts and colleagues at Kennaraháskóli Islands (Iceland University of Education) for their insights, support, and warm welcome. Their expertise with technology in teacher education and the opportunities I had to discuss the articles and purpose of the book helped me keep my plans focused while completing my Fulbright obligations, enjoying the countryside, and trusting in the Icelandic attitude that all will work out well in the end. I wish to thank Ólafur Proppé and Ingvar Sigurgeirsson for giving me the opportunity to become a member of the faculty. And I thank the many faculty and staff members who offered friendship and opened their homes to me during my visit. This birthday will never be forgotten. (I will stop there so as not to overstate the deep affection and appreciation I feel for these wonderful new friends.) And of course I especially wish to thank my very dear friend Sólveig Jakobsdóttir, whose keen mind and warm heart kept me going through it all. You were right, Sólveig: Þetta reddast!

Patricia L. Rogers, Ph.D.
Bemidji State University, Minnesota State Colleges and Universities (MnSCU) and Kennaraháskóli Islands
April 2001

Section I

Instructional Design:
An Overview of the Field

Chapter I

Teacher-Designers: How Teachers Use Instructional Design in Real Classrooms

Patricia L. Rogers
Bemidji State University
Minnesota State Colleges and Universities (MnSCU), USA

INTRODUCTION

If you are a practicing teacher at any level—primary, secondary, or higher education—you already know quite a lot about designing instruction. Your work, prior to teaching a course, includes finding out what your students already know when they walk into the first day of class and determining what knowledge you hope they will gain by the end of the course. You design activities that enhance their new knowledge and allow them to practice with it. You plan tests that help the students demonstrate their newfound understanding. Every time you teach the course, and even at some points during the course, you make changes based on "how things are going" and later on you think about "what happened" throughout the course. The next time you teach the course, it is (hopefully!) much improved.

That is, in essence, exactly what instructional design is all about. But instructional design practices proceed from a more formal and systematic way of thinking about the teaching and learning process. Such systematic thinking helps designers focus on each component of the design process that ensures a successful design for learning.

Of course, if you have any experience with instructional design you know that the field and the various models of design associated with it seem most appropriate for teams of people working on the course materials together. Once in a while, some of us are fortunate enough to have instructional designers, subject matter experts, graphic artists, programmers and so on available on our campus or in our school district to assist us with our technology-enhanced course. But most often, it the teacher alone who must rethink and redesign his or her course for technology-enhanced learning. And very often it is the teacher who must also prepare the materials for the Internet, interactive television, or some other delivery medium. They often do not have any background in instructional design theory or practices and have only just mastered the skills for using the delivery medium. These are the people I call "teacher-designers."

This book is intended to provide teacher-designers with models, examples, and ideas for the practical application of instructional design for technology-enhanced classrooms. Those teachers with more background in instructional design or those who are working on staff development projects in this area will find the book useful as a resource for designing at all levels of education. This chapter is an introduction to the background of the field of instructional design, offers insight into how people become comfortable with technology, and presents a design model adapted for teacher-designers that may help you think about how to design for technology-enhanced courses as you read through this book.

OBJECTIVES OF THIS CHAPTER

By the end of the chapter, readers will be able to:

- Compare and contrast formal instructional design and the teacher-designer approach
- Select appropriate media and teaching strategies for technology-enhanced instruction based on intended learner outcomes
- Apply a modified design model for designing materials for technology-enhanced instruction

LEVELS OF TECHNOLOGY ADOPTION

What is it about technology that makes some teachers run away in fear and others embrace every new instructional medium that comes along? Why have some teachers become "technology gurus" and others are still struggling with email? I have worked extensively with a five-part technology adoption hierarchical model first posed by Rieber and Welliver (1989) and later refined by Hooper and Rieber (1995) that has helped explain what is happening as teachers use and infuse technology in the classroom (Rogers, 2000). The model levels are familiarization, utilization, integration, reorientation, and evolution.

This hierarchy begins at the *familiarization* level, which is a very basic exposure to a new technology. *Utilization* is a level that teachers reach when they actually try a new technology in their classroom. These two lower levels of technology adoption represent teachers at their most vulnerable. At either of these stages, failure of the technology, lack of technical support help, or lack of additional training will likely result in the teacher dropping the technology.

The next level, *integration*, may actually be divided into two parts. At the early stage of this level, teachers use the new technology by choice rather than by other suggestions (often from school administrators!) and begin to use it for more than simple page-turning presentations. The later stage of this level marks a change in how the teacher actually thinks about his or her classroom. A reexamination of the teaching and learning context takes place.

Reorientation is a level that continues the process of rethinking the classroom environment. A new emphasis on teaching and learning, rather than a focus on the technology, predominates. The evolution level in technology adoption is typical of those teachers who are willing to try anything new, but only if it facilitates learning. Their concern is not the technology, but what it can do to improve teaching and learning.

I think you can see that, if you find yourself focused solely on the new technology you are required to use in your classroom, you are likely at an earlier level of the adoption hierarchy. Take heart! Things do get much better and easier as you use technology in your teaching. The best analogy I can think of is learning to drive a car. Think of how many things you had to know and do while first learning. Could you play the radio and drive? Could you carry on a conversation and drive? Not likely. Now what can you do? My guess is you hardly even think about driving and indeed never have much thought about the car itself while you travel down the road, listen to the news, munch on a candy bar, chat with someone in the back seat, and remember where you are going and how to get there.

It is exactly that way at the later stage of the integration level of technology adoption and the reorientation level: the technology as an instructional medium becomes so much a part of the teaching and learning context that you hardly know it is there. Just as you needed guided practice to get beyond focusing only on the car and beyond to a high level of automaticity in driving, so it is with infusing technology in teaching. Instructional design models provide that kind of guided practice in integrating technology into our teaching. And the models help you move quickly past just delivering lectures with PowerPoint to using a variety of technology characteristics to improve teaching and learning. As the authors in this book will demonstrate, all good instructional design models start with learning, not technology.

INSTRUCTIONAL DESIGN: AN APPLIED MODEL

Instructional Systems Design (ISD) has its roots in behaviorism and systems thinking (see Reigeluth, 1999). Formal models of instructional design usually describe a step-by-step prescriptive procedure for designing instruction. Materials based on such designs were often meant to be "teacher proof" in that all of the learner outcomes were "assured" because output from each element of the model was carefully linked to the others in a progressive, systematic process. Possibly the best example, and most widely used of these models, is the model proposed by Dick and Carey (1990). Indeed, this model, and subsequent similar models, has been in use by professional designers since its first appearance around 1985.

The Dick and Carey model, like others of its kind, has several specific elements. The elements are presented in a step-wise flow chart that is meant to be iterative at many points for revisions and refinements. I will briefly discuss this model here as a means of introducing it to those of you who are unfamiliar with the field. A more detailed overview of design models is included in Anne-Marie Armstrong's chapter of Section 5 in this book.

The first element is a needs assessment, which is meant to determine whether the need for instruction actually exists and what the nature of the instruction should be. Needs assessment is critical in most new design situations and particularly when new curriculum is being introduced. For formal instructional design, this almost takes on the characteristics of a market survey as well as an assessment of instructional need.

The second and third elements are a task analysis and an analysis of the learners and their characteristics respectively. These are often conducted at the same time to match tasks with learner skills. The goals of instruction are first identified. The goals are then broken into several large tasks that are broken into smaller component skills depending on the entry level skills of the targeted learners. And, true to ISD's connection to systems thinking, most task analysis models look very much like flow charts for computer programming. The analogy is the human/computer similarities in performing tasks and using inductive thinking.

The model next moves the designer into identifying performance objectives and developing assessment instruments. This makes sound pedagogical sense: you first document the objectives, written as measurable behavioral performance objectives based on the goals of instruction, and then decide how you will assess whether or not learning has taken place. Performance objectives and assessments are directly connected to behaviorism, though as you already know, matching the goals and objectives to assessments is good practice no matter which learning theories you follow. The problem many teachers have is keeping the goals and the skills you taught to meet the goals, and how students' progress through the materials is related to assessment. Many times, assessment instruments do not measure what was actually taught.

The next two elements are also considered simultaneously: selecting instructional strategies or methods and selecting or designing instructional materials. Since the model is based on a flow chart, you should interpret the selection of strategies and materials as being based on what has come before: analysis of goals, tasks, learners, objectives, and assessments.

The next element in the model is a formative evaluation of how the design is shaping up. Ideally, you would field test the materials with learners who are similar to the target learners. The materials are refined or changed as formative evaluation is conducted. Once the materials are complete and have been implemented, a summative evaluation is conducted. This "final" evaluation determines the efficacy of the materials and provides a basis for new versions.

Formal design models are useful for guiding a design team's procedures when developing instructional materials. Following the model ensures a systematic and thorough process that forces designers to focus on each element or on the theory behind the model (Richey, 1994) and how each element relates to all other elements of the model. However, formal design models and practices are not exactly practical for teachers who must follow a state-mandated curriculum, translate the curriculum into a course, design their own materials, teach the course, and assess student achievement and the effectiveness of the course.

A model I have developed to more closely follow what teachers actually do when designing instructional materials is presented in Figure 1. Notice the similarities to the more formal model, though the "flow chart" look of the model in Figure 1 is deliberate for ease of discussion. I actually see this model as being much more akin to various constructivist models first visualized by

Jerry Willis (1995). Constructivist models such as Willis's resemble Celtic knots in that they are more circular and reflective, indicating much more interaction and influence among the elements (Willis, 2000; Willis & Wright, 2000). Or they may be more spiral in shape (Rogers & Mack, 1996) indicating learner knowledge gains as one passes through basic knowledge to higher order thinking. However, past experience in working with teachers who are new to instructional design has shown that a more linear presentation of a design model is helpful in understanding the processes and discussing each element.

Focus on Curriculum Requirements

Rather than begin with an assessment of the need for instruction, this model assumes such analysis of the "student market" has been conducted and the teacher-designer is at the point of designing instruction, not looking for new educational markets. We can assume that teacher-designers in the preschool, primary, or secondary levels have been given a curriculum and may even have been given textbooks that must be worked into the course design. Teacher-designers in higher education have a bit more freedom to choose; however, courses must be designed as relevant and logical components of whole programs. Students in higher education may choose different programs or institutions if the course does not facilitate learning new skills and competencies (Rogers, In Press).

In addition to curriculum requirements, there are other circumstances and constraints that may be in place as you begin your design. Carefully consider the availability of hardware, software, access to materials, and requirements of your school. Keep all of that in mind as you move through the model. Someone designing a driving course may wish they had a simulator, but the reality may be that learners will get behind the wheel of a real

Figure 1: A modified instructional design model for teacher-designers

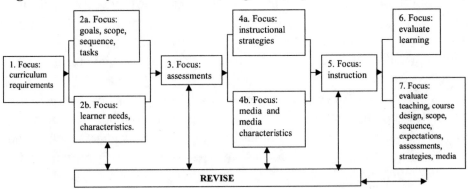

car sooner than later. Do not design for the ideal situation, design for the reality of your situation.

Focus on Goals of Learning and Learners

What kinds of learning outcomes are necessary for success in this course? Who are the learners and what do they already know? What do they need to know by the end of the course?

I have found that the most accessible and readily applicable way for teacher-designers to think about the goals of learning (and later how to match teaching strategies and instructional media to these goals) is to use Gagné, Briggs, and Wager's (1992) essential learner outcomes. Certainly, teachers know that we cannot easily segregate learning outcomes into neat categories such as those presented by Gagné, Briggs, and Wager, and in fact, they did not intend the outcomes to be thought of as discreet categories. But by thinking of categories of learning outcomes in terms of the kinds of learning we desire in a course or lesson, you will see that our selection of teaching strategies, media, and assessment instruments is more closely guided by the goals of instruction. Table 1 provides a brief overview of these outcomes with short definitions. For more information and background (and a very clear presentation of concepts), refer to Ana Donaldson and Nancy Knupfer's article in Chapter 2 of this book. I further recommend reading the *Principles of Instructional Design*, 2nd Edition (Gagné & Briggs, 1979) or the more recent *Principles of Instructional Design*, 4th Edition (Gagné, Briggs, & Wager, 1992).

Notice that teaching strategies and the instructional media must allow for certain kinds of practice and application of the new knowledge. Feedback on how a learner is progressing is essential and varies with each type of outcome (Sales & Dempsey, 1993). Thus, teacher-designers select strategies and instructional media based on the desired learning outcomes for the course or lesson.

If you are in one of those rare situations that require you to use one medium over another or include certain strategies over others, you will likely be faced with changing the learner outcomes! For example, I have had to teach courses at my university using two-way interactive television (video conferencing) due to the needs of distant learners, the availability of the medium (funded by the state), and past practices for distance delivery in rural Minnesota. Teaching with this medium requires much more than being a talking head on television! I use a variety of PowerPoint presentations, videotape, guest speakers, and texts as instructional media. I also use camera changes, close-ups and long shots, etc. to keep visual interest. And I require

Table 1: Overview of Robert Gagne's Essential Learner Outcomes

Outcome	Definition Examples	Strategies, Media, Learner Needs
Attitudes	Moral development, social development, and human interaction. Changes in attitudes are demonstrated by **preferring** or **choosing** options.	Teaching strategies should include human modeling and allow actual practice, instructional medium must include real practice and/or close simulations. Feedback with explanations is necessary.
Motor Skills	Movement of any kind, including: dancing, writing, welding, playing a game, etc.	Teaching strategies should allow actual practice. Instructional medium must include physical objects or close simulations. Feedback with demonstrations is necessary.
Verbal Information	Facts, spelling, basic terminology, reading and/or listening to learn.	Teaching strategies are usually teacher-centered (lecture is most common). The medium must present verbal information in written and/or oral form for non-readers. Feedback may be simple notice of correct or incorrect answers.
Cognitive Strategies	Thinking and learning strategies are **selected** or **adopted** by the learner.	Teaching strategies must allow learners to practice learning strategies. Instructional medium must allow learners to practice in an interactive environment. Feedback should be detailed and provide further information.
Intellectual Skills: Discriminations to Higher Order Rules (problem-solving, critical thinking)	Discriminate, identify, classify, and apply rules before problem-solving. At the upper levels of these skills, learners **generate new solutions or procedures**.	Teaching strategies must allow learners to practice learning strategies. Instructional medium must allow learners to practice in an interactive environment. Feedback should be detailed and provide further information.

students to dialogue during class. If these strategies resemble writing/ directing/acting in a film, you are correct. I was fortunate to have had a theatre background when faced with using this medium for the first time!

Our digital system has a "visual follows voice" feature, meaning the camera switches to each site by responding to sound. So, I set the ground rules for discussion by telling students to identify themselves by name and location anytime they wish to ask a question or make a comment. By the time the student is through speaking, the camera has switched to his or her site and we continue. I also train students to operate the cameras so that we can all have a close-up of a speaker at any site or a long shot of an entire classroom.

Before I added a Web site resource, we depended mainly on these real time meetings and used fax, email, or regular mail to exchange materials. Because I did not limit my strategies to straight lecture, I was able to design my courses to cover a wide range of desired learner outcomes not possible in a typical one-way television course or correspondence course. However, some of the more hands-on or small group projects I use in my campus-based course could not be used in the interactive television course. And I must add that this is not necessarily a negative issue: I simply had to be aware of the limitations of the medium as I thought about the learner outcomes for the course.

Focus on Assessments

How will students demonstrate their new knowledge? Traditional paper and pencil tests, norm or criterion-referenced tests, and informal assessments are all a part of determining the effectiveness of instruction. In technology-enhanced courses, there is often the added requirement to gain technology skills while learning about the other course content. Decide what it is you are assessing: is it knowledge gains in the content domain, technology skills, or both? If, for example, the assessment in an English class in on writing skills, the fact that a student's Web page for the writing project is poorly constructed should not determine the grade for the actual writing.

For courses designed specifically with technology-enhancements in mind, I recommend the use of rubrics (Campbell, Melenyzer, Nettles, & Wyman, 1999) along with other types of measures. Rubrics may be written to encompass the whole project, performance, or portfolio that includes the use of technology as well as the content knowledge gains. In other words, if skills for using the technology are infused in the course, the assessments should have some feature for evaluating the new technology skills.

Focus on Teaching Strategies and Instructional Media

How do teachers match instructional media to teaching methods? At times, it seems we are under some mandate to use certain kinds of strategies that are currently in vogue. At other times, we have so much freedom to choose teaching strategies but are required to use a specific instructional medium. In either case, this is the wrong approach to selecting teaching strategies or instructional technologies. However, as I mentioned earlier, there are times when some of these decisions are out of your hands (such as using interactive television or not).

Part of your task as a teacher-designer is to consider the entire context of your course design. Remember the first element of the model? Take into account the curriculum, environmental constraints, and expectations from your administration and peers. Carefully consider the goals of your course (the learner outcomes). Table 1 includes some suggestions for matching teaching strategies and instructional media to the learning outcomes. Notice that no specific technology is mentioned. Rather, you will want to select instructional media that has necessary characteristics to support the learning goals you have identified. You will select teaching strategies that facilitate learning through the use of the media. This point is discussed in more detail by several other authors in this book.

Focus on Teaching

At this point, you will stop designing and start doing! Contrary to formal design models that produce prototype materials ready for testing at this point, this applied design model suggests that you use the materials you have designed in the actual setting. Take careful notice of what "works" and what does not work in the classroom as you teach the first one or two lessons. This is the formative evaluation portion of your course design. Again, this is a bit of a departure from the prescriptive ISD models, but I believe it is much more realistic and applicable for teachers.

Focus on Evaluating Student Gains

Take a careful look at portfolio materials, tests, reflective papers, Web sites, and so on that were produced by students to demonstrate their knowledge gains. Use the rubrics you developed and shared with students to assess and evaluate student learning. Did they attain the goals you had in mind? Did students go beyond the course goals? Or did students get lost in learning technology skills?

If the answer to the latter question suggests that students spent more time focused on a technology rather than on the intended new knowledge, you have a problem. You should (a) reevaluate the entry level skills you assumed your students had when they began the course, (b) reevaluate the scope and sequence of your course lessons, and (c) determine the RELEVANCE of the new technology skills to the intended new knowledge.

Reexamining entry level skills is often the easier solution to design problems of this kind. If you find that you expected more skills up front, you will need to either add a section to your course to work on those skills or determine some prerequisites to your course. Be sure to get feedback from your students as to what kinds of skills they felt they needed to begin the course. A similar examination of the scope and sequence of your course may also be in order. Perhaps a critical step was misplaced or perhaps there was not enough emphasis on some aspect of the course, for example, building Web pages.

The last item you should examine is actually the most important: was the required technology skill relevant to the performance objectives? Did creating the Web page or adding a sound file make sense in terms of learning outcomes? I recently witnessed a case where a teacher had asked students in a math course to place their final solutions on a Web page for ease of viewing by campus-based and distance learning classmates. During the two days before the assignment was due, students crowded the computer lab until the wee hours of the morning struggling with an html editor.

In questioning those involved (the teacher and the exhausted technical support staff), use of the html editor had been introduced early in the course in two 45-minute lessons. The software was not used again until the last assignment was due. The teacher was very confused as to why students had such a hard time, given the html editor was "so easy" to use. When I raised the relevance question, most agreed that there was little connection made between the intended learning in math and the required presentation on a Web page!

Focus on Evaluating Teaching and the Entire Course

As you can see, evaluating student learning very quickly spills over into an evaluation of your own teaching, the scope and sequence of your course design, strategies selected, and supporting media. Ask hard questions about your own teaching. Use feedback from students on the use of technology for instruction as well as for learning and evaluation. A good structure for assessing your course might be to use Sara Dexter's eTIPS found in Chapter 3 of this book. And for sound, practical advice on how to evaluate e-learning, see Som Naidu's chapter of Section 4 in this book.

Revise, Revise, Revise

Even when using formal design models, the necessity of revising and refining the materials and course design is critical to useful and effective teaching. You are never completely finished with a course, particularly courses designed for technology-enhanced learning. It isn't only that the technology changes and more capabilities are added, it is also a matter of changing with the needs of your learners and the gains in new knowledge in your field.

Formal design models suggest that a summative evaluation is made once the course has been up and running (implemented) for a time. This step is sometimes skipped or is performed only once due to the short shelf life of most commercial instructional materials. Those educational materials that have been around for a while (e.g., *The Oregon Trail 3rd Edition* (2000), or *Where in the World is Carmen Sandiego?* (2000)) have been through many such evaluations, and the subsequent versions reflect careful attention to who is using the product and how well it sells.

Teachers using this modified design model, or any of the other models presented in this book, will find that they will rarely perform a summative evaluation on a single course but may in fact evaluate a whole program or subject area during periodic curriculum review processes. Indeed, skipping the summative evaluation step is precisely what happens as teachers actually work with their courses, though some courses, destined for sale to for-profit institutions, may have a summative evaluation before they leave the institution's control. However, teachers rarely have the luxury of carefully evaluating a course in such detail before it is time for the next class of learners.

PROMOTING COGNITIVE CHANGE IN E-LEARNING

We are in a business that is primarily concerned with the processes, conditions, and contexts of learning. Have you ever asked yourself: what is learning? The standard answer from educational psychology is that learning is a relatively permanent change in behavior as a direct result of new experiences. Cognitivists would say that learning is more than changes in behavior: learning is also connected to relatively permanent changes and increased activity in cognitive processes.

Designing for technology-enhanced or "e-learning" courses does not change the fact that we are still about the business of promoting cognitive change in learners (Bullen, 1998; Wild & Quinn, 1998). E-learning is the seamless infusion of technology in technology-enhanced teaching and learning, regardless of where the teachers and students are located (Rogers, In Press). Design models are used to help ensure that the educational context and all of the necessary elements for effective instruction have been considered. Yet, as noted above, most models (including the one presented in this chapter) appear to be very linear and rigid in their consideration of teaching and learning. Instructional media may still seem to be something outside or bolted on to teaching and learning.

If we really think about what is happening during a course, it seems that teachers and learners have access to a variety of tools and materials for thinking, learning, and teaching. Some of these are internal, others external.

But all of them are available to everyone concerned and all contribute to learning. If you need a graphic representation of this concept, Figure 2 is an approximation of the interaction of teaching, learning, thinking tools and the necessary enabling technologies needed to facilitate cognitive change in learners.

Teaching Tools

Teaching tools are the strategies and methods available and appropriate for the learning task. Teachers choose to use small group strategies for cooperative learning tasks, lecture/presentations for providing basic factual information, hands-on learning in apprentice situations, and so on. It is assumed that teachers have a large amount of internalized domain-specific knowledge that is to be shared with students either through direct instruction methods or through coaching and facilitating methods. Teachers select and use enabling and facilitating technologies to support their teaching methods. These technologies become part of the teaching tools.

Learning Tools

Students have internal and external learning tools that aid the cognitive change process. Learning tools such as internal motivation to learn (Keller, 1987), perceived self-efficacy and predicted success in the class (Salomon, 1984), and the amount and quality of knowledge (Perkins & Salomon, 1989) all contribute to the tools available to the learner in a new learning context. The external enabling and facilitating technologies provide a means to express or demonstrate new understanding and knowledge gains as well as serve as a source of new knowledge.

Thinking Tools

Thinking tools are employed by both teacher and learner. Thinking tools are the cognitive strategies selected by the learner to encode and recall new knowledge (Gagne, Briggs, & Wager (1992). They are the tools of knowledge construction (Jonassen, Carr, & Yueh, 1998 ; Perkins & Salomon, 1989) and motivation to learn.

Thinking tools include metacognitive skills, which is the conscious awareness of how one thinks and learns. An understanding of learner characteristics established in research to be critical to certain types of learning environments (such as field dependence/independence (Al-Saai & Dwyer, 1993), learner control (Arnone & Grabowski, 1992), and a variety of learning styles) influence the teacher-designer's teaching methods and choice of media in a given course.

Figure 2: A model for cognitive change

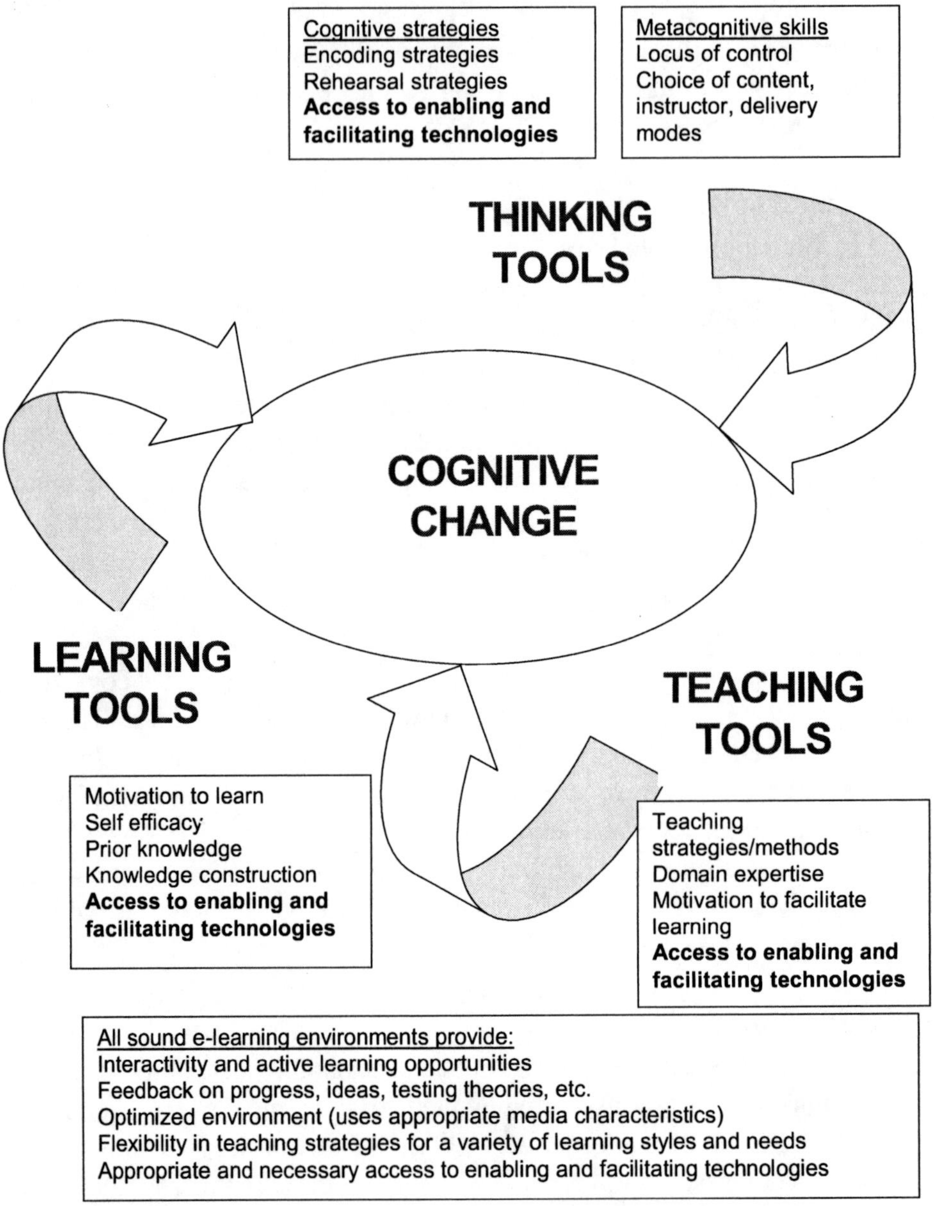

Cognitive strategies
Encoding strategies
Rehearsal strategies
**Access to enabling and
facilitating technologies**

Metacognitive skills
Locus of control
Choice of content,
instructor, delivery
modes

**THINKING
TOOLS**

**COGNITIVE
CHANGE**

**LEARNING
TOOLS**

**TEACHING
TOOLS**

Motivation to learn
Self efficacy
Prior knowledge
Knowledge construction
**Access to enabling and
facilitating technologies**

Teaching
strategies/methods
Domain expertise
Motivation to facilitate
learning
**Access to enabling and
facilitating technologies**

All sound e-learning environments provide:
Interactivity and active learning opportunities
Feedback on progress, ideas, testing theories, etc.
Optimized environment (uses appropriate media characteristics)
Flexibility in teaching strategies for a variety of learning styles and needs
Appropriate and necessary access to enabling and facilitating technologies

QUESTIONS FOR FURTHER CONSIDERATION

As you can gather from Figure 2, successful technology-enhanced learning requires that the facilitating technologies are actually part of teaching, learning, and thinking tools. Once a certain point in the integration level of technology adoption has been reached (Hooper & Reiber, 1995), such smooth infusion of technology into everyday classroom activities is achieved. If you were to create a graphic representation of your classroom technology infusion, would it resemble this figure or something else? How might you rethink the role of technology in your teaching? How would students describe technology use in your classroom?

As you read the rest of the book, think about this image of how new technologies become infused and integrated components in promoting and supporting cognitive change. Practice using the practical design model presented in this chapter (or any of the other models discussed in this book). Compare technology-enhanced lessons you previously designed without a model and those you create using a model. Compare and contrast the lessons. Has anything changed in your approach?

REFERENCES

Al-Saai, A. J. and Dwyer, F. M. (1993). The effect of visualization on field-dependent and field-independent learners. *International Journal of Instructional Media*, 20(3), 243-249.

Arnone, M. P. and Grabowski, B. L. (1992). Effects on children's achievement and curiosity of variations in learner control over an interactive video lesson. *Educational Technology, Research and Development*, 40(1), 15-27.

Bullen, M. (1998). Participation and critical thinking in online university distance education. *Journal of Distance Education*, 13(2), 1-32.

Campbell, D. M., Melenyzer, B. J., Nettles, D. H. and Wyman Jr., R. M. (1999). *Portfolio and Perfomance Assessment in Teacher Education*. Needham Heights, MA: Allyn and Bacon.

Dick, W. and Carey L. (1990). *The Systematic Design of Instruction* (3rd ed.). Glenview, IL: Scott, Foresman & Co.

Gagné, R. M. and Briggs, L. J. (1979). *Principles of Instructional Design* (2nd ed.). New York: Holt, Rinehart and Winston.

Gagné, R., Briggs, L. and Wager, W. (1992). *Principles of Instructional Design* (4th ed.). Englewood Cliffs, NJ: Prentice-Hall.

Hooper, S. and Rieber, L.P. (1995). Teaching with technology. In Ornstein, A. (Ed.), *Teaching: Theory into Practice*. Boston, MA: Allyn and Bacon.

Jonassen, D. H., Carr, C. and Yueh, H. P. (1998). Computers as mindtools for engaging learners in critical thinking. *TechTrends*, 43(2), 24-32.

Keller, J. M..(1987). The systematic process of motivational design. *Performance and Instruction*, 26(9-10), 1-8.

Perkins, D. N. and Salomon, G. (1989). Are cognitive skills context-bound? *Educational Researcher*, 18(1), 16-25.

Reiber, L. P. and Welliver, P. W. (1989). Infusing educational technology into mainstream educational computing. *International Journal of Instructional Media*, 16(1), 21-32.

Reigeluth, C. M. (Ed). (1999). *Instructional-Design Theories and Models: A New Paradigm of Instructional Theory*, 2. Mahwah, NJ: Lawrence Erlbaum Associates.

Richey, R. C. (1994). Design 2000: Theory-based design models of the future. In *Proceedings of Selected Research and Development Presentations at the 1994 National Convention of the Association for Educational Communications and Technology Sponsored by the Research and Theory Division*, Nashville, TN, February 16-20.

Rogers, P. L. (in press). Traditions to transformations: The forced evolution of higher education. *Educational Technology Review*.

Rogers, P. L. (2000). Barriers to adopting emerging technologies in education. *Journal of Educational Computing Research*, (22)4, 455-472.

Rogers, P. L. and Mack, M. (1996) A constructivist design and learning model: Time for a graphic. In *Proceedings of Selected Research and Development Presentations at the 1996 National Convention of the Association for Educational Communications and Technology* (18, Indianapolis, IN.

Sales, G. and Dempsey, J. (Eds.). (1993). *Interactive Instruction and Feedback*. Englewood Cliffs, NJ: Educational Technology.

Salomon, G. (1984). Television is "easy" and print is "tough": The differences investment of mental effort in learning as a function of perceptions and attributions. *Journal of Educational Psychology*, 76(4), 647-658.

The Oregon Trail (3rd Edition). (2000). [Computer software] The Learning Company.

Where in the World is Carmen Sandiego? (2000). [Computer software] Mindscape: The Learning Company.

Wild, M. and Quinn, C. (1998). Implications of educational theory for the design of instructional multimedia. *British Journal of Educational Technology*, 29(1), 73-82.

Willis, J. (1995). A recursive, reflective instructional design model based on constructivist-interpretivist theory. *Educational Technology*, 35(6), 5-23.

Willis, J. (2000). The maturing of constructivist instructional design: Some basic principles that can guide practice. *Educational Technology*, 40(1), 5-16.

Willis, J. and Wright, K. E. (2000). A general set of procedures for constructivist instructional design: The new R2D2 model. *Educational Technology*, 40(2), 5-20.

Section II

Foundations of
Instructional Design

Chapter II

Education, Learning, and Technology

J. Ana Donaldson
University of Northern Iowa, USA

Nancy Nelson Knupfer
Digital Horizons, USA

INTRODUCTION

The classroom is a jumble of bright colors and excited children. I enter as a guest into a world of noise, chaos, and learning. A reptile-enriched environment surrounds the children. There is a multitude of colorfully illustrated resource books; lizard-related images crowd each other on bulletin boards; and multi-hued plastic bins are filled with glassy-eyed stuffed reptiles. One youngster proudly introduces me to the class frog in a terrarium while another child shyly approaches and takes hold of my hand, offering to share a picture of an alligator that she has found on the Web.

My trek into the unknown world of a second grade class coincides with the final stages of a technological variation on a game of my youth, "20 Questions." A list of 18 negative, yet informative, responses to the e-mail game with an across-town second grade class is posted on the front chalkboard. The long list includes the following notations: " It doesn't have eyelids; It lives in a warm climate; There is something unusual about it." The 27 students on this end of the game are down to only two remaining responses to guess what type of lizard the other class has chosen as the "mystery reptile." There is a sense of urgency in the class as each eager student attempts to unravel the identity of the secret creature.

Two mop-headed, jean-clad boys eagerly sit at a solitary computer searching the Internet for information on Komodo Lizards and Flying Dragons. Other students are sharing a variety of animal picture books, looking for reptiles that will meet the criteria for the eighteen clues that they have posted. Three diminutive, pastel-clad girls are flipping through the pages of an encyclopedia while another pair is waiting their turn at the computer in order to view a CD-ROM that might reveal the elusive answer. Several students breathlessly approach both the teacher and myself to talk enthusiastically about what they consider to be the most likely candidate for the next response.

I take a moment to view the activity in the classroom. Every student is actively involved with collaborative research and discovery learning. They are using higher-level learning skills by applying a process of comparative logic and selection based on elimination. Yes, it is noisy, but more importantly, there is learning occurring. The energy and sense of involvement within this group of second graders is an example of what is possible in a student-centered, engaged-learning classroom environment. The classroom is abuzz with bright eyes and smiles, and the biggest smile is on the face of the teacher.

After months of teacher preparation, two second grade classes had joined forces to partner on a life science project, which integrated technology into the curriculum within an engaged-learning environment. This scenario represents one slice of an afternoon in the year long project supported by a grant from the Higher Education Cooperation Act (HECA) with Triton College in River Grove, Illinois. It is an example of what can happen when technology combines with pedagogy to actively engage the students in the learning process. All children had an active role and the technology was used to support an activity that otherwise would have been impossible to accomplish between the two schools.

OBJECTIVES FOR THIS CHAPTER

This chapter posits that technology can be used successfully in schools, but that it will be more likely to enhance learning if certain considerations are addressed and appropriate guidelines are followed. After positioning technology within the historical framework of evolving learning theory, the chapter explores some of the issues, controversies, and problems surrounding the use of technology in schools, then discusses some of the current trends and delineates some ideas for the future success of technology-enhanced education.

BACKGROUND

Technology has great potential to enhance education if appropriately applied. Yet debates rage on about whether it holds great promise, drains resources, or even presents dangers to our children (Armstrong & Casement, 2000; Cuban, 1986; Roszak, 1994; Sloan, 1985; Stoll, 1999). One educator stated, "We have allowed our schools to remain in the past, while our children have been born to the future" (Strommen & Lincoln, 1993, p. 1). Others take an opposite stance and claim that computer technology simply does not belong in the schools (Stoll, 1999). Indeed, Clifford Stoll (1999) believes computers are valuable in their own place, but that the educational technology hype has gotten in the way of good education that emphasizes critical thinking and good communication. There are strong arguments for both positions, yet the most accurate perspective surely lies somewhere in between.

As we discover more about the human brain, psychology, social dynamics of education, and the evolution of learning theories over time, we see that learning is a complex process. Naturally, there are outside factors such as politics, budgets, bureaucracy, opinions, and personalities that influence all sides of the debate. Perhaps we can make better decisions about learning environments if we understand some of the background and issues at hand.

Technology Timeline

The value of computers in education has been debated since the mid-1960s when mainframe computers first came to high schools. The invention of microcomputers in the 1970s changed the expectations about the role computer technology would play in the learning process. Yet successful technology integration in schools depends on educators' abilities to meaningfully incorporate new pedagogical tools. Truly, it is the teachers who are the gatekeepers of classroom activity, so simply providing resources will not guarantee the successful implementation of technology into education (Knupfer, 1989-90). Indeed, the process of implementation is more important than the actual innovation (Berman & McLaughlin, 1976; Cuban, 1986; Knupfer, 1989-90; 1993). This begs several questions. What has been done to help teachers and other key personnel to make good decisions about implementing technology? Are colleges of education doing a good job of preparing pre-service and in-service teachers to implement technology? Are professors of education receiving adequate training in order to support teacher training efforts? What are some of the obstacles that educators face as they try to implement technology in university teacher training programs, and K-12 schools? Should education change to accommodate technology and if so, why? How can technology best fit into the curriculum so that it makes a meaningful difference to learning? Is the price of technology worth the result in terms of learning gains? The questions are endless and very difficult to answer. Although the answers are not obvious, the questions are not new. As each new technological innovation has been introduced to schools, similar questions surely were asked.

Figure 1 places the introduction of school technologies since 1900 in perspective. Each era has been plagued by issues concerning teacher training and universities' lack of capacity for teacher preparation, yet each new innovation appeared with much optimism for radically changing teaching (Cuban, 1986; Kaufman, 1998; Mehlinger, 1996; Saettler, 1990). By 1920, classroom use of films had become a symbol of progressive teaching, just as computers are today. Yet we have learned that the films were often shown without proper introduction or follow-up activities and thus, their impact on meaningful learning was compromised. Further, teachers frequently depended on boys to run the projector, absolving themselves of the responsibility and promoting gender stereotypes (Knupfer, 1997). Similar implementation issues have plagued each new technology as it has been introduced to schools. Often there are overly optimistic and unrealistic expectations of the technology, followed by some disillusionment and massive curtailment or abandonment of the technology.

In the mid-1970s articles about computer literacy began to appear, primarily addressing the understanding of computer capabilities, applications, and algorithms. There also was some early discussion about social issues (Saettler, 1990; Popkewitz & Shutkin, 1993). The introduction of microcomputers in 1977 fostered the belief that teachers should learn computer programming. Preparation for authentic computer usage emphasized programming and learning about drill-and-practice type utilization (Anderson, 1983; Friedman, 1983; Uhlig, 1983).

Although microcomputers have been in schools for about 30 years, obstacles that impede the most effective implementation remain present. If computers are to gain a meaningful place in schools, the teachers must be

Figure 1: The evolution of classroom technology

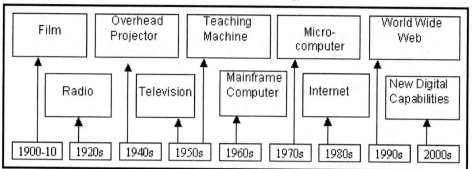

trained and certain obstacles need to be replaced with the supportive infra-structure necessary to successful innovation. A good place to begin is with a thorough understanding of learning theories and paradigm shifts. It is within this learning environment that all educational materials must fit if they are to be helpful to the students.

PARADIGM SHIFTS IN PSYCHOLOGY, TEACHING, AND LEARNING

Electronic technology has had a profound impact on our society, especially during the past 20 years. Computers have increased in power and speed faster than any other technology. Graphical user interfaces and multitasking software have combined to radically alter the possibilities for educational computing. Masses of people are using the Internet. Teachers and students have fast access to different kinds of information. We are in the midst of a major paradigm shift from "teacher" as the provider of information to facilitator of learning (Downs, Clark, & Bennett, 1995). As facilitators of learning, teachers are encouraged to learn with the students. But Strommen and Lincoln (1993) caution us that estrangement between students and teachers can develop when instructors present knowledge in a linear format to learners who exist in an interactive and exploratory environment. Thus reflective teaching becomes critical.

To best understand the evolution of teaching strategies, let us present some of the background information about learning theory. The progression from behaviorism to cognitive science to constructivism is important to understand because teachers' beliefs about how people learn will certainly influence how we apply instructional technologies.

Behaviorism

Behaviorism flourished during the 1950s and 1960s. Rooted in turn-of-the-century Russia, the experiments of Ivan Pavlov taught us that dogs could be taught to salivate when a stimulus, a bell, was paired with a food reward. Pavlov was able to gradually remove the reward and still get the dogs to salivate when the bell rang. He called this response the "conditioned reflex." John B. Watson (1912), an American psychologist, believed that conditioned reflexes could be the foundation for *all* behavior and he was the first to coin the term "behaviorist." Watson believed that behavioral descriptions were the only way to describe human learning because mental processes and states could not be observed.

Meanwhile, another American, Edward Thorndike, conducted experiments at Columbia University to investigate how different types of stimuli could affect human learning. He found that incentives and disincentives could influence learning and he coined the term "law of effect" to describe that phenomenon. His experiments emphasized associating an unknown term with something familiar, thus if beginning readers could see a new vocabulary word paired with a picture to match the word, then they could learn new vocabulary words by sight and memorization (Thorndike, 1936).

Like Watson, Harvard professor B. F. Skinner believed that mental processing was beyond the bounds of observation and so he set up experiments to alter behavior by external conditions. He coined the term "operant conditioning." Skinner believed that all learning, human or otherwise, was composed of a basic set of three elements that he called the "conditioned operant." The three elements of the "conditioned operant" were the discriminative stimulus, the response, and the reinforcing stimulus (Skinner, 1938). Skinner also used the commonly accepted term "technology of education" to refer to the field of study about the process or techniques of education (Skinner, 1968). Many people do not realize that the term "technology of education" historically refers to a field of study about teaching methods and have mistakenly thought that "educational technology" meant only education with computers.

While most teachers are not pure behaviorists today, the effects of behaviorism remain in some common educational practices. For example, writing objectives, whether they are called behavioral objectives, learning objectives or performance objectives, stem from behaviorism and theoretically involve some observable evidence that learning has occurred. Within educational computing, the drill-and-practice type of software certainly relies on behaviorism. This type of approach is good for rote memorization, for example math facts, but it is not good for higher level cognitive processing such as understanding the concepts of numerical operations.

Behaviorism also led to "programmed instruction" which does not mean a computer program, but a *sequence of events* organized to lead the learner through specific steps. The mechanical "teaching machine" of the 1950s was based upon programmed instruction and relied on the "conditioned operant." Programmed instruction depended heavily upon three important parts: presenting the information in small steps; requiring frequent, overt responses; and building on those steps by rewarding correct responses; it led to the first examples of computer-assisted instruction. While this type of learning can be effective for certain kinds of tasks, the programs tend to be inflexible and limited in value. Even though the types of software we have today can at first appear quite sophisticated, they often do no more than allow learners to receive small pieces of information, enter a response, and get simple feedback.

Cognitivism or Information Processing Psychology

Human thinking is much more complex than a set of behaviors. At the beginning of the 20th century, Frenchman Alfred Binet became very interested in ways of measuring human intelligence. Binet and his colleague, Théodore Simon, developed the first intelligence quotient (IQ) test in order to sort out and place children appropriately (Gardner, 1983). The IQ testing gained immense popularity and even though there was strong debate over its value to predict success beyond the classroom, it was used heavily throughout a large part of the century.

Around 1920, Swiss psychologist Jean Piaget began his working career in Simon's laboratory and became interested in why children made errors on the IQ tests. Piaget believed that the accuracy of a response was less important than the lines of reasoning and assumptions the children followed to reach a conclusion. So he developed a theory of developmental stages of intelligence (Piaget,1952; 1969) that eventually overshadowed the popularity of the IQ testing. The four stages include:

- Sensorimotor—at age 0-2 the child's perception of self is separate from the rest of the world
- Preoperational—at age 3-7 the child begins to see object permanence but has difficulty understanding some concepts due to simplistic thinking, and often makes errors in such things as object size and volume
- Concrete operational—at age 7-11 the child can engage in complex thinking
- Formal operational—beginning at age 12, the child can engage in abstract thinking

Piaget believed that children constantly try to make sense of the world and in so doing construct hypotheses and generate knowledge. He had great influence on teachers of young children because these instructors tailored the curriculum and teaching methods to meet the perceived mental readiness of the children's age group.

Cognitive science evolved out of the need to understand how people think and thus researchers began to study what is called the "human information processing model." This model assumes that people use a variety of different systems to learn. The sensory system of seeing, hearing, smelling, and so on receives stimuli from the environment. Then a system of attention and controls determines which information is noticed and processed. If it is processed, the information goes into working memory, which is a short-term memory. Some information is forgotten at that point and other information is stored in long-term memory, at a particular address in our minds, so that it later can be retrieved and remembered (Aschcraft, 1994).

Learning involves much more than receiving information and storing it into memory. It also involves thinking, analyzing situations, drawing logical conclusions, developing strategies, producing products, reacting to interpersonal situations, and so forth. While behaviorists stress the importance of training and repetitive practice, cognitive psychologists stress the importance of practicing in realistic situations and the ability to learn strategies for solving problems by thinking them through. For example, David Ausubel (1963) noted the importance of relating new material to prior learning and suggested the use of "advance organizers" to give students a clue about forthcoming information. He also suggested the need to position information in relation to other information and developed a set of classification schemes that later were developed into schema theory by others (Aschcraft, 1994).

Schema theorists stress the importance of prior knowledge in order for students to comprehend new material. Teachers should know that holistic approaches to teaching reading and language arts depend on student's prior learning in relation to the new material, and thus depend on schema theory. If, for instance, first graders are engaged in an online story writing project with another class of first graders, then it is likely that some of the vocabulary words used might be familiar to some children but not to others. Children of this age are emerging readers and when they come to words they don't know, they might use phonics or contextual clues to decode the new words. Teachers who anticipate this will provide a supportive learning environment in which the schema is assessed prior to the activity and throughout the exercise period. Teachers who use this approach should be careful to assess the children's current schema for the subject at hand and then use care to present material of appropriate complexity. For example, if third graders in East Lansing, Michigan and Pretoria, South Africa engage in an online project to compare climates and daily weather conditions, they would need to know something about seasons and the earth's movement in relation to the sun, along with basic information about differences in Celsius and Fahrenheit measurements, general concepts about precipitation, enough math and graphing skills to make some comparisons, and so forth. If a group of sixth graders, ninth graders, or college students engaged in a similar exercise, they would be able to handle increasingly complex questions about the climatic comparisons. In all cases the teachers should ensure that the students have the prerequisite information necessary to understand their project prior to embarking upon it and then follow through with appropriate individual, small group, and large group activities to clarify, reinforce, and position the learning within a meaningful context.

Cognitive psychologist Robert Gagné delineated five kinds of "learning outcomes," along with a hierarchy of teaching strategies intended to help meet the learning outcomes (Gagné, 1964; 1984; 1985; Gagné & Briggs, 1979; Gagné & White, 1978; Wager & Gagné, 1988). The outcomes of learning represent the type of performance the student is expected to show as a result of learning:

- Intellectual Skill–enables learners to do something that requires cognitive processing. It is *procedural knowledge* that is separated into the further varieties of using concepts, skills, and procedures, such as learning a higher order rule during problem-solving.
- Cognitive Strategy–skills by which learners exercise control over their thinking and learning. These strategies help learners to determine which intellectual skills to use and when to use them.
- Verbal Information–sometimes referred to as *declarative knowledge* because learners must be able to use language to declare or state an answer using a verbal form.
- Motor Skill–involves the process of refining skills by doing something with the muscles of the body. For young children, this could be something like learning to write the letters of the alphabet or the numbers from one to ten.
- Attitude–motivation to make certain choices or decisions. Attitudes can be influenced in the instructional process so learners will shift their personal choices, such as developing a love of reading books or always trying to do their best.

In order to support these learning outcomes, Gagné developed a hierarchy of external instructional events that emphasized things teachers should do to best promote the desired learning outcomes from the students. This hierarchy is generally referred to as the "Nine Events of Instruction." These are:

- Gain the learner's attention
- Inform the learner of the objective
- Stimulate recall of prerequisite information
- Present the stimulus material
- Provide guidance
- Elicit the desired performance
- Provide feedback to the learner about correctness of the response
- Assess the learner's performance
- Enhance retention and transfer of learning

Many teachers and instructional designers have used the *learning outcomes* and *events of instruction* to design learning activities for students. Instructional designers who develop mediated materials for learning have relied heavily on those guidelines for product development. Several successful pieces of instructional computer software have utilized the nine events in order to analyze and provide feedback to learners in the tutorial mode. Unfortunately, many teachers learn the nine events of instruction but use them individually, rather than as a support mechanism for the desired learning outcomes.

Critical Thinking

As cognitive processes were studied, there eventually emerged an emphasis on critical thinking skills, which are viewed as higher level, deeper thinking processes that lead to better understanding through logic, analyzing, inferring, judging, planning, and problem-solving (de Bono, 1971; Ennis, 1989; Pea & Kurland, 1987; Resnick & Klopfer, 1987). Critical thinking began receiving significant attention in the 1970s because it was seen as an extension of learning beyond rote memorization, repetition, and regurgitation of facts (Paul, 1992). Teachers began asking their students to justify answers and explain why they came to certain conclusions. The scientific process was introduced into schools so students could begin to develop hypotheses and then discover results. If we revisit the earlier example about the online climate comparison study between Michigan and South African third graders, we would expect the students to study the background information, then develop a hypothesis that states what they would expect to find before beginning to

Table 1: Gardner's seven types of intelligence

Type	Attributes	Who
Linguistic	Sensitivity to sounds and meanings of words; Language abilities	Writer, Orator Literature teacher
Musical	Sense of rhythm, pitch, and melody; Appreciation of musical expressions	Musician, Singer Composer
Logical-Mathematical	Using logical and numerical patterns; Deductive reasoning	Mathematician Scientist, Logician
Spatial	Ability to perceive visual objects even when manipulated and transformed; Spatial memory	Artist, Sculptor Architect Mathematical topologist
Bodily-Kinesthetic	Control of bodily movements; Proprioceptive abilities	Athlete, Dancer, Actor, Skilled artist
Interpersonal	Understanding and dealing with the moods, temperaments, motivations, and behaviors of other people	Counselor Social Worker Salesperson
Intrapersonal	Understanding one's own feelings, motivations, needs, strengths, and weaknesses	Guiding one's own behavior

gather data about the daily weather. Once they gather the data, then they would determine if the evidence from the data supports their hypothesis.

Many researchers have offered variations on the concept of critical thinking. For example, Walters (1990) believes that the basic components of critical thinking are most likely to be useful only if they are used in combination with imagination, insight, and intuition. Litecky (1992) defines critical thinking as a process by which we actively examine our thoughts in order to better understand content and make meaning of our world, which suggests an alliance with constructivist thinking.

One example of the complexity and challenge of higher order thinking is explained in Howard Gardner's theory of multiple intelligences (Gardner, 1983; Gardner & Hatch, 1989). This currently popular theory posits that there are seven different kinds of intelligence, each to be used characteristically as noted in Table 1.

Most people use all of these types of thinking at various times and, due to individual differences, possess different levels of skill in the various areas. When people engage in complex learning tasks, they use various combinations of these types of thinking.

Constructivism

Neither behaviorists nor cognitivists have been able to fully understand and explain human learning, so there is yet another interpretation currently underway, called "constructivism." Because constructivism is still emerging as a field, the research yields some different explanations about it. In general, students "construct" their own sense of the world, their own perceptions of themselves as learners, and their own interpretations of critical information, thus being actively involved in shaping the learning process (Duffy & Jonassen, 1992; Savery & Duffy, 1995). Constructivism stresses the importance of critical thinking skills.

In contrast to constructivism, instruction in the United States emerged historically from an objectivist tradition. The term "objectivism" was coined by George Lakoff (1987), who posits that the world is real and it is composed of entities, properties, and relations. The goal of objectivism is to strive for complete, correct, and in-depth understanding of predetermined meanings. Evaluation within objectivist instruction is based on the degree to which learners understand the meanings among the entities, properties, and relations. While the constructivist epistemology agrees that the world is real, it does not agree that full and complete meanings are predetermined. Constructivist epistemology posits that meaning is not predetermined, but instead constructed by the learners as they experience life and share knowledge, so there can be many different interpretations about the meaning (Brown, Collins & Duguid, 1989; Duffy & Jonassen, 1992). If, for example, the third graders who are comparing weather conditions between East Lansing, Michigan and Pretoria, South Africa are asked to investigate the potential impact of the climatic differences on the lives of the children, they will look at the data differently. They likely would be encouraged to go beyond the obvious climatic facts to asking more questions of the other group of children and interpreting their answers in order to draw some conclusions about living in each city.

Behaviorism and cognitive information processing are unique but share some common ground in the objectivist epistemology. Behaviorism utilizes the stimulus-response method for transferring specific knowledge, so an instructor would focus on optimizing knowledge transfer. Cognitive science depends on the mental manipulation of symbols to understand the meaning, so an instructor would strive for the most efficient mode of transferring the specified knowledge. In contrast, the constructivist instructor draws from the convergence of several ideas about learning in order to create the best situation in which the students will be able to construct their own meaning, in discovery mode, rather than learn preconceived knowledge. As learners gain experience, they develop their own set of understandings and meanings, thus constructing their own knowledge internally. So each person might learn something different from the same set of external experiences. Constructivist epistemology posits that while the world is real, human interpretation of experiences is essential to constructing individual knowledge. Concepts can emerge when learners interact with each other and share their ideas. Thus in the extended example of the potential impact of the climatic differences on the lives of the children in Michigan and South Africa, the online discussion that happens among the children becomes more extended and in-depth.

While the constructivist theory has gained recent popularity, it is not completely new, but rather has emerged as a convergence of some underlying ideas that have been around for several years. For example, experientialism (Lakoff, 1987), relativism (Perry, 1970), semiotics (Cunningham, 1987), intertextuality (Morgan, 1985), social interaction (Vygotsky, 1978) and the connectionist approaches to cognitive science (Rummelhard & McClelland, 1986) all influence the constructivist theory. Constructivism supports Vygotsky's belief that social interaction about ideas precedes internalization of those ideas. In other words, when students experience and discover important concepts by thinking on their own and within socially meaningful situations, they learn and remember more about those concepts than they would if a teacher simply presented the same concepts as facts. At the heart of Stanley Pogrow's (1988a; 1988b; 1993) Higher Order Thinking Skills (HOTS) program is the idea that all students can learn if they are engaged in a meaningful dialogue between teacher and students and among students. But teachers must become skilled in the techniques of questioning and responding. Pogrow (1998b; 1993) warns that computers do not teach, rather teachers' conversations with students plus guidance promote learning. Therefore the quality of dialogues can quickly deteriorate to rote learning if the teachers are not trained in productive questioning techniques.

Referring again to the extended example about the potential impact of the climatic differences on the lives of the children in Michigan and South Africa, we would expect the teacher to avoid questions that would call for a "yes" or "no" answer. Instead, teachers would ask stepwise questions that encourage active thinking and construction of knowledge. Such questions would not have right or wrong answers but instead would build upon a series of logical questions and conclusions, probing deeper with each successive level of questions. While such an exercise might begin with charting temperatures and discussions of the earth's movement in relation to the sun, it could predictably advance to logical conclusions about the climate in each area and its impact upon local culture, such as comparisons of the school calendar and holidays, popular sports, local food production, seasonal school uniforms, clothing styles, folklore about the solar system or weather conditions, preferred transportation styles, and so on.

Engaged Learning Theory and Technology Implementation

There is an increasing amount of literature on the advantages of implementing an *engaged* (also termed a constructivist) learning environment along with the integration of technology into the classroom (Dwyer, Ringstaff, & Sandholtz, 1990a; Faison, 1996; Jonassen, 1996; Strommen & Lincoln, 1993; White, 1995; Wilson, 1996). According to Faison (1996), technology-utilizing teachers in a student-centered learning environment have discovered that most students possess increased enthusiasm, motivation, and self-esteem. There is increased student-group interaction, shared responsibility, and interdisciplinary study. Students are more receptive to exploring information and are more willing to take risks when problem-solving. Further, students can extend the learning to greater breadth and depth of information.

An engaged learning approach is not new. The groundwork was begun in this country a century ago with the work of John Dewey. The emphasis of Dewey's pedagogical theory was focused on the learner along with the learner's importance within society. "Teachers began with the concepts that they wanted children to learn and planned the activities accordingly" (Tanner, 1997, p. 26). Dewey valued the teacher as a guide rather than a leading force. "Dewey had faith in teachers' professional judgment to a degree equaled by only a few of his peers and rarely exceeded to this day" (Tanner, 1997, p. 10).

Piaget (1969) defined engaged learning (constructivism was his term) as a way of explaining how people come to know their world. Many believe that a "constructivist process" orientation to technology education is critical (Dwyer et al., 1990a; Strommen & Lincoln, 1993; White, 1995; Wilson, 1996). "The constructivist view of learning asserts that learners 'construct' their own meaning/knowledge from the information they acquire. This differs from the traditional view which assumes a teacher can 'deliver' knowledge to a learner" (Dwyer et al., 1990a). The emphasis in this learning process redirects the focus away from the teacher and toward the student.

Engaged learners use a constructivist approach to solve their tasks. They are critical thinkers and are highly involved with their tasks. They take a problem-based approach to their tasks and they collaborate to solve instructional problems. Engaged learners are strategic thinkers who are responsible for their own learning and seem to be energized by the excitement of inquiry and discovery. Technology in the engaged learning situation can by used for a wide variety of activities, each of which merges with the whole in the meaningful way. Looking again at the example about the potential impact of the climatic differences on the lives of the children in Michigan and South Africa, the extended questions posed by the teachers and other third-grade students could be very effective in the electronic situation and would have the

benefit of allowing students time to investigate and reflect prior to responding. Such an investigation would take on an entirely different flavor if the
students were doing it by paper mail. Certainly the electronic medium enables
momentum and therefore encourages enthusiasm and progress that is far
different from what would otherwise be possible.

The projects that become possible with the electronic media are limitless,
yet few teachers take full advantage of the potential. Over time, three of the
biggest reasons given for this are lack of teacher training, lack of time, and lack
of access to computers (Becker, 1991; Knupfer, 1987; Willis & Mehlinger,
1996). These combine with poor training, lack of skills among higher
education faculty, and inadequate infrastructure and support on campuses
(Barksdale, 1996; Spotts & Bowman, 1995) to make a serious situation across
all levels of school. While technology is not appropriate for all educational
activities, teachers who can imagine the potential of applied technology in
specific situations can certainly find a meaningful fit for at least some limited
yet powerful applications.

ISSUES, CONTROVERSIES, AND PROBLEMS

Throughout nearly a century of implementing technology in the schools,
the past thirty years have been the most controversial. Perhaps this is because
technological change has outpaced most school implementation and teacher
training efforts. The controversies have been many and have ranged the gamut
from concerns about finances and administration to infrastructure, learning,
safety, power and control, information access, equity, and rapid change.

Need for Teacher Training and Supportive Infrastructure

Much of the current literature about technology in education expresses
concern about inadequate teacher training and supportive infrastructure
within the school environment. These are not new phenomena; they have
emerged repeatedly as each new type of educational technology was made
available to educators (Cuban, 1986). As various technologies have been
introduced to schools, teacher training and supportive learning environments
have been substantial and ongoing issues.

While many people use the term *technology* interchangeably with *computers,* in reality there are many other types of technologies that can be used
separately or in combination with computers for instructional purposes,
although today's microchips do control many of the surrounding technological devices as well. As each different technology has been invented, there
have been waves of attempts at fitting it into the educational process. Even if

we were to contain our discussion to telecommunications, there would be many types of technologies to consider, for example telephone, fax, radio, television, two-way interactive video, e-mail, and so on. Yet most of the attention since the early 1980s has focused on computer technology and within the 1990s until today has narrowed in scope to concentrate on the Internet. Each new stage of technology seems to be pushed by interested parties to become the newest focus of attention in the schools. While advocates for educational computing claim sometimes thoughtful and other times grandiose ideas, study after study reveals that teachers lack adequate training and support to successfully implement computers for meaningful instruction (Becker, 1991; Becker & Sterling, 1987; Knupfer, 1989-90; Kozma, 1991; Stoll, 1999; Willis & Mehlinger, 1996). The Office of Technology Assessment (OTA) recognizes the role of technology in school reform and yet agrees that many studies confirm teachers are unprepared to meet the challenge (OTA, 1995).

A serious look at demographic information shows that new teacher attrition rates are skyrocketing and that within the next decade an additional three million children will need to be educated (Office of Postsecondary Education, 1997). It is critical that teachers are prepared for these children. There is no doubt that technology has a meaningful role in terms of learning, but the questions abound concerning whether or not teachers will have the necessary infrastructure in place for appropriate implementation.

The popularity of the Internet, including the World Wide Web (WWW or Web), has sparked renewed interest in microcomputer usage in schools. As newer technologies appear in substantially increased quantities, American schools continue to face the dilemma of inadequately prepared teachers. "It is apparent that, although American K-12 schools have computer technology resources, K-12 teachers do not have meaningful strategies with which to integrate their classroom use effectively" (Willis, 1995, p. 1). An OTA report stated, "The most direct and cost-effective way to educate teachers about technology is through the pre-service education they receive in colleges of education or other institutions" (OTA, 1995, pp. 166-167). Yet questions remain about the ability of teacher education programs to prepare K-12 teachers to meet the challenges of the new cyber world (Mehlinger, 1996; Uhlig, 1983; Willis & Mehlinger, 1996).

There are some exemplary programs available to review teacher technology preparation curricula, yet there is an incredible amount of work ahead. Uhlig (1983) reminds us that technology literacy is a dynamic and continuous process. It is not enough merely to create technology-enhanced classrooms. It is imperative to address faculty development for professors of teacher education (Guffey, Rampp, & Bradley, 1998; La Follette, 1992).

One of the best ways for pre-service teachers to achieve technology literacy is by watching their instructors model the use of technology in college classrooms. Yet the typical higher education situation is notoriously far from ideal due to lack of training, support, and resources, combined with an old structure of course requirements and heated debate about the value of technology for learning. Faison (1996) warned that many college professors consider technology use to be a separate course. This is not surprising when one considers the historical pattern of technology training in higher education. Yet any other view would require change, which seems to come about as a very slow process. One such revolutionary teacher education program is described by Barbara Bridges in Section 5, Chapter 11 of this book.

Power, Control, Access, Equity and Choice

There remain some issues of knowledge, power, control, access and equity that need resolution before things can go smoothly in a technology-rich learning environment. When resources and training are in short supply, there must be ways to collaborate to share them. There can be jealousies or competition among teachers within an institution as a result of differential knowledge, skill, or access to a scarce resource. Certainly some teachers feel a bit out of control if the students are determining the flow and the outcome of the lesson. In order to feel more comfortable, the teachers will need enough access to the technological resources to become proficient at using the technology in a meaningful way and have the support necessary to allow them time to collaborate in planning interdisciplinary activities with their colleagues.

When some teachers and students have access to the technology and others do not, a digital divide ensues. Who has the opportunity to use the technology and how it is used is critical in overcoming inequities. Furthermore, teachers must be alert to the quantitative and qualitative nature of potential inequities. Quantitative inequity exists when funding, limited amounts of equipment, or access preferences for limited groups, such as advanced students, restrict access inequitably. Yet qualitative inequities can be just as dangerous. "Qualitative inequity involves intangible attitudes and institutional biases that presumably pose a greater long-term threat to equal access and use" (Knupfer, 1987, p. 84). Qualitative inequities might emerge if certain groups of students use computers to engage in higher level cognitive learning while other students are limited to more simplistic or rote tasks. Perhaps one of the most difficult issues of equity involves learners with special needs. For example, students with physical limitations that make it difficult to use computers can sometimes be ignored rather than accommodated.

A difficult idea to adjust to is the notion that knowledge is dynamic and not static. This notion impacts the way that knowledge is acquired and utilized in classroom. Teachers must recognize this when designing assignments and assessing students' work. For example, the process of locating information can be more important than the final result, and the result can be different for different students. While the Web is full of information, much of the information is difficult to find and of poor quality. This means that good teachers will help students find information from various resources, not limited to online search techniques. Furthermore, safe and responsible use of the Internet is imperative.

Technology changes the way people access information, so questions arise about the usefulness of current textbooks. Is it possible to save money by purchasing fewer textbooks or is it a lot more expensive to use electronic media to access information? Perhaps the question we should be asking is not whether computers can replace textbooks but how computers can accompany and complement books and other instructional materials. Which combinations of materials are best utilized for which tasks? How should teachers choose the most appropriate media from among the many options that would support each educational goal? For example, a survey of available resources about recycling glass might yield some very good resources that are not Web-based. But if a teacher predetermined the Web as the medium of choice, then the materials found on the Web would need to be used whether they were of good or mediocre quality for the task at hand. How can teachers locate online resources and make good decisions about the different kinds of distance technologies available? How can these resources best be used to enhance education? How can we implement computer technology within a reasonable budget and without depersonalizing the educational process? Better yet, how can we implement computer technology for engaged learning that supports the existing curriculum and without diluting current valuable classroom learning? What type of infrastructure is needed to do so in a time-efficient and cost-effective way?

Unfortunately, technology is costly and needs frequent updates. The expense and continuous evolution require administrators to understand the potential strengths and weaknesses of using technology in schools. It is not acceptable for administrators to make decisions about technology based upon guesswork or the prestige factor. Enough information is available for administrators to get sound advice and make good decisions about technology plans. Yet even with a good infrastructure, technology infusion will bring change, which inevitably involves a certain amount of discomfort and resistance. There is nothing wrong with that. It would be far more worrisome if teachers blindly implemented technology in shallow ways that would inevitably degrade the learning.

Opposition to Technology in the Classroom

Never before has the goal of technology enhancement been more strongly proclaimed among school administrators. Schools are advertised and judged according to the perceived value of their computer holdings and distance education efforts. Unfortunately, we rarely hear about the content of what is accomplished with technology. Amid the cry for increased technology in education, the technology hype, there exist several voices raised in opposition.

A feature article in the *Atlantic Monthly* vigorously questions the idea of a classroom that minimizes the real, physical world in favor of an unreal, "virtual" world (Oppenheimer, 1997). Oppenheimer questions the value of technology in education and asks what might be lost as a result of the technology push: "There is no good evidence that most uses of computers significantly improve teaching and learning, yet school districts are cutting programs—music, art, physical education—that enrich children's lives to make room for this dubious nostrum" (p. 45).

Kaufman (1998) cautions us against viewing computers as the ultimate panacea to "do for education and learning what the printing press did for society ... cheaper, faster, better" (p. 63). We definitely should be concerned about unrealistic expectations that focus on the *means* of delivery and not on the *content* and *quality* of the instruction.

Clifford Stoll (1999) is one of the most vehement objectors to blanket use of technology in schools. He recognizes the high potential value of computer technology if it is applied to an appropriate task, but he points out that most schools are implementing technology for the wrong reasons, so it becomes misused and counterproductive. Even the idea of using the public address (PA) system into classroom loudspeakers is offensive to Stoll. He views them as an unnecessary disruption to teaching. Perhaps he has a point: Are PA systems and telephones in classrooms disruptive to learning? Probably so, if they disrupt an important dialogue or emerging idea, and most certainly that will happen if they are used excessively. On the other hand, if a PA system or telephone can enhance communication with other classrooms and it is used appropriately, then it ceases being a liability and instead enhances the classroom environment.

The arguments against using technology in the classroom are many. They range from issues concerning administration and budgets, to increased teaching duties and time constraints, to curriculum priorities and harmful effects on students. Certainly the technology is not completely harmful, nor is it likely to be helpful if not properly implemented.

The potential advantages of a cyber-classroom must be balanced with the needs of the students, and therefore the teachers must be a part of any technology integration plan. Too often the primary emphasis is placed on administrative issues or technology acquisition and connectivity, with little cognizance or emphasis on the student needs. In order for technology to serve the learners, it must be used in a way that enhances learning. Perhaps Stoll (1999) says it best: "My skepticism grows from a love for computing, from a wish to make our technological world better suited for people, rather than people better suited for machines" (p. xiii).

Semantics plays a role in the opposition to the integration of technology. The term "computer as tool" misleads many school administrators to equate computers with classroom supplies such as pencils and paper clips, thus dismissing the choice without having to understand its capabilities (Morton, 1998). Dismissing "the idea of 'computer as tool' permits the ignorant to justify their decision to reject it" (p. 23).

We live our daily lives surrounded by technology that has become an integral part of our existence. But instead of adopting Papert's (1993) approach of integrating technology as a child's own interactive learning extension, administrators and school boards often see computers as expendable items on the budget. Further, teachers often see it as nonessential, but rather something for students to do in their extra time after completing the important academic tasks. Thus, the fast workers often get more time on computers while slow, careful workers may not get any chance at all.

Regardless of preferences, the fact remains that computers are entering our nation's classrooms. But simply filling classrooms with computers will not improve instruction. While none of the technologies should be viewed as the ultimate panacea, they certainly can enrich the educational process if used appropriately. Meaningful use of the technologies to support the curriculum holds great possibilities. But technology is not the total experience, for it is simply a resource with the potential to support learners in a rich learning experience (Sasha, Hay, & Duffy, 1998).

SOLUTIONS AND RECOMMENDATIONS

A friend relates the following true story…. A fifth grade teacher returned a book report to one of his students with a prominently positioned scarlet C in the upper right corner. When the tearful student questioned the grade, the curt response was that the child's interpretation was incorrect and that it did not agree with the teacher's most learned understandings. The next day the normally quiet and unassuming young girl militantly marched into class and demanded an A on her paper, stating that the author agreed with her interpretation. "I e-mailed the author and she said that my interpretation was correct." She got her A.

The very relationship between students and teachers is being challenged in many of our nation's classrooms, partly because the emerging technologies empower learners. In the past, schools have been places where people in authority decided what would be taught, how it would be taught, and in what sequence. The new technologies provide students timely access to information that once was under the control of teachers (Mehlinger, 1996).

Educational reform must include changing teachers' beliefs and practices to a certain degree. Students working collaboratively and teachers assuming the role of facilitators characterize a constructivist, student-centered learning environment. Such an environment is inherently active and engaged, so the students likely will be talking excitedly and productively. Unfortunately many teachers and their school principals do not know this. The Apple *Classrooms of Tomorrow* research study discovered that classroom movement and noise conflicts with many teachers' traditional beliefs in the sanctity of classroom quiet and order (Dwyer et al., 1990b). Yet this is not surprising because many creative teachers have been criticized on annual evaluations by principals who have nothing more meaningful to say than the students were too noisy during collaborative work sessions; go figure. While schools of the past rewarded compliance, Peterson and Hart remind us that schools of the future have better things to attend to:

> Placing emphasis on control, objectivity, managing facts, testing, technology, behavior, and grading (without the corresponding development of the affective, psychological, and spiritual) disconnects, trivializes, and deadens the learning process. We recognize a great learner (and a great teacher) as one who is enlivened, exploring, seeking growth and appropriate challenge rather than compliance and sameness. (Peterson & Hart, 1997, p. 189)

This is the spirit that must be introduced into classrooms and the nation's teacher preparation programs. Fitting the technology into old methods of teaching will not work to achieve the greatest accomplishments, but modifying methods of teaching can be difficult for many people. Rather than view technology as disruptive to the learning process, a better perspective considers the need for engaged learning and educational change both with and without technology, as appropriate. Students can indeed make the adjustment and are likely to do so enthusiastically, but it does take a bit of risk taking for everyone involved. Students and teachers must dare to do things differently, to share their answers among themselves and create communities of educators. The friction of learning actively and collaboratively is exciting and yet uncomfortable for some people.

Regrettably, the paradigm shifts in teaching and learning have evolved in contrast to some of the initial attempts to implement computer technology in schools. For example, sending full classes of students to computer labs under the direction of teacher aides who implement drill and practice programs or teaching word processing mechanics without the benefit of a meaningful classroom task do not support the paradigm shift to engaged and meaningful learning strategies. Prior beliefs about the way people learn, and further, how they learn with technology are now being questioned. Initial implementation efforts relied heavily on programming and drill and practice activities that have turned out to be of limited value. Engaged learning with mixed media can support the kind of learning that stimulates cognitive processes and encourages students to achieve more than teachers expect. To effectively implement technology, teachers must find creative ways to support the curriculum, and truly extend learning in a unique, safe, and meaningful way.

Too often, key individuals in the community have a limited view of technology as a "noun." They view it is a thing to be possessed and used as if it were a remedy for all of the school's ills. Computers can easily be perceived as hammers, and all classroom challenges become the nails. Effective technology integration should be viewed as a "verb," constantly evolving, supporting, and functioning to enhance the classroom adventure.

Grant opportunities abound for various types of technology innovation. Grants are available to schools from the federal and state governments, non-governmental organizations, private companies, local school districts, universities, and so on. Often the grants are for development projects that allow teachers to receive training and then develop materials for classroom usage. Teachers frequently have the opportunity to team up on grant projects, either within their own school or between schools of various levels.

Foremost among things that could enhance technology-assisted learning is a focus on teacher preparation at both the pre-service and in-service levels. In order for the technology to be implemented in a meaningful way, teachers must understand the possibilities and have the necessary support to follow through appropriately. This includes a much deeper understanding than simply knowing how to run computer programs, search the Web for information or construct homepages on the Web. Further, using computers for teacher productivity is much different from implementing technology as a whole into meaningful learning situations for students. To fully utilize technology for the benefit of students, educators must heed the past, both in terms of learning theory and technology implementation.

Using Technology to Facilitate Engaged Learning

According to Bloom's Taxonomy, knowledge is the lowest level of cognition, followed by comprehension, application, analysis, and finally synthesis of information. If teachers strive to provide rich learning experiences that reach the higher levels of cognition, then we should be able to test the experiences against these levels of cognition. So students who simply must locate isolated facts on the Web do not enjoy the same high level, cognitive challenge as students who accomplish meaningful tasks within a problem-solving context. If a lesson requires students to solve a problem using information that they can only find on the Web, then they are likely to use the Web productively. For example, if students must locate information, summarize key points, put the information in context, compare it to other information through analysis, and eventually draw conclusions by synthesizing the information, then the learning will have been extended to a higher level. These are the kinds of activities that engage the learners.

FUTURE TRENDS

Based on current trends, we can safely predict that technology of the future will be more integrated, interactive, and intelligent. Integration will continue to escalate through the development of advanced multimedia systems. Interactivity will occur with increased distance learning and Internet interaction. Individualized knowledge bases will address the learning styles of each student (Mehlinger, 1996). It will be imperative for teachers to keep abreast of technological changes to empower their students. "Teachers who are responsible for today's children are responsible for tomorrow's Cyberspace citizens" (Wakabayashi, 1997, p. 47).

Through worldwide access to a variety of resources and fellow learners, we are learning that knowledge is not finite. Teachers do not have all of the answers and perspectives are becoming global. Instruction can become more individualized to adapt to various learning styles (Mueller & Mueller, 1997).

The impact of technology cannot be ignored. Mehlinger (1996) has termed it a "technology revolution in our schools" and viewed it as "the transformation of schooling through the use of technology" (p. 12). Papert (1993) viewed this impact in terms of evolution. He argues that students have attained a new kind of sophistication about technology and have gone beyond that to expand their methods of research and ways of learning.

Computers can be utilized in various ways to enhance learning within classrooms. They can be used in a local mode to run programs or CDs or in a distant mode to connect to the Internet for communication with people or to search for information outside of the classroom. Computer technology itself is just one of a variety of instructional media. The example at the beginning of this chapter described children who were engaged in collaborative learning. They used the Internet to communicate via e-mail with another class, search the Web for scientific information, and run a CD encyclopedia. In addition, the children used books, the chalkboard, visual displays in the classroom, paper, and pencil. While no one medium supported all of the tasks, and no one child had the burden of finding all of the solutions, the combination of media enhanced the richness of the lizard-mystery challenge and helped to distribute the tasks among all of the children.

Among the numerous choices of classroom activities that utilize technology, some have been particularly popular and promising. These include using multiple media, communicating with people outside of the immediate school, engaging in extended learning opportunities, gathering resources electronically, increasing global awareness, and expressing ideas more visually. Instructional television (ITV) has come a long way since it was first introduced in 1953 and is seen by some districts as a vehicle for accommodating teacher shortages. E-mail is ubiquitous in many curricula; learning partners are especially effective in the classroom for establishing key pals, doing collaborative activities, or engaging in role-playing opportunities with other students. Students are being offered the opportunity to express themselves visually through the new technologies, for example by giving school announcements or school news using video transmission and creating presentations using various software.

As we plan for the future, it seems prudent to heed the words of Kaufman (1998), who cautions us against viewing technology as a panacea to solve all our educational problems, and Oppenheimer (1997), who reminds us that research about the effectiveness of technology as an educational tool must continue. Others warn that many administrators view bringing technology into the school setting as being limited to the physical installation of hardware and software without regard to the supportive training, staff, and maintenance that are essential to a supportive infrastructure (Knupfer, 1989-90; Morton, 1998). Technology in itself is not the ultimate answer but when used appropriately, in concert with learning theories, it can enhance the instructional experience beyond what has been possible in the past.

CONCLUSION

Technology and the expectations of the new millennium surround the students of today, yet many classrooms still are without educators trained to integrate the technology into the curriculum. Universities and school districts must strive to better prepare technology-using teachers. Many teacher educators are not able to model technology integration. Despite their vital role to pre-service teachers, universities do very little to help professors progress in this area. While individual professors and classroom teachers might struggle to keep abreast of the technological changes, that is not enough; they cannot fight an uphill battle without the necessary institutional infrastructure. The rush to place a computer in every classroom in the nation is not the answer either. The technology itself is of limited use; it is not a magical wand that is capable of unleashing a new reality for both students and teachers. Educators who use technology for tasks of little meaning are likely to see little gain and possibly even pay a heavy toll in wasted effort, while those who focus on meaningful integration will certainly harvest the rewards.

Any local plan to implement technology for meaningful learning must consider the history of technology in education, its link with learning theory, and training opportunities for classroom teachers, professors of teacher education and administrators who make the decisions about support systems. Specifically, this training should emphasize meaningful integration of technology to enhance learning rather than hardware and software skills. It is imperative that innovation efforts also consider the overall scope of expenditures, timeline, access to resources, equity, evaluation, and above all, reasonable goal-setting for appropriate student activities to support the curriculum through engaged learning experiences.

We hope that technology will eventually be seen as an integral part of the instructional flow, rather than peripheral components. In such a view the technology takes on a meaningful role in the learning process rather than an optional activity. When administrators make informed decisions about technology, then the expenditures might very well prove to be a worthwhile investment. Until these things happen, the usefulness of computer technology in the classroom will not meet its full potential.

Failing to implement technology in a meaningful way that supports learning has some deep implications, because other instructional programs will certainly suffer along the way. Wasted technological resources have come at a high cost to schools districts in terms of support for other areas. For example, humanities education such as music, art, and language programs are typically cut in order to provide funding for technology. Our children need the humanities as well and technology usage should not be seen as a tradeoff or superfluous activity, but rather a tool that supports humanity and learning.

Something nearly "magical" happens when technology is combined with teaching in an atmosphere of engaged learning and discovery. We repeatedly have seen the resulting empowerment of students when combined technologies are added to the classroom equation. The transformation within classrooms when this magical moment occurs is a quality of spirit-energized learning that motivates and enhances any classroom environment.

QUESTIONS FOR FURTHER CONSIDERATION

Based on theories of learning:

1. How might you implement active, engaged learning experiences for students?
2. How does technology extend learning in a meaningful way?
3. How can technology be used to stimulate higher level thinking skills?
4. How would you and your students evaluate learning with and from technology?
5. In what ways can Web site developers improve sites for better curricular integration?
6. What practical, useful role could distance education serve in schools?
7. What would you suggest as the best strategy for improving technology training for K-12 teachers?
8. Suggest ways for universities to help professors of teacher education improve technology components of teacher education programs.
9. How can we know if technology is really effective in improving instruction?

We conclude this chapter with a resource list of Web sites filled with practical, meaningful project ideas for teachers and students (see Appendix A, Practical Web sites for students and teachers). As you utilize these sites, please ask yourselves how the various projects encourage active, engaged learning experiences for students. How can each of the sites best be used to stimulate higher level thinking skills? Finally, how can you extend some of these ideas to help educators make better decisions about meaningful use of technology?

REFERENCES

Anderson, C. A. (1983). Computer literacy: Changes for teacher education. *Journal of Teacher Education*, September-October, 34(5), 6-9.

Armstrong, A. and Casement, C. (2000). *The Child and the Machine: How Computers Put Our Children's Education at Risk.* Beltsville, MD: Robyn's Lane Press.

Aschcraft, M. (1994). *Human Memory and Cognition.* New York: Harper Collins.

Ausubel, D. (1963). *The Psychology of Meaningful Verbal Learning.* New York: Grune & Straton.

Barksdale, J. (1996). Why schools of education are still sending you staff you'll have to train in technology. *Electronic Learning,* 15(5), 39-45.

Becker, H. J. (1991). How computers are used in United States schools: Basic data from the 1989 I.E.A. computers in education survey. *Journal of Educational Computing Research*, 7(4), 385-406.

Becker, H. J. and Sterling, C. (1987). Equity in school computer use: National data and neglected considerations. *Journal of Educational Computing Research*, 3, 289-311.

Berman, P. and McLaughlin, M. (1976). Implementation of educational innovation. *Educational Forum*, 40(3), 345-370.

Brown, J. S., Collins, A. and Duguid, P. (1989). Situated cognition and the culture of learning. *Educational Researcher*, 18, 32-42.

Cuban, L. (1986). *Teachers and Machines: The Classroom Use of Technology Since 1920.* New York: Teachers College Press.

Cunningham, D. (1987). Outline of an educational semiotic. *The American Journal of Semiotics*, 5, 201-216.

de Bono, E. (1971). *New Think.* New York: Avon.

Downs, E., Clark, K. and Bennett, J. (1995). *New Directions for Teacher Education in the Information Technology Age.* Available on the World Wide Web at: http://www.coe.uh.edu/insite/elec_pub/html1995/0810.htm.

Duffy, T. M. and Jonassen, D. H. (Eds). (1992). *Constructivism and the Technology of Instruction: A Conversation.* Hillsdale, NJ: Lawrence Erlbaum Associates.

Dwyer, D. C., Ringstaff, C. and Sandholtz, J. H. (1990a). *Teacher Beliefs and Practices Part I: Patterns of Change* (Report No. 8). Available on the World Wide Web at: http://www.atg. apple.com/technology/proj/acot/full/acotRpt08full.htm.

Dwyer, D. C., Ringstaff, C. and Sandholtz, J. H. (1990b). *Teacher Beliefs and Practices Part II: Support for Change* (Report No. 9). Available on the World Wide Web at: http://www.atg.apple.com/technology/proj/acot/full/acotRpt09full.htm.

Ennis, R. H. (1989). Critical thinking and subject specificity: Clarification and needed research. *Educational Researcher*, 18(3), 4-10.

Faison, C. L. (1996). Modeling instructional technology use in teacher preparation: Why we can't wait. *Educational Technology*, September-October, 36(5), 57-59.

Friedman, D. (1983). The impact of educational computing on teacher education. *Journal of Teacher Education*, September-October, 34(5), 14-18.

Gagné, R. M. (1964). Problem solving. In Melton, A. W. (Ed.), *Categories of Human Learning*. New York: Academic Press.

Gagné, R. M. (1984). Learning outcomes and their effects: Useful categories of human performance. *American Psychologist*, 39, 377-385.

Gagné, R. M. (1985). *Conditions of Learning*. New York: Holt, Rinehart and Winston.

Gagné, R. M. and Briggs, L. J. (1979). *Principles of Instructional Design* (2nd ed.). New York: Holt, Rinehart and Winston.

Gagné, R. M. and White, R. T. (1978). Memory structures and learning outcomes. *Review of Educational Research*, 48, 187-222.

Gardner, H. (1983). *Frames of Mind*. New York: Basic Books.

Gardner, H. and Hatch, T. (1989). Multiple intelligences go to school: Educational implications of the theory of multiple intelligence. *Educational Researcher*, 18(11), 4-10.

Guffey, J. S., Rampp, L. C. and Bradley, M. J. (1998). *Curriculum and Technology: Integration Through Modeling*. (ERIC Document Reproduction Service No. ED 418 075), August.

Jonassen, D. H. (1996). *Computers in the Classroom*. Englewood Cliffs, NJ: Prentice Hall.

Kaufman, R. (1998). The Internet as the ultimate technology and panacea. *Educational Technology*, January-February, 63-64.

Knupfer, N. N. (1987). *A Survey of Teachers' Perceptions, Opinions and Attitudes Regarding Instructional Computing: Implications Regarding Equity*. Doctoral dissertation. University of Wisconsin-Madison.

Knupfer, N. N. (1989-1990). The teacher as a critical component of computer education and school change. *Journal of Computing in Teacher Education*, Winter, 6(2).

Knupfer, N. N. (1993). Teachers and educational computing: Changing roles and changing pedagogy. In Muffoletto, R. and Knupfer, N. N. (Eds.), *Computers in Education: Social, Political & Historical Perspectives*, 163-179. Cresskill, NJ: Hampton Press.

Knupfer, N. N. (1997). Gendered by Design. *Educational Technology*, March, 37(2), 31-37.

Kozma, R. (1991). Learning with media. *Review of Educational Research*, 61(2), 179-211.

La Follette, J. J. (1992). Instructional technology and teacher education. *Canadian Journal of Educational Communications*, Summer, 109-122.

Lakoff, G. (1987). *Women, Fire, and Dangerous Things*. Chicago, IL: University of Chicago Press.

Litecky, L. (1992). Great teaching, great learning: Classroom climate, innovative methods, and critical thinking. In Barnes, C. A. (Ed.), *Critical Thinking: Educational Imperative*. San Francisco: Jossey-Bass.

Mehlinger, H. D. (1996). School reform in the information age. *Phi Delta Kappan*, February, 400-407.

Morgan, T. (1985). Is there an intertext in this text?: Literary and interdisciplinary approaches to intertextuality. *American Journal of Semiotics*, 3, 1-40.

Morton, C. (1998). The modern land of Laputa: Where computers are used in education. In Hirschbulh, J. J. and Bishop, D. (Eds.), *Computers in Education*, 22-25. Guilford, CT: Dushkin/McGraw-Hill.

Mueller, R. J. and Mueller, C. L. (1997). *The Cognitive Revolution and the Computer*. DeKalb, IL: Northern Illinois Printing Services.

November, A. (1999). The skills of freedom. *Ties Magazine*, January-February, 1, 24, 28.

Office of Postsecondary Education. (1997). *Shaping the Profession That Shapes America's Future: Initial Ideas for Teacher Development Across America and the Reauthorization of Title V of the Higher Education Act* (report in progress). Washington, DC: U.S. Department of Education.

Office of Technology & Assessment [OTA]. (1995). *Teachers and Technology: Making the Connection* (Report No. OTA-EHR-616). Washington, DC: U.S. Government Printing Office.

Oppenheimer, T. (1997). The computer delusion. *The Atlantic Monthly*, July, 45-62.

Papert, S. (1993). *The Children's Machine: Rethinking School in the Age of the Computer*. New York: Basic Books.

Paul, R. W. (1992). Critical thinking: What, why, and how. In Barnes, C. A. (Ed.), *Critical Thinking: Educational Imperative*. San Francisco: Jossey-Bass.

Pea, R. and Kurland, D. (1987). On the cognitive effects of learning computer programming. In Pea, R. and Sheingold, K. (Eds.), *Mirrors of Minds: Patterns of Experience in Educational Computing*, 147-177. Norwood, NJ: Ablex.

Perry, W. (1970). *Forms of Intellectual and Ethical Development in the College Years: A Scheme.* New York: Holt, Rinehart and Winston.

Peterson, T. and Hart, T. (1997). Pedagogy for the soul: Revisioning of spirit in education. *Educational Horizons,* Summer, 75(4), 187-191.

Piaget (1952). *The Origins of Intelligence in Children.* New York: International Universities Press.

Piaget, J. (1969). *The Mechanisms of Perception.* London: Routledge and Kegan Paul.

Pogrow, S. (1988a). A thinking skills approach to enhance the performance of at-risk students: Experience from the HOTS program. *Educational Leadership,* 4(7), 79-85.

Pogrow, S. (1988b). The computer coverup. *Electronic Learning,* 7(7), 6-7.

Pogrow, S. (1993). A learning drama approach to using computers with at-risk students. In Muffoletto, R. and Knupfer, N. N. (Eds.), *Computers in Education: Social, Political and Historical Perspectives,* 207-217. Cresskill, NJ: Hampton Press.

Popkewitz, T. and Shutkin, D. (1993). Social science, social movements, and the production of educational technology in the U.S. In Muffoletto, R. and Knupfer, N. N. (Eds.), *Computers in Education: Social, Political and Historical Perspectives,* 163-179. Cresskill, NJ: Hampton Press.

Resnick, J. B. and Klopfer, L. E. (1987). Toward the thinking curriculum: An overview. In Resnick, L. B. and Klopfer, L. E. (Eds.), *Toward the Thinking Curriculum: Current Cognitive Research.* Washington, DC: Association for Supervision and Curriculum Development in cooperation with the North Central Regional Educational Laboratory.

Roszak, T. (1994). *The Cult of Information* (2nd ed.). Berkeley, CA: University of California Press.

Rummelhard, D. and McClelland, J. (1986). *Parallel Distributed Processing.* Cambridge, MA: MIT Press.

Saettler, P. (1990). *The Evolution of American Educational Technology.* Englewood, CO: Libraries Unlimited, Inc.

Sasha, A. B., Hay, K. E. and Duffy, T. M. (1998). Grounded constructions and how technology can help. *TechTrends,* March, 43(2), 15-23.

Savery, J. and Duffy, T. M. (1995). Problem based learning: An instructional model and its constructivist framework. *Educational Technology,* 5, 31-38.

Skinner, B. F. (1938). *The Behavior of Organisms.* New York: Appleton Century Crofts.

Skinner, B. F. (1968). *The Technology of Teaching.* Appleton Century Crofts.

Sloan, D. (Ed.) (1985). *The Computer in Education: A Critical Perspective.* New York: Teachers College Press.

Spotts, T. and Bowman, M. (1995). Faculty use of instructional technologies in higher education. *Educational Technology*, 35(2), 56-64.

Stoll, C. (1999). *High-Tech Heretic: Reflections of a Computer Contrarian.* New York: Anchor Books, a Division of Random House.

Strommen, E. F. and Lincoln, B. (1993). *Constructivism, Technology, and the Future of Classroom Learning.* Available on the World Wide Web at: http://www.ilt.columbia.edu/ilt/papers/construct.htm.

Tanner, L. N. (1997). *Dewey's Laboratory School: Lessons for Today.* New York: Teachers College Press.

Thorndike, E. (1936). Autobiography. In Murchison, C. (Ed.), *A History of Psychology in Autobiography*, 3. Worcester, MA: Clark University Press.

Tirozzi, G. N. (1998). Partnerships in today and tomorrow. *On Common Ground: Strengthening Teaching Through School-University Partnership,* Winter, 6-7.

Uhlig, G. (1983). Dimensions of technology literacy in teacher education. *Journal of Teacher Education*, September-October, 34(5), 2-5.

Vygotsky, L. (1978). *Mind in Society: The Development of Higher Mental Processes.* Cambridge, MA: Harvard University Press.

Wager, W. and Gagné, R. M. (1988). Designing computer-aided instruction. In Jonassen, D. H. (Ed.), *Instructional Designs for Microcomputer Courseware,* 35-60. Hillsdale, NJ: Lawrence Erlbaum Associates.

Wakabayashi, I. (1997). From Internet user to cyberspace citizen. *Educom Review*, July-August, 46-55.

Walters, K. S. (1990). Critical thinking, rationality, and the vulcanization of students. *Journal of Higher Education*, 61(4), 448-467.

Watson, J. (1912). Psychology as the behaviorist views it. *Psychology Review*, 20, 158-177.

White, C. (1995). *The Place for Technology in a Constructivist Teacher Education Program.* Available on the World Wide Web at: http://www.coe.uh.edu/insite/elec_pub/html1995/0821.htm.

Willis, E. M. (1995). *What If We Teach Integration, Not "Computers"?* Available on the World Wide Web at: http://www.coe.uh.edu/insite/elec_pub/html1995/098.htm.

Willis, J. W. and Mehlinger, H. D. (1996). Information technology for teacher education. In Sikula, J., Buttery, T. J. and Guyton, E. (Eds.), *Handbook on Research on Teacher Education*, 978-1029. New York: Simon & Schuster Macmillan.

Wilson, B.G. (1996). *Constructivist learning environments: Case studies in instructional design.* Englewood Cliffs, NJ: Education Technology Publications.

APPENDIX A: PRACTICAL WEB SITES FOR STUDENTS AND TEACHERS

The African-American Mosaic

A Library of Congress resource guide for African-American history and culture. http://lcWeb.loc.gov/exhibits/african/intro.html.

The Amazing Picture Machine

To help locate pictures, maps, and other graphic resources on the Internet. http://www.ncrtec.org/picture.htm.

Celebrate the Year of the Ocean

Eighteen activities for students to practice math, geography, science, and language skills while learning about the world's oceans. http://www.education-world.com/a_lesson/lesson060.shtml.

The Educational Resources Information Center (ERIC)

This index has links to the 17 ERIC clearinghouses, ERIC catalog, U.S. Department of Education, National Library of Education, and several other resources. http://www.accesseric.org:81/home.html.

Eduscapes

A great resource for engaged learning projects and teacher assistance. http://eduscapes.com.

The Electronic Zoo

Specializes in resources for veterinarians and animal lovers. It is an online compendium of information about animals, animal care, and veterinary medicine, featuring links to indexes, organizations, mailing lists, discussion groups, and so on. http://netvet.wustl.edu/e-zoo.htm.

Emerging Technologies in Science, Education, and Business

The course is designed for students interested in understanding new technologies and scientific methods for use in education and/or the workplace. http://www.ncsa.uiuc.edu/EP/index.html.

The Exploratorium

As a virtual museum visit, this site is both fun and educational. San Francisco's Exploratorium hosts this interactive site that can be used by children and adults. The site includes links to interactive online exhibits. http://www.exploratorium.edu/.

The Global Schoolhouse

Links kids around the world, creating a "connected" learning community. The site includes educational resources for parents and teachers, while K-12 students will find contests, online publications, and cyberfairs that have been created just for them. http://www.gsh.org/.

Handbook of Engaged Learning Projects

Classroom projects designed by K-12 teachers to demonstrate engaged learning and effective use of technology. http://www-ed.fnal.gov/help/index.html.

Internet Use in the K-12 Classroom

A valuable and very useful site. http://www.indiana.edu/~eric_rec/comatt/Websites.html.

Journey North: A Global Study of Wildlife Migration

Uses data supplied by schoolchildren to track the migratory habits of different wildlife. A wonderful way to integrate computers into the science classroom. http://www.learner.org/jnorth/.

Kathy Schrock's Guide for Educators

A classified list of useful Internet sites for enhancing curriculum and teacher professional growth. It is updated daily. http://school.discovery.com/schrockguide/.

Kid's Web

A kid-friendly version of the Web, simple to navigate with appropriate K-12 targeted information. Includes four subsections: arts, sciences, social studies, and miscellaneous. http://www.npac.syr.edu/textbook/kidsWeb/.

The Knowledge Loom: What Works in Teaching & Learning

Created to help locate promising practices in education and identify those of use to your school. http://knowledgeloom.org/.

LD Online

Guide to learning disabilities for parents, teachers, and children. Contains over 5,000 links useful to teachers working with disabled students, including adaptive technology, government, rehabilitation, and more. http://www.ldonline.org.

LearningVista.com—The Original Kids Web

Biology and Life Sciences, General Biology, Evolution, Genetics and Molecular Biology, Animal Species, and lots of dinosaurs. http://www.kidsvista.com/Sciences/biology.html.

Librarian's Ready Reference Guide to the Internet

An updated database of useful information for librarians, teachers, and students. http://www.winsor.edu/library/rref.htm.

NASA's Quest Project

Provides support and services for schools, teachers, and students seeking to fully utilize the Internet and its underlying information technologies as a basic tool for learning. http://quest.arc.nasa.gov/.

Patrick Crispen's Roadmap96

A free, 27-lesson Internet training workshop. A very popular online workshop. http://Webreference.com/roadmap.

The PEP Registry of Educational Software Publishers

A compendium of links to over 1,000 publishers and their products. A good place to locate product information prior to purchasing. http://www.microWeb.com/pepsite/Software/publishers.html.

Primary and Secondary School Internet User Questions

Contains links to information on the E-rate and teacher training in advanced technology. Technology planning committees will find a wide array of information on funding, getting connected, and technology use in classrooms. http://cosn.org/.

Reinventing Schools: The Technology is Now

An excellent site from the National Academy of Sciences. http://www.nap.edu/readingroom/books/techgap.

The SchoolNet Software Review Project

An excellent and comprehensive database that evaluates science, mathematics, language arts, and social studies software programs for K-4 classrooms. Teachers can use it for planning content area lessons and units, while technology planners can use this as a resource in their technology integration plan. http://www.enc.org/rf/ssrp/.

Science Museums, Exhibits and Family Sites

This Web index includes links to science museums and family sites where visitors can access exhibits, schedules, and museum information. This is a great reference for science and math teachers, as well as parents and students. http://www.ilt.columbia.edu/k12/livetext/curricula/science/exhibits.html.

The Space Science Laboratory

NASA's Marshall Space Flight Center maintains this colorful and fascinating site devoted to all aspects of science that relate to space travel and exploration. http://www.ssl.msfc.nasa.gov/.

Teachers Helping Teachers:

A Web site created by teachers, for teachers. http://www.pacificnet.net/~mandel.

TechWeb

Technology News Site with daily updates. TechWeb will return related articles published in any one of over 20 online and computer magazines. http://www.techWeb.com/.

TERC Science and Math Education

This site links to a growing collection of educational resources and services for mathematics, science, and technology educators. Hub services can help you join or start a networked community, publish on the Internet, or conduct custom information searches. http://hub.terc.edu.

The Thinking Fountain

Valuable to children interested in learning and discovering new things about science. Parents, science teachers, and children can explore this site together and submit their own science experiments and findings. http://www.sci.mus.mn.us/sln/.

U.S. Department of Education

An award-winning Web site. It provides links to Department-funded or affiliated sites and services. http://www.ed.gov/.

Web 66: A K-12 World Wide Web Project

A comprehensive Web resource for educators offered by the University of Minnesota. http://Web66.coled.umn.edu/.

The Web 100

The Web's best 100 classroom sites: Education and Reference. (Updated hourly). http://www.Web100.com/listings/education.html.

Tools For Web Searches

- Altavista http://www.altavista.digital.com
- Ask Jeeves http://www.askjeeves.com
- Dogpile http://www.dogpile.com
- Go http://www.go.com/
- Google http://www.google.com
- Hotbot http://www.Hotbot.com
- Lycos http://www.Lycos.com
- Netscape http://www.Netscape.com

Section III

Designing for Learners in Primary and Secondary Education

Chapter III

eTIPs–Educational Technology Integration and Implementation Principles

Sara Dexter
University of Minnesota, USA

WHY A SET OF PRINCIPLES TO GUIDE TEACHERS ABOUT INTEGRATING AND IMPLEMENTING EDUCATIONAL TECHNOLOGY INTO THE K-12 CLASSROOM?

In this chapter of the section, I present a set of educational technology integration and implementation principles, or eTIPs. These principles are offered as an explanation of the conditions that should be present in order for educational technology integration to be effective. The principles are an elaboration of two premises: First, that the teacher must act as an instructional designer, planning the use of the technology so it will support student learning. Second, that the school environment must support teachers in this role by providing adequate technology support. Thinking about these principles while deciding whether or how to integrate technology can help a teacher to take an instructional design perspective while also taking the "technology ecology" of the setting into perspective.

Objectives for this Chapter of the Section

I will begin by discussing these principles more generally. I then offer a specific explanation of each principle and describe what it would look like in a best practice environment. At the end of this chapter I offer questions to ask while following these principles when considering technology integration. I also suggest other ways these principles can be adapted and used to help create the conditions that allow effective educational technology integration.

At the end of this chapter of the section, the reader should be able to apply the eTIPS to his or her own teaching context. The eTIPS questions and examples provide a structure for designing in any K-12 setting.

EDUCATIONAL TECHNOLOGY INTEGRATION AND IMPLEMENTATION PRINCIPLES

Two Dimensions

These principles are organized into two dimensions: classroom and schoolwide. The classroom principles expand upon the premise that effective technology integration requires the time and attention of teachers in the role of instructional designers. Educational technology does not possess inherent instructional value: a teacher designs into the instruction any value that technology adds to the teaching and learning processes. Thus, the three classroom eTIPS prompt a teacher-designer to consider what they are teaching, what added value the technology might bring to the learning environment, and how technology can help to assess student learning. Together these three principles guide a teacher-designer through the important phases of designing instruction and also in considering technology as a part of that learning environment.

Part of what makes teachers' integration activities feasible or not is the level of technology support at a school. The three schoolwide principles focus on technology support features that are present in high-quality technology support programs, the presence of which are correlated to teachers' increased uses of educational technology. These principles describe the implementation environment necessary to support teachers. Together they will help teachers to evaluate the level of access and support available to them in their integration work, which may help to determine whether or not, given their amount of planning time, a particular integration goal is realistic.

Classroom Level Principles

Learning outcomes drive the selection of technology. In order for learning outcomes to drive the selection of technology, teachers must first be clear about their lesson or unit's student learning outcomes. This is an important first step in determining whether or not the educational technology available can be a support to teaching and learning. It will allow teachers to be more efficient as they search for available, appropriate technologies because they will quickly eliminate those that do not support their learning outcomes.

The learning outcomes teachers might plan for their students might focus on acquisition of facts or higher level thinking in a specific curricular area, more general procedural skills, specific technical skills, or some combination of these. While educational technology can support any of these types of outcomes, some educational technologies may be more appropriate for certain outcomes than for others.

For the technology under consideration for use, teachers must also consider the cognitive demands it places on the user. Does it require them to recall facts, like in drill and practice software? Does it require the user to provide content information and represent their understanding, as tool software (such as a database) does? Or does it require the user to represent their knowledge in a symbolic form, as with a programmable calculator? Any one of these technologies requires the user to respond in different ways, thereby supporting very different learner outcomes but perhaps also adding to a learner's outcomes.

When learning outcomes drive the selection of technology in a classroom, the educational technology will be a better fit for teaching and learning, supporting the achievement of the designated outcomes. The conditions for effective technology integration are enhanced further when teachers across a school all work together to enact this principle: Technology use is linked to larger goals and outcomes at the grade level, department, school, district, or state level. Processes for selecting and purchasing technology are linked to these curricular goals. A variety of educational technology, i.e., software titles, Web sites, and peripherals, are present, correlated to grade levels, and characterized by the type of outcomes they support.

Technology use provides added value to teaching and learning. The phrase "added value" is used to designate that the particular packaging, delivery method or combination of services in a product bring extra benefits than one would otherwise receive. Here, I use the phrase to communicate that the use of technology brings added value to the teaching or learning processes when it makes possible something that otherwise would be impossible or less viable to do.

For teaching, adding value might mean individualizing instruction or making it more responsive to student's questions and interests, or providing additional resources of information so instruction is more real world, authentic, and current. Educational technology can also aid teachers in providing "scaffolds" that support learners as they move from what they already know and can do to what they are learning, for example, by aiding the visualization of or quick reference to information. Educational technology can also help teachers to create social arrangements that support collaborative as well as independent learning by facilitating communication and interaction patterns. This might aid students in carrying out reflection or deliberation themselves or with others. Teachers can also use educational technology to support additional opportunities for learners to practice, get feedback, or allow for revision or reflection. Thus, it supports knowledge acquisition and practice, so learners become more fluent in their knowledge.

Added value for learning might mean educational technology that supports the accessing of data, processing of information, or communicating of knowledge by making these processes more feasible (see Table 1).

Educational technology can aid students' accessing information or representing it in new ways. It can increase access to people, perspectives, or resources and to more current information. Many times, software's interface design allows learner interaction or presents information in a multi-sensory format. Hyperlinks can allow learners to easily connect to related information. Built-in indexes and key word searching support learners by easing their search through a large amount of information to find what is relevant. These features all add value by increasing access to data or the users' control during that access.

In terms of processing information, added value might mean that the educational technology supports students learning-by-doing or aids them in constructing mental models, or making meaning, by scaffolding their thinking. For example, a database can allow students to compare, contrast, and categorize information through query features. By asking students to create products with tool software, it requires them to think more deeply about the material in order to represent it with that tool (Jonassen, 2000). For example, to create a concept map students would have to analyze and then categorize information, synthesizing it from multiple sources. The resulting concept map would show what they understood to be key and subordinate ideas. When students designed the layout of a hypermedia, multimedia document this representation would have required them to think about the best media to represent the content on their topic and then analyze and synthesize this information. When word processing text, students can represent their analysis and categorization of information through its formatting and positioning, for example, by using multiple levels of headings, tables, or other visual clues to visually represent main and subordinate ideas.

Educational technology can also add value to students' ability to show and articulate to others about what they have learned. For example, the World Wide Web is a medium through which it is relatively easy for students to communicate with others around the world. Whether to their peers or outside experts, with educational technology students are able to create more authentic and professional communication and in the style and format appropriate for the topic.

Using educational technology in a classroom to add value to teaching and learning by adding, extending, or changing what teachers or students do inherently increases the effectiveness of technology. When teachers work together on this principle in a department, grade level, or school it will ensure that students will learn to use technology to help them find information, organize or analyze it, and then tell others about what they have learned. Software and hardware being considered for purchase would be evaluated according to the value that it adds to teaching and learning, ensuring that only the most effective materials are selected for purchase.

Table 1: Added value summary for accessing data, processing information, and communicating knowledge

Task	Added Value
Accessing Data	• Multi-sensory • Greater amounts of data • Searching and "mining" capabilities • Timeliness of the information • Relevance of the information
Processing Information	• Self-paced • Individual attention • Remediation • Practice to the point of fluency • Visualizing information • Develop process or skill capabilities • Organize and categorize information
Communicating Knowledge	• Publish information to an audience • Communicate in authentic format, style • Communicate findings and understanding to others

Technology assists in the assessment of the learning outcomes. Planning for the assessment of students' learning outcomes is a key component of designing instruction. At times, teachers will want to collect and return to students formative data to let them know about their learning progress. Almost always, teachers will want to collect summative information about students' achievement of the learning outcomes. Technology can assist teachers in collecting both formative and summative data that will help them understand how students are meeting or have met the learning outcomes for that lesson or unit.

Some software or hardware actually collects formative data during its use, and some technologies also provide help in the analysis of the information. Generally, these are software programs designed to assess student learning, such as tutorial or drill and practice software. Some of these programs, through screens or printouts of information, or other feedback mechanisms, support student's self-assessment of their learning. When students are working on learning procedural knowledge, they need opportunities to practice and develop their skills. Their progress as they work toward a product can easily be captured through software features such as tracking changes or by asking students to use the "Save As" feature to freeze earlier versions of their work. These in-process products could help teachers to provide feedback to students for their revision and reflection, thereby aiding teachers' formative assessment practices.

In addition, educational technology is an aid to summative assessment, especially performance assessments where students are to produce products that allow them to show what they know and can do. Products students produce through software, whether a database, "mind map," multimedia or word processed report, or a Web site, demonstrate what they have learned about both the content of their product, the procedural knowledge required to produce it, and their ability to communicate. The capabilities a product might demonstrate include the skills of editing, analysis, group collaboration, or the operation of the software itself.

When teachers use educational technology to assist them in the assessment of students' progress toward or obtainment of learning outcomes it makes technology an even more effective instructional tool. It will help students to prepare for their future to be asked to create computer-produced products, to become accustomed to showing their progress through such products, and to describe how these products demonstrate what they know. If this principle were employed consistently within a grade level, department, or a school, teachers would become more skillful at determining what can be learned about students' process skills, his or her progress, and learning through their technology products.

School Level Principles

I now turn to the principles of technology implementation that are associated with the overall school technology environment, which is shared by all the teachers at the same school. While this means that these principles are usually beyond the control of any one teacher, as a group the teachers at a school can, and do, influence the decisions and priority-setting that would put these principles into place. These school level principles are conclusions from the findings of Dexter, Anderson and Ronnkvist (In Press), who describe the quality technology support conditions that are associated with increased teacher and classroom uses of technology.

Ronnkvist, Dexter, and Anderson (2000) report that technology support encompasses both technical and instructional domains. In both of these domains, teachers need facilities, staff support, incentives, and opportunities to provide feedback (see Table 2).

In the school-level educational technology implementation principles I have simplified and collapsed these domains and resource types to the following three eTIPs.

Ready access to supported technology is provided. Teachers must have convenient and flexible access to and technical support for appropriate educational technology in order for them to utilize it in their classrooms. Perhaps of all the principles, this one is the most self-evident. Without available and working educational technology, it can hardly be utilized in a classroom. But, the two key words in this principle are *ready* and *supported.* Ready access means the technology should be close to where teachers need to use it and that it is scheduled flexibly, so that teachers have an opportunity to sign up for it when it is relevant for classroom work. Here, support specifically refers to the technical domain, like troubleshooting help and scheduled maintenance.

The idea of ready access should raise for the teacher questions about whether or not the students could be grouped together to work with the educational technology, if it could be a station through which students rotated, or if all students need to have simultaneous access to the educational technology. Ultimately, the access has to be practical. It must be ready enough that working through the logistics of providing students access to the technology does not outweigh the added value it provides.

Dockterman (1991) describes several possibilities for how to effectively use one computer in a classroom. The instructional uses he describes include using the computer as a presentation tool, as a discussion generator, and as a station to which cooperative groups circulate. Other sources for one-computer classroom ideas are found in most educational technology magazines for practitioners.

Table 2: Technology support content by resource type used to deliver technology services to teachers

Resource Type	Technical Domain
Facilities	• Network and Internet access, hardware, software
Staff assistance and necessary services	• Technical support, help desk, network services
One-on-one personal guidance, help	• Computer experts for trouble-shooting
Professional development	• Operating equipment, general software, etc.
Incentives	• Release time; free hardware, software and network access; anticipation of expert status
Resource Type	**Instructional Domain**
Facilities	• Content-area specific software, communications access to pedagogical expertise
Staff assistance and necessary services	• Instructional expertise and background of people providing support
One-on-one personal guidance, help	• Guided practice, consultation for curriculum integration
Professional development	• Pedagogy, models implementation strategies
Incentives	• Release time, support focusing on instructional content

Means, Olson, and Singh (1995) describe the advantages and disadvantages of a variety of computer placement configurations: Computer labs usually provide enough machines for one student to one computer access. However, scheduling their use and having to move to the lab's location can hamper the integration of the computer with the content under study. Where labs are staffed, scheduling and support of its users contributes to a positive experience; however, this can be a negative experience if relying on the lab staff results in less engagement by the teacher. An advantage of equipment distributed throughout regular classrooms is that it gets the equipment to the where the teachers and students do their work. But because of budget constraints, it might be difficult for the school to provide enough equipment to make student groups feasible in size or to use them as stations through which students would rotate. More mobile computers, such as laptops or desktop computers on carts, can aid in bringing a critical mass of computers to the classroom. However, it does require scheduling and coordination of equipment between staff members. Additional time must be allowed to move and setup the equipment.

The other key idea in this principle is that there is technical support. Many teachers are able to provide simple troubleshooting on their own. Those who cannot, or when the problem is more complex, must have access to technical support. Most schools have some level of technical support available, although the frequency and level of expertise varies widely (Ronnkvist, Dexter, & Anderson, 2000). Teachers must individually assess whether or not the level of support available to them serves as an adequate safety net. For example, if technical support is through a staff member who comes to the school only once a week, a teacher would have to determine if s/he could wait that long to continue the activity should a problem arise that s/he could not fix. Of course, no matter what the level of access, a backup plan is essential for all technology-integrated activities.

Ready and supported access at a school obviously adds to the effectiveness of technology, making possible teachers' basic, working access to technology. When a school makes it a priority to provide ready, supported access, the distribution of hardware and software resources is based on instructional priorities; if instructional priorities change, the hardware and software resource distribution is revisited. For example, computer labs might be dismantled if teachers decide they would benefit from classroom-based access to computers. Schools that work toward this principle also provide trained, reliable technical support at the most frequent level of access that can be afforded.

Professional development is targeted at successful technology integration. Technology professional development is key to teachers' learning to integrate technology effectively into the classroom (CEO Forum, 1999). The learning needs can be thought of as, one, about learning to operate the software, and two, about learning to use software as an integrated, instructional tool. Too often, teachers' learning opportunities are limited to the operation of the software. Teachers must have frequent opportunities to simply learn how to operate the educational technology but also have learning opportunities that address more than these basic skills; this eTIP emphasizes the entire instructional domain shown in Table 2. Possible formats for learning include access to shared resources, training modules, mentoring, face-to-face classes, or online, asynchronous professional development courses or net-seminars. Whatever the format, the target of professional development for technology must be an opportunity for classroom teachers to examine their goals of instruction and related educational technology resources so they may construct an understanding of educational technology as an instructional tool.

Specifically, these extended learning opportunities should guide teachers in the instructional design I have laid out in the three classroom educational technology integration principles. By having sufficient time to explore educational technology and having their technological imagination sparked by examples of it in use, teachers can identify which materials match their learning outcomes (eTIP #1). Professional development sessions should also provide frameworks or criteria that can aid a teacher in determining whether or not an educational technology resource brings any added value to teaching or learning (eTIP #2). Likewise, through examples and discussion, teachers should have opportunity to consider how might educational technology aid the formative or summative assessment of students' learning (eTIP #3).

Professional development targeted at successful technology integration at a school increases the effectiveness of technology by ensuring that teachers' learning needs are met with both "how to operate" and "how to integrate" sessions. Because technology integration should be in support of specific outcomes and add value to and assist in the assessment of those outcomes, the professional development sessions would ideally be specific for grade levels and customized to match the outcomes they teach. This means that overall, curriculum connections should often be the central focus of technology professional development sessions and facilitate sharing or instructional planning time.

Teachers reflect on, discuss, and provide feedback about the role of and support for educational technology. This principle describes a professional collaborative environment for integrating and implementing technology. In such an environment technology use would be more effective because the school organization would recognize the contribution individuals make to the collective knowledge of the school (Marks & Louis, 1999). And the entire staff would work toward consensus about the school's performance, in this case with technology, and how they could improve it (Marks & Louis, 1997). A collaborative professional community would serve as the vehicle for school-wide knowledge processing about technology integration and implementation, increasing the likelihood of reflective dialogue, sharing of instructional practices, and generally increasing collaboration on new practices.

When a school staff has habits of discussing the ways technology is used and supported, they will identify ways to make the technology environment at the school more conducive to effective use. Such collaboration might come from a number of sources; for example, if teachers from all grade levels or subjects were represented on a school's technology committee. When school leaders systematically seek input from teachers and these ideas are used to guide future goals for and decisions about educational technology, this feedback can assist in planning for future educational technology purchases and be used to improve the quality of technology support. When technology integration is regularly discussed among colleagues, they are likely to develop shared goals for technology use. When teachers are asked to reflect on the role of technology in their classroom, it is likely that they will recognize ways to become more effective integrators. Teachers can self-assess their use against shared schoolwide goals as well as set personal goals for their technology uses.

When technology integration is underway at a school where teachers' interactions are characterized by professional collaboration, it increases the likelihood of all the other eTIPs being in place, and thus the effective use of technology. In a collaborative environment teachers share their successes, or failures, at matching technology to outcomes. They can talk about their hopes or fears for whether technology will add value to their classroom, and what was revealed or obscured about student performance. A school that works to learn from all its members uses input from technology novices and experts alike to create high quality technology support.

QUESTIONS FOR FURTHER CONSIDERATION

In the following section, I present questions to prompt teachers' awareness of and work towards each of the educational technology integration and implementation principles (eTIPs). I designed them to be used by teachers while planning instruction in order to guide their thinking through the additional issues and questions that are raised when integrating and implementing technology.

After determining the lesson or unit objections, consider the following additional issues and questions about the appropriateness of integrating technology into the instruction.

Questions for eTIP 1: Learning Outcomes Drive the Selection of Technology

- Which objectives or standards does the technology complement and support? Are these mainly content area objectives or process skills?
- What is the cognitive demand on the learner as they use the technology?

After determining your lesson or unit objections, the following questions guide teachers' thinking through adding value by integrating technology.

Questions for eTIP 2: Technology Use Provides Added Value to Teaching and Learning

- How does using the technology add to what the teacher or students can do? Compared to other resources, what added value does the technology bring to the teacher or students' work?
- What are the costs and benefits? Do students have sufficient skills with the computer's operating system to use the technology? What menu items or operational skills do students need to use the technology? Will developing the necessary prerequisite skills require extensive instructional time? Would all students need these prerequisites or could students be grouped with an "expert"? How does the time required for the integration of the technology balance with the instructional goals and objectives?
- Would using the technology require the teacher to overcome inordinately difficult logistics (i.e., to secure sufficient electrical outlets, tables, or chairs and space for the computers)?

After determining the lesson or unit outcomes and that educational technology would add value to students' work towards those outcomes, these next questions can guide teachers' thinking through how integrating technology could help assess student learning.

Questions for eTIP 3: Technology Assists in the Assessment of the Learning Outcomes

- What criteria will be used to evaluate student work? In the assessment, will students' capability with the software also be assessed?
- How can the students' technology-supported work help you learn what they know and can do?
- How does a technology-supported performance demonstrate progress toward specific content standards?

These next questions can help teachers to determine whether or not the access to educational technology is ready enough that the added value provided by the capabilities of the educational technology outweighs the effort required to work through any logistics.

Questions for eTIP 4: Ready Access to Supported Technology is Provided

- What technology will the students or teacher need to complete the task?
- Are enough of the technology resources available during the time frame you will need them?
- Are the resources available in locations and configurations that fit your

time and space needs?
- Does the level of availability of the technology resources suggest that students will work individually or in groups for the different tasks or components of the lesson?
- Who is available to assist with the setup and troubleshooting of the technology resources? How quickly can they respond if you need assistance?

The following questions can guide teachers as they determine any learning needs they have for the technologies they are considering using.

Questions for eTIP 5: Professional Development is Targeted at Successful Technology Integration

- What professional development or instructional support might you need to implement this technology integration?
- Are there online resources, classes, or individuals that could show you how to operate the technology?

The questions below could be used to guide teachers' thinking through the additional issues and questions that are raised by integrating and implementing technology in a collaborative professional community.

Questions for eTIP 6: Teachers Reflect, Discuss, and Provide Feedback about the Role of and Support for Educational Technology

- With whom can you talk or share to gather insight about your integration experiences?
- How can you capture your integration experiences to share them with others?
- How will you make your integration experiences more public, so others can learn from you?

CONCLUSION

In addition to helping teachers recognize and plan for effective technology use, the educational technology integration principles (eTIPs) can be adapted for other purposes. For example, job candidates might use them as a framework to organize questions to ask during an interview and to determine whether or not they might like the technology environment at the school site, if offered a job. Generating indicators for the presence of each principle could be used as a checklist by a school technology team to conduct a needs assessment. Teachers could use them to determine the kinds of input and guidance to provide during technology planning or evaluation efforts.

Overall, these educational technology integration and implementation principles point out the two key aspects of teachers designing effective integrated instruction: the technology use must match and support teaching and learning, and the larger school environment must provide support for the logistical and learning demands technology integration puts on teachers.

ACKNOWLEDGMENTS

The author would like to acknowledge the Ed-U-Tech (see http://education.umn.edu/edutech) at the University of Minnesota project staff members and collaborators Marc Johnson, Rachel Brown, Aaron Doering, Christine Greenhow, Gary Burns and Greg Sales for their contributions to the ideas represented in the eTIPs. Their conversation at project meetings, contributions to presentations, and feedback on this chapter made it a better piece of work than it otherwise would have been. I am grateful for their collaboration.

REFERENCES

CEO Forum on Education & Technology. (1999). School technology and readiness report: Professional development: A link to better learning, February 22. Available on the World Wide Web at: http://ceoforum.org/reports.cfm?RID=2.

Dexter, S., Anderson, R. E. and Ronnkvist, A. (In Press). Quality technology support: What is it? Who has it? and What difference does it make? *Journal of Educational Computing Research.*

Dockterman, D. (1991). *Great Teaching in the One-Computer Classroom.* Watertown, MA:Tom Snyder Productions.

Jonassen, D. H. (2000). *Computers as Mindtools for Schools: Engaging Critical Thinking* (2nd ed.). Columbus, OH: Prentice-Hall.

Marks, H. M. and Louis, K. S. (1997). Does teacher empowerment affect the classroom? The implications of teacher empowerment for instructional practice and student academic performance. *Educational Evaluation & Policy Analysis*, 3, 245-275.

Marks, H. M. and Louis, K. S. (1999). Teacher empowerment and the capacity for organizational learning. *Educational Administration Quarterly*, 5, 707-750.

Means, B., Olson, K. and Singh, R. (1995). Beyond the Classroom: Restructuring Schools With Technology, September. *Phi Delta Kappan*, 69-72

Ronnkvist, A. M., Dexter, S. L. and Anderson, R. E. (2000). Technology support: Its depth, breadth and impact in America's schools. *Report from the Teaching, Learning and Computing: 1998 survey*. Available on the World Wide Web at: http://www.crito.uci.edu/tlc/html/findings.html.

Chapter IV

Teaching in the Digital Age: "Teaching as You Were Taught" Won't Work

Gay Fawcett and Margarete Juliana
Kent State University, USA

INTRODUCTION

Playing school. It's a part of childhood. Children don't have to be taught to do it; they just do it. The pretend "teacher" gathers her pretend "students" in the basement, on the back porch, or on the school playground and they reenact what they know so well. Some of those "pretend" teachers grow up to be "real" teachers, and they continue to reenact what they know so well— models of teaching and learning that have predominated in the United States for nearly a century. For years that worked, but it won't work now. Teachers can no longer look backward for models of teaching; the digital age demands that they look forward and create new models.

A year 2000 survey by the National Center for Education Statistics found that only one teacher in ten felt "very well prepared" to integrate technology into his/her classroom (Teacher Use of Computers and the Internet in Public Schools, 2000). Teachers typically respond to this lack of preparation in one of three ways. First, many teachers simply ignore the technology. Nearly 40% of teachers surveyed said their students don't use computers at all (Trotter, 1999). A second response is to "play school" with the technology, reenacting old models of teaching that don't take advantage of the capabilities of technology to help students learn in new ways. A third response is to look forward and create new models of teaching and learning. Unfortunately, this is an uncommon response, not because of teacher incompetence, but because of a system that does not encourage or reward such risk-taking.

A FRAMEWORK FOR IMPROVEMENT

In order to teach effectively in the digital age, teachers must realize that "teaching as you were taught" will no longer work. We believe that teachers will come to this realization when faced with three things: (1) research, (2) instructional models, and (3) success stories. We are creating all three in the Ameritech Electronic University School Classroom at Kent State University. The purpose of this chapter is to share our research, success stories, and instructional model with you as a scaffold to help you look forward and create your own new models of teaching and learning.

Ameritech Electronic University School Classroom

The Ameritech Classroom opened in Spring 1998 and is housed in the newly renovated Moulton Hall at Kent State University. The purpose of the Classroom is to provide a technology-based classroom for K-12 students and a research laboratory for college faculty and education majors. The Classroom is comprised of an observation room and two classrooms, each equipped with up-to-date computers, AMX integrated systems, extensive peripherals, and a support team. The Classroom is "school" for students for a half day, every day as they complete six to twelve week units of study. The teachers choose which instructional units they will teach within the Classroom. Most units reflect an interdisciplinary examination of a particular K-12 curricular topic.

Researchers in the one-of-a-kind, attached observation room study the impact of technology on teaching and learning. Their findings are shared widely with educators, legislators, and pre-service teachers so that the lessons learned can benefit large numbers of teachers and students. We anticipate that the understandings generated by this exciting classroom concept will contribute greatly to the development of technology-based knowledge and skills that will be of value in meeting the educational needs of our nation's children.

Research. The research agenda for the Ameritech Classroom was established by a statewide (Ohio) network of researchers who determined that the questions below must be examined in order to fill gaps that currently exist in research regarding the impact of technology on teaching and learning.

- Under what conditions can technology be used by students for problem solving, inquiry, and critical thinking, and what is the impact of such use on student learning?
- Under what conditions do pre-service teachers learn to make decisions about effective uses of technology for higher order thinking?
- What alternative assessments can be used to measure student learning when technology is used for higher order thinking?

A sampling of the questions currently being explored include the following: (1) How do Internet communication technologies facilitate learner interaction and promote learning through collaboration and authentic learning contexts? (2) What is the nature of teacher-student interactions in a technology-rich classroom? (3) What is the nature of online communication between deaf students and hearing students? (4) How do students identified as learning disabled learn in a technology-rich classroom when paired with non-learning disabled peers? While it is too early to draw definite conclusions, we are encouraged with preliminary findings that indicate the potential for technology to improve teaching and learning.

Instructional Model

Constructivism. Ameritech Classroom teachers meet for a full week in the summer and then monthly after school to prepare for their visit to the Classroom. During these sessions they design units of instruction that will provide opportunities for students to use technology for high level thinking and real world problem solving.

The entire instructional model is based on our conviction that unless teachers examine their deeply held beliefs about teaching and learning, technology-based instruction will make no more difference than any of the dozens of other educational reform efforts that have come and gone. Thus, the workshop begins with small groups working together to list as many educational bandwagons as they can. Needless to say, there is no shortage of ideas. We then discuss why we are so "change adept" (we can do it!) but so "change inept" (we just can't do it well!) (Phillip Schlechty, personal communication, May 23, 1999). We caution that unless we spend time examining how we teach and how children learn, and what the implications are for technology-based instruction, we run the risk of adding one more bandwagon to the list.

The video *Private Universe* (Sadler & Schneps, 1988) sets the stage for the examination of current research on the brain and how humans learn. The video offers a series of interviews with Harvard graduates and faculty as well as with eighth grade students regarding the cause of the seasons. Most teachers who view the video are astounded at the inaccurate understanding the interviewees have "constructed" of this science concept and how difficult it is to convince them otherwise.

The stage is set for discussion of current learning theory. Teachers are often surprised to learn that the popular educational term *constructivism* is not synonymous with discovery learning, student centered learning, or hands-on projects. Instead, as the video illustrates, constructivism is about how human beings *construct* meaning by putting new information with their existing knowledge. Whether doing a science experiment, listening to a lecture, or reading a book, students are always constructing meaning (Brooks & Brooks, 1993; Sylwester, 1995). The teachers discuss practical ways to find out what existing knowledge students have and how to continually check their new constructions. Strategies such as journals, KWL, group discussions, and anticipation guides are demonstrated by the teachers and by the instructors. Later these strategies will be integrated into the units they develop.

Inquiry. A great deal of time is spent in gaining an understanding of the difference between *inquiry* and *questions* (Lindfors, 1999; McKenzie, 2000; Short & Burke, 1991). Jamie McKenzie's definition of essential questions guides the process: "These are the questions that touch our hearts and souls. They are central to our lives. They help to define what it means to be human" (2000, p.14). It is a difficult concept for teachers who have been trained to ask questions with tidy answers, but the meaning becomes clearer when examples are provided, such as the following from actual classrooms:

- Why were slaves black and not white? (fifth grade students studying the Civil War)
- Whose America is it anyway? (high school students studying immigration)
- Could the nations of Europe be the United State of Europe? (high school students studying European history)
- What does it mean to be a good friend? (first grade students studying family and friends)

In collegial groups the teachers develop essential questions for their units that become the center of all the activities, lessons, and assessments of the unit. Fred Newmann's (1996) characteristics of inquiry serve as a guide to ensure that the questions will lead to authentic student achievement:

- The question builds on an established knowledge base. That is, in order to be answered students must draw on solid academics such as mathematics, history, English, etc.
- Pursuing the question leads to deep understanding of an issue. It will require more than memorization of facts that will be forgotten soon after the test.

- Answering the question requires the learner to elaborate in some way rather than just give a brief answer. S/he will have to write, discuss, enact, perform, etc.

A few examples of guiding questions that the Ameritech Classroom teachers have developed include the following:

- How do patterns affect our lives? (learning disabilities class unit on patterns in math, poetry, the natural world, and human habits)
- Do I dare give up my bear? (a third grade unit on risk-taking)
- Could it happen here? (a high school unit on the Holocaust)

Unit development. With this foundation in place, the teachers are ready to develop a unit. Using Grant Wiggins framework for a unit design (Wiggins & McTighe, 1998), the teachers first define the desired results for their units. They have online access to the state curricula and are reminded that inquiry does not mean "anything goes." Once they define the results, they define what would constitute acceptable evidence that the students had achieved those results. Evidence could be anything from a traditional test, to a project, a debate, or a performance. The key is that students strive for deep understanding. Next, the teachers plan learning experiences and instruction that will promote that understanding.

Only at that point in time do the teachers consider the technology—what will they need to help students learn? Using a combination of prior experience, conversations with their colleagues, expert advice, and research on technology alternatives, the teachers incorporate a variety of technologies to suit their unit plans. Each teacher's effort to create a thorough unit plan supported by technology rather than dictated by it results in noteworthy successes. The classroom experiences described next, ranging from second grade to high school, illustrate how this instructional model is implemented.

SUCCESS STORIES

Anne and Roosevelt Kids

At-risk students: the term conjures up images of disaffected kids who are, at best, reluctant to be in school. A unique program in Kent City Schools (Ohio) ninth grade class is seeking to challenge these students to connect with learning through a curriculum tailored to support and encourage them to make learning personally relevant. Though this five-teacher team had used computers in their classroom for writing and some Internet searching, they had not used it as intensively as they planned in the Ameritech Classroom.

How the unit was designed. The unit under investigation was the Holocaust. Anne had taught this unit for five years as a standard unit for the ninth graders in her high school. Though viewed as a language arts unit, a primary objective of the unit was to heighten students' awareness and understanding of prejudice and discrimination. Anne's essential question was "Could it happen here?"

Although Anne and her students used technology in their home school, they had not incorporated the use of technology as comprehensively as they would in the Ameritech Classroom. Anne knew the unit would change fundamentally through her decision to fully use the Ameritech Classroom facilities. First, it became more student-directed. Anne had been teaching the class in lecture format prior to this experience. Her redesign of the Holocaust unit included having students pick their own topics of inquiry. This occurred after initial discussions and readings about the events before, during, and after World War II. Anne knew that student selected topics would hold more interest than if she assigned them. The students would also show greater commitment to researching their topic areas.

Next, Anne knew that traditional tests she normally gave would not fit this technology intensive and student-directed design. She provided her students a list of potential formats for final projects, but students were not limited to the list. Students were also given an overview of the various technologies to be used for their projects by the Ameritech Classroom technology specialist. Students then chose a format and various technologies to begin designing their final projects as they continued to research the topic they had chosen to investigate.

Students' final projects reflected a variety of project topics and formats. Peer evaluation was used and students assessed each other's final projects using a teacher-created rubric. Final interviews with Anne and a team-teacher revealed that the students learned as much as students in prior years had learned, but because of the student directed approach and variety in presentation options, the students' interest level was higher, as was their commitment to the projects. This interest level was evident in some of the connections the students made about their chosen topics and a personal understanding of their world. One student's PowerPoint presentation about the resistance movement ended with two side-by-side photos. The first picture was of a group of armed men from the resistance movement during WWII. Beside it was another picture of a group of armed men from the Black Panthers. The student questioned why people viewed these two groups so differently if both groups were dedicated to resisting oppression. This connection was inspired by the student's own reflection of his knowledge of the events of these periods of history.

How technology was built into the unit. Multiple technologies were used throughout the experience. Information about the Holocaust came from book-marked Web sites and Web searches conducted by the students. Several students used PowerPoint and explored the flexibility of the program. (One student designed a presentation on the Jewish ghettos with modern day popular music about living in a ghetto as background.) In one project about the children of the Holocaust, a student created original artwork (using a graphics tablet) and wrote original poetry. Still another small group project focused on video interviews with students back at the home school about issues concerning the medical experiments conducted during the Holocaust.

What made this a "success story." Anne, the lead teacher for this unit, was nervous about students' success within a more independent learning environment, but she was convinced about the design changes when she saw the hard work and dedication these students devoted to their projects. The students made connections between the world of World War II Germany and Holocaust suffering and their own personal worlds. Multimedia became a bridge between their personal modern world and historical events as it was used to create original work. Observers could see the quiet concentration of the students and the proud ownership of their work when it was presented at the end of the unit.

Bunny—I'll Never Teach the Same Again!

Bunny, a veteran third grade teacher, was no scared rabbit when she emerged from the technology intensive teaching experience in the Ameritech Classroom, and neither were her students. In fact, she was amazed at how confident her students were as they progressed through their six-week unit in which they used a wide variety of technology to learn about weather and its effect on our everyday lives. Follow-up interviews showed that this confidence continued in their school classroom after the Ameritech Classroom experience.

How the unit was designed. Bunny's integrated unit on weather employed the question "How does weather affect our lives?" to guide the students' learning experience in the Ameritech Classroom. Unlike her typical classroom experience, Bunny had students do most projects in cooperative pairs. Bunny elicited some student choice on topics and on the choice of partners. Classmates often critiqued one another's presentations of projects, while Bunny used rubrics to assess the completed projects. As Bunny made clear, she did not have significant experience in allowing student choice, partner projects, and non-traditional grading.

How technology was built into the unit. Because this class spent up to 80 minutes a day driving to and from their home school to the Ameritech Classroom, they took advantage of the Alpha Smart word processors. These small units enable simple text word processing that is later downloaded to computer. The World Wide Web (WWW) was used extensively as a resource for weather related topics. The teacher used the Elmo™ document camera as she read books aloud and showed weather maps from the newspaper. Students also used the Elmo™ for their presentations. Students used three programs extensively, Microsoft Word, PowerPoint, and KidPix, throughout their Ameritech Classroom experience. Digital cameras were used to capture relevant images to illustrate their presentations.

What made this a "success story." Bunny challenged her students and herself to use technology to go beyond the limits of her traditional teaching and their traditional learning. Her third grade students surpassed her prior expectations and broke the boundaries she unconsciously set about children's learning. Bunny was convinced that technology became a catalyst for her to see how responsive and independent students could be toward learning and sharing their knowledge with classmates.

Teacher Team and Brown Middle School Seventh Graders

As one of the first classes in the Ameritech Classroom, the Brown Middle School students became known as the "Ameritech Kids." Hand picked to come to Kent State University to experience nine weeks in a technology-immersed classroom, these students experienced a learning environment outside of their normal routine of bells, crowded hallways, and interruptions of thought. The teachers had worked together for over 20 years and proved to be a superlative team ready to capitalize on the opportunities that technology and other resources made available to them.

How the unit was designed. The unit "The Planet Under Stress" provided the backbone to their essential question of "How do we live in a planet under stress?" The interdisciplinary unit included a variety of lessons to investigate global problems. Small group and cooperative work promoted team problem solving. Lots of student choice in the areas that the students wanted to investigate, coupled with choice in how they presented their findings, made student involvement and interaction quite high.

How technology was built into the unit. This teacher team was determined to get everything possible out of the Ameritech Classroom experience. Though they came to the classroom with some experience with computers (mostly Macintosh), they were somewhat nervous about the prospect of handling a technology-immersed classroom. They drew on prior experience they had with technology and sought creative ways to use what they had at their disposal. For example, Pat, the science teacher, used the microscope and TV connection to see Daphnia organisms used for a population study. This data was then graphed in Excel. Students took advantage of the many multimedia tools available for final projects by using video, digital cameras, and the Elmo™ document camera to present findings in a variety of formats. Hyperstudio and PowerPoint figured prominently in many of the students' final projects.

What made this a "success story." The teachers started with the units of study and with the curriculum and then began to imagine the variety of ways in which technology could enhance the units. Students were encouraged early on to become teachers as well as learners. Intellectual sharing became a hallmark in the classroom, whether that was content, concepts, or technical expertise. Teachers could sense a palpable pride students had in their work as individuals and in small group projects. Each new project became an opportunity to work toward a "personal best." Additionally, teachers fostered caring interactions between students. They could sense that working in teams was something new to some students and saw it as an opportunity to help students broaden their interpersonal skills and to personally mature.

Kellie's Second Grade Students

How do you get second graders interested in the Mayflower's historic journey?—by focusing on the children, whose pivotal roles during that first winter ensured the survival of the Pilgrims. Just as the Mayflower's children were pioneers in their day, Kellie's second graders pioneered learning in innovative ways. Kellie, the driving force behind this innovation, believes that children learn best when given age appropriate content, rich classroom conversations about the topic's issues, and a variety of resources to express themselves.

How the unit was designed. Kellie's unit was interdisciplinary, including science, social studies, math and health. She was especially adept at providing a variety of literacy activities using the technology, which heightened students' understanding about what constitutes good writing. This was evident in the students' interest in and concern about their own writing. Rather than being satisfied with writing just to satisfy their teacher's need for written work, these second graders applied their growing understanding about the writing process to a variety of projects.

Students learned specifically about the Mayflower experience through the Peanuts' video *This is America, Charlie Brown - The Mayflower Voyages* (Paramount, 1989), the book *On the Mayflower* (Waters, 1996), read aloud by

Kellie, and student searches on Yahooligans. Kellie included group discussion and brainstorming about Mayflower topics and had student pairs decide on a topic of interest. An interactive Web-based tour of the Mayflower further helped children choose a topic on which to focus. The students worked in pairs to make a KidPix show about the experiences of the people of the Mayflower voyage and their difficult first winter.

How technology was built into the unit. Technology was used for a vast variety of literacy purposes. Students used the Alpha Smarts to journal about their class experience. They used email to write each other and to send email to parents and other adults in their lives. An online dictionary and electronic card site provided yet more opportunities for students to practice reading and writing using their Mayflower-related vocabulary words.

Students used paper and pencil to develop the storyboard for their Mayflower KidPix show, for which each student pair recorded a narration. The software program Inspiration provided opportunities for the students to create Web diagrams about the Pilgrim children's responsibilities, and the Venn diagram allowed them to compare and contrast their life experiences with those of the Pilgrims.

What made this a "success story." Kellie's dynamic and fluid teaching style encouraged her children to be thoughtful about learning. She modeled a comfort with technology and encouraged students to share skills and knowledge freely. Most important, Kellie was very comfortable with expanding her students' growing literacy skills through technology. She did not pass up an opportunity to allow the children to use technology to explore reading and writing as well as other subject areas. She made it clear to the students that though reading and writing may take effort, it was a worthwhile effort. The students' work was high quality. They used complex sentences and concentrated on details such as spelling corrections. They didn't hesitate to redo or refine their work if they believed it was necessary. This effort was heightened by Kellie's conferencing with the students and having them critique their own work and make suggestions for improvement.

CONCLUSION

Because teachers cannot "teach as they were taught," they need support in their growing professional challenge of being teachers in the digital age. This support is a significant goal of the Ameritech Electronic University School Classroom. Teachers are provided opportunities to use a growing body of research about teaching and learning as a starting point to discuss their beliefs about teaching and learning. Ample time is built in to talk with their colleagues and to reflect on how teaching practices affect the way they construct learning in their classrooms.

Teachers are then given opportunities to work with their colleagues to develop unit plans that will provide meaningful learning opportunities for their students. Teachers keep the state curricula objectives in mind as they develop essential questions, lesson plans, and acceptable assessment criteria for their upcoming experience in the Ameritech Classroom. Lastly, they think about the various technologies that will be used to support their students' learning goals.

As we work with Ameritech Classroom teachers, they continually tell us how important it is that they have time to dialogue with other teachers about their successes and struggles with integrating technology into teaching and learning. Indeed, in the important national *Teaching, Learning and Computing* study, researchers found that teachers who are involved in the teaching lives of their peers are more likely than other teachers to be constructivist in beliefs, practice, and computer use (Riel & Becker, 2000).

QUESTIONS FOR FURTHER CONSIDERATION

The following questions are provided as a starting point for teachers seeking a framework for such discussions with their colleagues.

Research
- What are three classic research studies that could inform how we use technology?
- How would the findings from those studies play out in my classroom?
- What question could we investigate as a group of practicing teachers that would help us learn how to use technology effectively with our students?

Instructional Models
- What are three key principles of learning that we can apply to technology-rich instruction?
- What can technology help our students do that they could not do otherwise?
- What do we need to keep doing, stop doing, or change in our teaching?

Success Stories
- What success stories do we have to tell?
- Who needs to hear our stories?
- Whose stories do we need to hear?

We believe that with such structured collegial conversations, teachers will look to the future and create new models of teaching and learning for the digital age.

REFERENCES

Brooks, J. G. and Brooks, M. G. (1993). *The Case for Constructivist Classrooms*. Alexandria, VA: Association for Supervisions and Curriculum Development.

Caine, R. M. and Caine, G. (1997). *Education on the Edge of Possibility*. Alexandria, VA: Association for Supervision and Curriculum Development.

Lindfors, J. W. (1999). *Children's Inquiry: Using Language to Make Sense of the World*. New York, NY: Teachers College Press.

McKenzie, J. (2000). *Beyond Technology: Questioning, Research and the Information Literate School*. Bellingham, WA: From Now On Press.

Newmann, F. M. & Associates. (1996). *Authentic Achievement: Restructuring Schools for Intellectual Quality*. San Francisco, CA: Jossey-Bass.

Paramount Pictures (Producer). (1989). *This is America, Charlie Brown–The Mayflower Voyages* [Videotape]. Paramount Pictures.

Riel, M. and Becker, H. (2000). The beliefs, practices, and computer use of teacher leaders. Paper presented at the *Meeting of the American Educational Research Association*, April, New Orleans, LA.

Sadler, P. M. (Producer) and Schneps, M. H. (Director). (1988). A private universe [Film]. Available from Annenberg/CPB, 1-800-LEARNER or http://www.learner.org/catalog/pricelist.php.

Short, K. G. and Burke, C. (1991). *Creating Curriculum: Teachers and Students as a Community of Learners*. Portsmouth, NH: Heinemann.

Sylwester, R. (1995). *A Celebration of Neurons: An Educator's Guide to the Human Brain*. Alexandria, VA: Association for Supervision and Curriculum Development.

Teacher Use of Computers and the Internet in Public Schools. (2000). Washington, D.C.: U.S. Department of Education, Office of Educational Research and Improvement.

Waters, K. (1996). *On the Mayflower*. New York: Scholastic Press.

Wiggins, G. and McTighe, J. (1998). *Understanding by Design*. Alexandria, VA: Association for Supervision and Curriculum Design.

Chapter V

Constructing Technology Learning Activities to Enhance Elementary Students' Learning

Diane L. Judd
Valdosta State University, USA

INTRODUCTION

This chapter of the section presents four technology-integrated activities as models for elementary teachers to enhance their curriculum. During the last three years, in-service and pre-service teachers have implemented all of these activities with elementary students.

Objectives for This Chapter of the Section

The purpose of this chapter of the section is to assist elementary teachers to integrate technology into their curriculum through instructions and models of activities and projects. The extension suggestions and supporting information for each activity are provided to assist teachers in designing activities for their students, their learning objectives, and their curricula. The goals of these activities are to encourage and support teachers in their use of technology and to promote students' engagement in learning through productivity and creativity.

The four technology-integrated activities include: Playing Musical Computers with Creative Writing; What's the Connection?; Be an Artist, Paint a Picture-Story; and Where in the World is...? All of the activities encourage students to be creative and to develop a product by using problem solving and thinking skills.

The first activity is Playing Musical Computers with Creative Writing, which encourages students to develop a creative writing project with the inspiration of clip art. This activity can be an easy way for teachers to begin the integration of technology into their curriculum because of the ease of implementation. The second technology-integrated activity, What's the Connection?, is created through the use of concept webbing in a word processing program. This versatile activity could be developed and implemented as a curriculum project or an assessment product.

The third activity, Where in the World is...?, assists teachers in the process of integrating social studies, mathematics, and technology for their students. This activity also includes links to resources to aid teachers in their search for informational Web sites. In the fourth activity, students paint a picture using a paint program (e.g., Microsoft Paint, 1997). The completed picture can be pasted on a page in a word processing program and a story or content information can be added to go with the picture.

Each technology-integrated activity includes a quick reference table, an illustrated example of the activity, a sparking suggestion table, and an Internet resource site. The quick reference table summarizes the directions for easy reference in planning and teaching each activity. An illustrated model is provided as an example of the completed activity. The sparking suggestion tables can be used by teachers as springboards to modify presented activities and to spark ideas for designing activities that would enhance their curriculum. An Internet resource site has been developed for each activity to provide additional assistance and includes directions and examples of the activities.

This chapter has two main objectives. The first is that the teacher will understand how to integrate technology into the curriculum. The second objective is that the teacher will understand how to design activities to enhance the curriculum for his or her students.

BACKGROUND INFORMATION

The pressure to integrate technology into the curriculum has been felt by many educators. The public and educational administrators often place the burden of proof of integrating technology into the school's curriculum on classroom teachers (Glenn & Carrier, 1986; Johnson, 1997; Wiburg, 1995).

To decrease and alleviate these technology related pressures, educators are seeking ways to modify or change teaching methods that include the integration of technology into the curriculum.

Teachers are moving away from delivering all the information to their students to assisting students as facilitators in activities to acquire new knowledge (Collis, Knezek, Lai, Miyashita, Pelgrum, Plomp, & Sakamoto, 1996). Researchers have noted these changing trends in education and have investigated the uses of educational tools and the variations of educational philosophies in classrooms. The worldwide Information Technology in Education and Children (ITEC) study gave reflective insights concerning these changes by stating that learning has moved away from traditional indoctrination to cognitive constructivism (Collis et al., 1996). The ITEC study emphasized that computer usage is also changing. "Children initiate use of and actively employ computers as tools for problem solving, data retrieval, discovering principles and rules of natural and social phenomena, measuring natural phenomena, and controlling robots and machines" (p. 121).

A constructivist learning environment is defined by Wilson (1995) as "a place where learners may work together and support each other as they use a variety of tools and information resources in their pursuit of learning goals and problem-solving activities" (p. 28). Constructivism is a basic principle of the Piagetian theory, and its doctrines assert that "individuals of whatever age acquire understandings of the world about them primarily through an analysis of their own actions upon the world" (Lambert & McCombs, 1998, p. 413).

Seymour Papert, who worked with Piaget, combined the constructivist theories with the use of technology. Papert believes that computers in a technology learning environment are used as a tool "to manipulate, to extend, to apply to projects" (1980, p. 2) and that a computer could allow a child to enhance and control his or her learning. In the technology enhanced learning environments studied by Collis and Lai (1996), they report that students participated more in student-centered interactions, and the students were also more enthusiastic about computer-based lessons than other lessons.

The projects and activities in this chapter were developed from my research in learning processes and my studies of educational technology. As a result, the design principle of the presented activities places the focus on the learner to use thinking and problem-solving skills to be creative and productive.

An advocator of keeping students at the center of learning, Judi Harris (2000) described enriched Internet activities and computers as tools that "should be used in service of students' learning needs" (p. 11). Keeping with the Judi Harris spirit, I am hopeful that this chapter will help guide pre-service and in-service teachers to design technology-enhanced activities that will meet the needs of their students.

HOW TO BEGIN DESIGNING FOR ELEMENTARY STUDENTS

Integrating technology into the curriculum can be compared to many other tasks where often the hardest part of the task is just getting started. The first activity, "Playing Musical Computers with Creative Writing," usually provides a smooth beginning and a successful experience for students and teachers. All the activities in this chapter were developed to be easily duplicated and to serve as models for teachers to design activities to enhance their curriculum.

Pre-service and in-service teachers have commented that the examples of the activities they have developed were helpful to use as models when they were teaching their lessons. I believe it would be beneficial for teachers to develop models or examples before presenting the activities. As a result, teachers will have examples to share with their students, and the teachers will also be able to discuss the activity processes from their personal experiences. Teachers may be able to anticipate learning concepts and/or difficulties that their students could encounter while working on the activities.

Playing Musical Computers with Creative Writing Activity

The Playing Musical Computers with Creative Writing activity has proven to be an effective way for teachers to begin integrating technology into their curriculum. Teachers usually report that it is an easy activity to implement and most students enjoy the activity.

This activity is comprised of two parts: picture selection and creative writing. Students begin this activity by opening a blank page in a word processing program, such as Microsoft Word 2000 (1999). During the first part, the students select a designated numbers of pictures (i.e., four, five, six) from clip art or a picture file and paste them on the blank page. The students selecting the pictures can give the page a title and list their name as the person who selected the pictures. The pictures can be selected at random or based around a theme (e.g., animals, transportation), or a subject area (e.g., science, social studies).

After all the students copy and paste their pictures, the teacher explains that they are going to play musical computers by moving to a different computer where one of their peers has selected pictures. If this activity is conducted in a computer lab or a classroom with several computers, the teacher may give a time allowance, such as 20 seconds, to find a computer. This seems to increase the level of excitement. After moving to a computer with pictures that were selected by a peer, the student then writes a creative story that includes all the pictures selected by their peer, Figure 1. Students can add their name as the author of the writing project.

The previous directions are for implementing the activity for two or more computers. This creative writing activity can also be used when students have access to only one computer. Students can rotate and take turns doing this activity. First, a student selects the pictures on the class computer. Then another student writes a creative story and selects pictures for the next student.

The quick reference table (Table 1) gives at-a-glance directions for the Playing Musical Computers with Creative Writing activity. These brief directions are also included on the Web resource site for this activity at http://chiron.valdosta.edu/djudd/elementary1.html.

The sparking suggestion table (Table 2) provides additional suggestions of ways that teachers could use to modify the Playing Musical Computers with Creative Writing activity. This table was also developed to assist and encourage teachers to custom design activities that would enhance their curriculum.

In addition, the Web resource site at http://chiron.valdosta.edu/djudd/elementary1.html was designed and developed for the Playing Musical Computers with Creative Writing activity. This Web site includes brief directions and links to examples to assist teachers.

Figure 1: Sample page for musical computers and writing activity

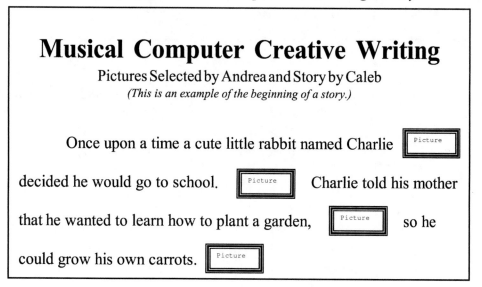

Table 1: Quick reference for Playing Musical Computers with Creative Writing activity

Quick Reference for Playing Musical Computers with Creative Writing
1. Open a word processing program to a blank page.
2. Peers select 6 pictures from clip art.
3. Change computers.
4. Write creative story to incorporate selected pictures.
5. Print and share creative stories with peers in class.

Table 2: Sparking suggestion table for Playing Musical Computers with Creative Writing activity

Suggestions to Spark Ideas for Your Class Using Playing Musical Computers with Creative Writing Activity
Change the number of pictures for creative writing to match the level and needs of students. **Example:** The teachers may want young or lower level students to select only four pictures.
Develop a picture gallery from pictures relating to specific subject areas. **Example:** A social studies teacher could select relevant pictures from clip art program on China or the rain forest.
Have students emphasize a particular part of speech when writing. **Example:** Students could print out their stories and underline all of the adjectives or exchange papers with a peer and find the adjectives in the peer's story.
Printed stories could be bound together to make a class book. **Example:** A class book of stories about China or a collection of students' creative stories.
Build-a-Story, a progressive writing activity. Students can take turns going to the computer to add a section to the story. Together the students can build a class story. **Example:** The story could center on a class field trip or topic in a subject area (e.g., If I Lived in Brazil, I Would …).

The assortment and selection of pictures usually inspire the students to write creative and interesting stories. Students can print their stories and share them with their peers in small groups or with the whole class. The students could also make copies of their stories and share them with younger students in their school.

What's the Connection?

What's the Connection? is a versatile activity in its usage in the classroom. It can be easily adapted to integrate technology with science, social studies, and language arts. The What's the Connection? activity can also be used to introduce, to develop, or to assess a topic in a subject area. This activity is implemented by using a program that can develop a concept Webbing map (e.g., Inspiration, 1999). Microsoft Word 2000 (1999) also has the capability to develop Webbing through the use of its drawing tools.

To begin this activity, open a drawing or Webbing program, such as Microsoft Word 2000 (1999). The illustrated example described was developed using Microsoft Word 2000 (1999). Since drawing tools will be needed, select the drawing toolbar, View > Toolbars > Drawing.

The example presented illustrates the concept Webbing used as an assessment tool for students. After studying the history of Cuba and its relations with the United States, the teacher can draw, label and connect keyword ovals with arrows, Figure 2.

The Webbing file is then saved as a document template. To do this go to File > Save As > (opens pop up window), give your file a name, Save As type: > select Document Template. This allows the file to be saved as a template and can be used over and over again without students changing the original template. The students will be able to use the template to add their work and save it as a separate document.

When using this as an assessment activity, the students can write the connection information in the boxes (e.g., John F. Kennedy and Cuba's connect-

Figure 2: A sample of concept Webbing

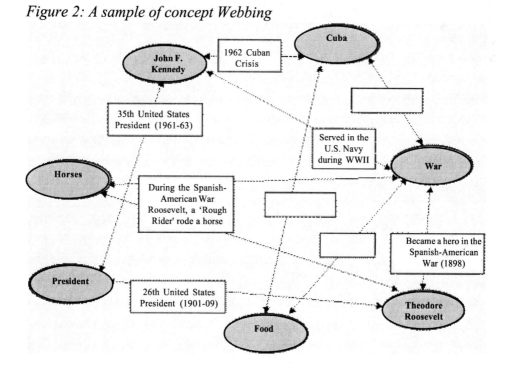

ing information box contains the 1962 Cuban Crisis), Figure 2. The students' concept Webbings can be saved and printed for sharing or evaluating.

The quick reference table, Table 3, gives at-a-glance directions for the What's the Connection? activity. These directions are included on the Web resource site at: http://chiron.valdosta.edu/djudd/elementary2.html.

The sparking suggestion table, Table 4, provides ideas for a variety of ability levels and curriculum areas to use in classrooms. Teachers can select and develop the What's the Connection? activity that is best for their students.

The Web resource site at: http://chiron.valdosta.edu/djudd/elementary2.html includes the quick reference directions and examples of the What's the Connection? activity. The students' concept Webs could be printed and shared in class or published on the Internet to share with others around the world.

Be an Artist, Paint a Picture Story

The Be an Artist, Paint a Picture Story activity has been implemented by in-service and pre-service teachers with kindergarteners through middle school grade students. During the past couple of years, I have received positive reflections and comments from teachers that have worked with the Be an Artist, Paint a Picture Story activity.

This activity incorporates both a drawing program and a word processing program. The example for this activity was developed by using the Microsoft Paint (1997) program and the Microsoft Word 2000 (1999) program. These programs work well and are commonly available to teachers and students. In the past, teachers have used several other writing and drawing programs with this activity and their students have developed wonderful products.

The Be an Artist, Paint a Picture Story activity is a good example of where a previously developed model by teachers seems to be beneficial for teachers and students. The firsthand experience by teachers makes it easier to explain and anticipate problems that their students may encounter.

Table 3: Quick reference for What's the Connection?

Quick Reference for What's the Connection?	
1.	Open Microsoft Word 2000 (1999) program.
2.	Select Drawing Toolbar (View > Toolbars > Drawing).
3.	Draw ovals and label.
4.	Save as a template (File > Save As > Document Template).
5.	Students open template in Microsoft Word 2000 program.
6.	Students draw connecting lines with boxes to write relationship information.
7.	Students save and print their concept Webs.

Table 4: Sparking suggestion table for What's the Connection?

Suggestions to Spark Ideas for Your Class Using What's the Connection? Activity
🖥 Change the number of keyword ovals to match the level and needs of students. **Example:** Teachers may want to have fewer keyword ovals for young or lower level students and additional ovals for older or higher level students.
🖥 Teachers may want to draw connecting arrows and information boxes for students, or students could develop their own concept Web on the topic to illustrate their understanding. **Example:** The concept Webbing can be as complete or incomplete as the needs of the students.
🖥 The concept Webbing could be used as an introduction to a topic to establish the material that the students already know to the new material to be presented. **Example:** When studying the U. S. Space Program, a concept web could link the information the students already know about space to prepare them for their future knowledge.
🖥 As students are working on topics they could organize their ideas and information in concept Webs. **Example:** After researching and finding information on the Internet about certain animals and their natural environment, students develop a concept Web of animals and their natural environments; this could include science, social studies, and technology.

Students begin this activity by opening a drawing program, such as Microsoft Paint (1997), which comes on many computers today. To open the Microsoft Paint (1997) program select Start >Programs >Accessories >Paint. It might be helpful to students before they start the activity to give a brief demonstration of the each of the drawing tools in the program (e.g., painting with the spray can, using the eraser).

The students can paint a picture of a creative writing story, a favorite book, or a selected topic in a curriculum area (e.g., animals that hibernate). Additional suggestions and examples are listed in the table of sparking ideas, Table 6. After the picture is completed, it can be copied and pasted in a word processing program to add a story or descriptive information to the picture. To select the picture and to copy it, begin by clicking on the "Select Button," the button with a rectangle on the Paint toolbar. Then drag crossbar to encompass the picture you want to copy and then Edit >Copy. After copying the picture, it is ready to paste in your word processing document.

Open a word processing program and paste the picture. Then stories or information can be written to go with the pictures. Links to examples of the picture stories developed by pre-service teachers at Valdosta State University to use as models for lessons with elementary students can be seen at http://chiron.valdosta.edu/djudd/elementary3.html. The quick reference guide for Be an Artist, Paint a Picture Story (Table 5) is also on the Web site.

Figure 3: Paintbrush picture

When combining the art in the picture story activity with writing of almost any topic in all subject areas, the possible suggestions and ideas seem infinite. A few suggestions are listed in the sparking idea table (Table 6) to assist teachers to design paint story activities to go with their curricula.

Teachers have reported that even students that are reluctant to write are motivated to write during this picture story activity. This activity is fun to share with peers, with younger students, or with the world when published on the Internet.

Where in the World is...?

The last activity, Where in the World is...?, effectively integrates social studies, mathematics, and technology through the development of fun and learning-based products. This activity could be implemented with a variety of subject objectives (e.g., understanding and comparing weather and facts of cities around the world) and group sizes (e.g., whole group, small groups or individuals).

Where in the World is...? includes several activities in its completed product. Teachers can decide if all or part of the activities would be best for their students. The first section includes searching and reporting information

Table 5: Quick reference for Be an Artist, Paint a Picture Story

Quick Reference for Be an Artist, Paint a Picture Story
1. Open Microsoft Paint (1997) program.
2. Paint a picture of a favorite book, a creative story, or a selected topic.
3. Copy picture and paste it into Microsoft Word 2000 (1999) program.
4. Add story to picture in Microsoft Word 2000 (1999).
5. Students share their picture stories with peers or with other classes.
6. Students can develop picture story class book or publish it on the Internet.

Table 6: Sparking suggestion table for Be an Artist, Paint a Picture Story

Suggestions to Spark Ideas for Be an Artist, Paint a Picture Story
🖥 My Favorite Book. **Example:** Students can select their favorite book or story for this activity.
🖥 A Page Out of History. **Example:** Students tell about an interesting event in history and paint a picture of the historical event (i.e., the first person walking on the moon). The students' pages could become the class history book.
🖥 My Creative Story. **Example:** Students write a creative story and paint a picture about the story.
🖥 Science in the Making. **Example:** Students can paint anything in nature (i.e., animals, plants, solar system, rain forest) and write descriptions to go with their pictures.
🖥 Worldwide Social Studies. **Example:** Students could select a country in the world to paint and describe its people, customs, or special events.

about the students' cities (e.g., geographical information, interesting facts, and places to visit in their cities). The second section consists of a search on the Internet of weather temperatures that can be obtained from a linking weather Web site.

The first step is to select two cities. As mentioned above, the teachers can establish guidelines for city selections that will enhance their curricula (e.g., cities in different sections of the United States, or cities in certain countries). Facts about the cities and their geographical information can be located through a search on the Internet.

The information gathered can be organized in a table in a word processing program, such as Microsoft Word 2000 (1999). When using the Microsoft Word 2000 (1999) program it is easy to add pictures from clip art or other sources and paste in the Word document.

The next section of this activity is a comparison of the weather of the two cities selected. The weather search can be conducted at several different weather information Web sites. The Weather Channel at http://www.weather.com/ has an enormous amount of weather information for numerous cities in the United States and around the world.

The weather information of the selected cities is entered into a table in a spreadsheet program. I particularly like the Microsoft Excel 2000 (1999) program because it is easy to use and readily available. The weather information can be entered in Microsoft Excel 2000 (1999) using the format in Table 7.

The Microsoft Excel 2000 (1999) Chart Wizard helps to develop a graph that illustrates the comparison temperatures of the two cities. The weather chart can be copied and pasted on the Word document with the information and facts about the cities.

The quick reference directions are listed in Table 8, the quick reference table. This information can also be found on the Web site for this activity at http://chiron.valdosta.edu/djudd/elementary4.html.

Table 9, the sparking idea table, gives suggestions to assist teachers in developing this activity to enhance their curricula and to address the needs of their students.

The students' information can be printed and developed into a class book about cities around the world. The information can be used in a class game, Where in the World is...? A student could give the information and facts about a city and the other students could try to name the city. After the city is named the students could point out the city's location on a map.

Table 7: Example of a spreadsheet for weather data

Cities	Monday (date)	Tuesday (date)	Wednesday (date)
Athens, Greece (Lows)	49	50	45
Athens, Greece (Highs)	61	60	55
St. Petersburg, Russia (Lows)	25	30	32
St. Petersburg, Russia (Highs)	30	37	39

Table 8: Quick reference for Where in the World is ...?

Quick Reference for Where in the World is...?
1. Select two cities in the world.
2. Search for facts and information about selected cities.
3. Organize information in table in Microsoft Word 2000 (1999) program.
4. Add pictures from clip art or Internet.
5. Search for weather information about selected cities.
6. Enter weather information in Microsoft Excel 2000 (1999) program.
7. Make comparison weather graph with Microsoft Excel 2000 (1999) Chart Wizard.
8. Copy and paste weather graph on Microsoft Word 2000 (1999) document.
9. Students print their Microsoft Word 2000 (1999) documents or publish them on the Internet.

Table 9: Sparking suggestion table for Where in the World is ...?

Suggestions to Spark Ideas for Your Class Using Where in the World is...? Activity
Select cities with the same name, but which are located in different countries to research and compare. **Example:** Students could compare Rome, GA (USA) and Rome, Italy; Cairo, IL (USA) and Cairo, Egypt.
Change the number of cities to match the level and needs of students. **Example:** Teachers may want to compare a larger number of cities with higher level students or research only one city with lower level students.
The size of the group (i.e., whole group, small groups, individuals) to research cities could vary according to students' needs. **Example:** Whole group could work well if the class has access to a converter that is connected from the computer to the class TV screen. This could also be a good way to introduce the activity to the whole class.
The cities could be from designated areas in the world or from the selected states or regions in the United States. **Example:** After studying certain countries or as an introduction to countries, students could select their cities from the designated countries. This could be used as part of the introduction or review of countries.
Students could select cities they have visited. **Example:** The student could become an expert on their cities and share their collected information and their experiences of when they were in the cities.

FUTURE TRENDS

In the future, I believe the public and educational administrators will not only continue to place demands on educators, but will place even higher demands on educators to integrate technology into their curriculum. Many states are requiring colleges and universities to include at least one educational technology course in their teacher education programs. Some states are beginning to mandate that when teachers renew their teaching certificates, it must include certification in technology training. This trend is encouraging and in some situations is forcing educational systems and university systems to develop the necessary courses or in-service workshops to address the pre-service and in-service teachers' needs.

When discussing educational technology in reference to the future, it usually means that the discussions will center on new technological developments that often bring about change. I believe some of the technological developments in the future will evolve into changes that will assist educators, and could include the development of improved computers, connections, software, and Internet information. Together, the improved computers and connections will be directed toward "friendlier" or easier to use computers in the classroom and at home. The improved software and Internet information will aid in the development of integrated technology activities and projects at all levels of education.

Technology-wise, the future looks bright for teachers because of the increased technology training from universities and school systems and the possible advancement of technology hardware and software. In addition, it should also be noted that many factors are involved in the successful integration of technology into the curriculum. Time is a major factor in this technology integration formula. Teachers need time to do the technology training, time to explore the educational technology possibilities, time to develop integrated activities, and time to expand the integrated activities to meet the needs of their students, their learning objectives, and their curricula. This is an area of study that hopefully research will continue to explore and provide information to assist educators.

Although it is evident that integrating technology is a relatively new field of study, recent research results could be beneficial to teachers, administrators, and teacher educators. The educational technology research has made progress in the past, but our technology is advancing at a rapid rate. We will need to extend our research to include the new technologies and their effectiveness in our learning processes.

CONCLUSION

This chapter provides information especially for teachers that want to begin integrating technology into their curriculum. Most of the integrated activities were designed to assist elementary teachers who are at the beginning stages of integrating technology into their curriculum. At the same time, the sparking ideas were developed to allow teachers at any stage of their technology integration to design activities for the needs of their students.

It is evident that teachers will continue to be pressured to include technology as an integrated part of their curriculum. As noted earlier, teachers usually have the burden of proof that students are successfully using technology to enhance their learning. To help relieve this burden, the integrated activities in this chapter are developed to assist elementary teachers to design activities to yield products that illustrate not only the integration of technology, but also its enhancement of the elementary curriculum.

QUESTIONS FOR FURTHER CONSIDERATION

- After learning about technology-integrated activities in this chapter, which activity would you select to enhance your curriculum? Why?
- Explain how you would design the activity to meet the needs of your students, teaching objectives, and curriculum?

REFERENCES

Collis, B. A., Knezek, G. A., Lai, K., Miyashita, K. T, Pelgrum, W. J., Plomp, T. and Sakamoto, T. (1996). Reflections. In Collis, B. A., Knezek, G. A., Lai, K., Miyashita, K. T, Pelgrum, W. J., Plomp, T. and Sakamoto, T. (Eds.), *Children and Computers in Schools*, 113-137. Mahwah, NJ: Lawrence Erlbaum.

Collis, B. A. and Lai, K. (1996). Information technology and children from a classroom perspective. In Collis, B. A., Knezek, G. A., Lai, K., Miyashita, K. T, Pelgrum, W. J., Plomp, T. and Sakamoto, T. (Eds.), *Children and Computers in Schools*, 43-67. Mahwah, NJ: Lawrence Erlbaum.

Glenn, A. D. and Carrier, C. A. (1986). Teacher education and computer training: An assessment. *Peabody Journal of Education*, 64(1), 67-88.

Harris, J. (2000). Online to learn or in line with standards. *Learning and Leading with Technology*, 28(3), 10-15.

Inspiration 6. [Computer software]. (1999). Portland, OR: Inspiration Software, Inc.

Johnson, D. L. (1997). Integrating technology in the classroom: The time has come. *Computers in the Schools*, 13(1-2), 1-5.

Lambert, N. M. and McCombs, B. L. (1998). *How Students Learn Reforming Schools Through Learner-Centered Education*. Washington, DC: American Psychological Association.

Microsoft Excel 2000. [Computer software]. (1999). Microsoft Corporation.

Microsoft Paint. [Computer software]. (1997). Microsoft Corporation.

Microsoft Word 2000. [Computer software]. (1999). Microsoft Corporation.

Papert, S. (1980). *Mindstorms: Children, Computers, and Powerful Ideas.* New York: BasicBooks.

Wilburg, K. M. (1995). An historical perspective on instructional design: It is time to exchange Skinner's teaching machine for Dewey's toolbox? In Schnase, J. L. and Cunnius, E. L. (Eds.), *Computer Support for Collaborative Learning,* 385-389. Mahwah, NJ: Lawrence Erlbaum.

Wilson, B. G. (1995). Metaphors for instruction: Why we talk about learning environments. *Educational Technology,* 35(5), 25-30.

Section IV

Designing for Learners in Higher Education

Chapter VI

Designing Discussion for the Online Classroom

Lin Y. Muilenburg
University of South Alabama, USA

Zane L. Berge
University of Maryland, Baltimore County, USA

Learners need opportunities to reflect on the new material, discuss their tentative understandings with others, actively search for more information to throw light on areas of interest or difficulty and build conceptual connections to their own existing knowledge base. We were looking in our design for ways in which the WWW could be used to encourage learners to become more active in their learning and to interact and collaborate with others in the learning process. (Brown & Thompson, 1997, n.p.)

We hear approaches like this time and again, a seeming mantra for educators teaching either online or in-person, whose underlying philosophy is a social constructivist approach. Indeed, the underlying assumptions taken in this chapter concerning discussion used in teaching is that of inductive, autonomous, active, collaborative learning for students. We want to go beyond saying discussion teaching can be "a good (i.e., effective) method if implemented right" and explore instructional design issues in a way that may help the planning of discussion teaching online.

Discussion teaching is a "teaching/learning strategy that emphasizes participation, dialogue, and multi-way communication. The discussion method involves the teacher and a group of learners addressing a topic, issue, case study, or problem; and exchanging information, experiences, ideas, opinions, reactions, and conclusions" (Heming, 1996, n.p.). As an instructional strategy, the purposes of discussion include allowing students to: interact with more capable peers; articulate and reach a more critical, informed understanding about the topic under consideration, elaborate on and challenge ideas, and hear and incorporate multiple perspectives, while motivating students through active learning environments (Brookfield & Preskill, 1999; Heming, 1996; Powers & Dutt, 1995). Brookfield and Preskill (1999) list fifteen benefits of discussion. Some of the more salient for this article are:

- Helps students recognize and investigate their assumptions
- Encourages attentive, respectful listening
- Helps students become connected to a topic
- Shows respect for students' voices and experiences
- Affirms students as cocreators of knowledge
- Develops habits of collaborative learning
- Helps students develop skills of synthesis and integration
- Leads to transformation (pp. 22-23)

Even given the above benefits, the quality of in-person classroom discussion can be limited by many variables, including the amount of time available for interactions, domination by a few highly vocal students, the number of students participating, students' willingness to talk in public, the lack of time for reflection, the lack of knowledge about what causes effective discussion, and poor planning.

Many instructors have found that the benefits of classroom discussions can be realized and the limitations ameliorated through the use of carefully designed and managed online discussion. Online discussion here means a discussion for purposes of teaching and learning that is computer-mediated communication (CMC) (Santoro, 1995). While this discussion can be real time (e.g., synchronous chat), the emphasis here is on discussion via asynchronous conferencing, since in this form of CMC the nature of online discussion allows learners to respond at a convenient time that best suits them. It allows students time for reflection before responding to the topic or problem, or to seek clarification or help from others (Brown & Thompson, 1997). Numerous "lessons learned" articles have been written on the use and moderation of online discussion in which many stumbling blocks are noted. Online discussions present their own set of challenges, advantages and disadvantages, yet there is very little information in the literature regarding the systematic design of online discussion (Collins & Berge, 1996).

Objectives for This Chapter of the Section

The purpose of this chapter of the section is to provide some background information on "discussion teaching" as it relates to online discussion. Suggestions are made for a systematic design model that can be used in planning a course, or an individual lesson, that is based primarily on asynchronous, online discussion. The model, with some slight modifications, may also be used to design other types of technology-enhanced learning materials.

INSTRUCTIONAL DESIGN FOR ONLINE DISCUSSION

Table 1 outlines the Instructional Design for Online Discussion (ID-OD) model for designing a course or lesson that relies on discussion as the primary method. Although the model is presented in a linear format for ease of reading and explanation, it is certainly possible to conduct certain tasks in a different order. As the model is presented, it would appear that an entire course or series of lessons would be designed and developed prior to any implementation. As just one example of a different approach, some instructors or instructional designers may prefer to design the content for one module or lesson and run that one lesson through the remainder of the design, development, implementation and evaluation process before moving on to lesson number two. The ID-OD model is intended to point out important elements in the process, not to constrain designers in a lockstep fashion. It also models a process that is pragmatic and sensitive to a lack of time and resources often required in real-world instructional design situations.

Analyze

One of the first responsibilities in any instructional design process should be to analyze the context and situation. There are many different areas that can be analyzed, and the extent of the analysis depends somewhat on time and resources. At a minimum, designers should conduct an *instructional analysis* and a *learner analysis*.

The purpose of an instructional analysis is to determine the primary instructional goals and objectives (Schreiber, 1998). The scope and sequence of the content must be determined and the content chunked into appropriately sized instructional modules. Possible learning activities and the style or mode of presentation need to be considered.

Table 1: Instructional Design of Online Discussion (ID-OD)

Phase	Analyze	Tech Reality Check	High-level Design	Interactivity Design	Develop	Implement	Evaluate
Activities	Instructional analysis Learner analysis Does online discussion make sense?	Institutional technology inventory Student technology inventory Technology support availability	Modularize content, objectives, assignments Select evaluation methods Plan for tech training	Vary learning activities and discussion formats to maximize interactivity	Instructional materials and discussion questions Evaluation materials Tech training materials	Moderate discussion	Formative Evaluation: Revision on the fly Summative evaluation: Was the discussion effective?
Outputs	Content scope and sequence, Instructional objectives	Organizational tasks, Timelines, Responsibilities	Module plan, Evaluation plan, Tech training plan	Interactivity plan for each module	Completed course materials	Course delivery	Revise plans and materials as needed

In a learner analysis there are three critical areas to consider: 1) general characteristics such as age, gender, educational background, socio-economic status, job or position, and culture; 2) specific entry competencies (the knowledge and skills learners possess or lack); and 3) learning styles such as anxiety levels, preferred mode of perception (visual or auditory), and areas of aptitude (Heinich, Molenda, Russell, & Smaldino, 1996): "effective discussion leaders know their students. They know which students have which skills and perspectives and will often use this information to decide whom to call on to keep, or get, the discussion moving in the appropriate direction" (Center for Teaching and Learning (CTL), 2000, n.p.).

A key activity in the analysis phase that is often taken for granted is to answer the question: "Does online discussion make sense?" Is the discussion method a good match for the overall goals and objectives of the course, for the content, and for the learners? If the answer to any of these is "No," then you can spend all your time and allocate all your resources to this project, with disappointing results. Use online discussion only when it makes a valuable contribution to the desired outcomes of the course as indicated by the analyses.

Technology Reality Check

Some instructional design models may consider the "Tech Reality Check" part of the analysis phase as a "resource analysis." Online discussion is relatively new; therefore, we are treating these activities with special attention.

A reasonable first question to answer in this phase is, what technology is available? Find out if your organization has already chosen a particular software and hardware system that you should use. If not, perhaps someone else in your organization is already conducting online discussions and you can learn what program they are using for that purpose. The options for software on which to conduct online discussion are growing constantly and there are many free and low cost programs available. Make sure that the program you choose has the features you need and has a good record of performance.

It is important to consider the capabilities of the technology and the expertise of the users and of the developer/instructor. For small group discussions, and for novice users, a very simple conferencing software with minimal features may be the best option. Be careful not to overwhelm participants with complex capabilities that are not needed.

Determine the level of technical support that is available in your organization. Can someone teach you and your students how to use the program you have chosen? Is there funding for training or is there training already available? Who will be responsible for assisting students who have technical problems—24 hours a day, seven days a week? Are there instructional designers or Web developers available to help you prepare your course materials?

After you have answered the many issues raised above, ask the bigger question: What level of sophistication makes sense? If you are completely on your own with no support, utilizing online discussion for the first time, employ technological minimalism (Collins & Berge, 2000). You may have to limit the number of discussions that you design and keep the discussion formats relatively straightforward until you have built an experience base. Remember, this is a reality check. If you are flush with experience, resources, and time, then you can work on expanding your repertoire of discussion formats and increase the level and variety of interaction in your online discussions. At the conclusion of this phase, you should draft the organizational tasks to be completed, create timelines, and assign responsibilities to members of the project development team.

High Level Design

There are three main areas that need to be addressed during the high level design phase: 1) determining the evaluation methods that will be used; 2) planning for the technology training of the instructor and students; and 3) articulating the design that students will experience with the content, objectives and assignments for the instructional modules.

Plan for evaluation. Evaluation of the students, the instructor, and the course materials must be conducted. Because online learning is a new experience for many students and instructors, clear expectations for course requirements must be articulated. Seat-time in the classroom cannot be used as a measure of participation. Instead, required participation in the online discussions is recommended. You must determine how frequently students should participate in discussions, and what the criteria are for evaluating posts. Is there a required format for papers or projects? Where and how should assignments be sent to the instructor? Administering traditional paper and pencil tests raises concerns about cheating, although students can be required to be proctored for exams. Timed, Web-based quizzes and exams are one option, but technical problems can disadvantage some students. Many instructors find that project-based assignments and portfolios are a more effective assessment solution.

Evaluating student satisfaction, the quality of the instructor, and course materials will probably require the development of some customized instruments. Although some organizations have standard evaluation tools that are administered at the end of a course or training session, they were probably developed for use in a traditional setting and may not address important issues in online learning. If a course is offered totally online, administration of surveys or other data gathering instruments must be carefully planned. If you phone students or send instruments via email, anonymity is a concern. Mailing a questionnaire or having students complete a Web-based version may be a better choice. There are Web-based programs available for creating online surveys that automatically compute statistics and report the results, which are great time-savers.

Plan for training. The importance of training students in the use of the technology that will be used in an online course or lesson cannot be overstated. For many students (and faculty) there is a steep learning curve for conferencing software and file management procedures, such as creating directories and files for email storage and uploading and downloading assignments. Training can be provided prior to the start of the course or incorporated into the course objectives. Whatever the choice, technical training should be provided before any course content modules.

In addition to technical skills for operating the software, students also need to know what they can expect from you regarding participation, feedback and assistance with problems, such as how and when should students contact the instructor, how quickly can learners expect to receive a response from the instructor, rules for participation, and Netiquette must also be established, which sets the tone for a positive learning environment (Rohfeld & Hiemstra, 1995).

To summarize, the plan for training should include at a minimum: clear, non-technically written training regarding the use of the technology (e.g., handbook, video); access to a support person, usually 24/7, to quickly solve problems and reduce student frustration levels; a troubleshooting guide for minor problems; and student exercises in the first week or two that demand students are "checked out" on the technologies needed to complete the course (Agostinho, Lefoe, & Hedberg, 1997).

When planning for online discussions, keep in mind that it takes more time online to achieve the same objectives as it does in an in-person setting. For this reason Eisley (1999) recommends running several slowly evolving discussions simultaneously. Divide material into topics suitable for two week discussions. Assign readings, interviews, observations, etc., for each topic, and then discuss these assignments during the conference.

Design for Interactivity

Interaction is considered key to effective learning (Keegan, 1990), positive learner attitudes (Thompson, 1990), and the success of distance education (Moore, 1989). A great deal of time and effort is expended on the development of learning materials such as electronic course notes and syllabi for online courses, but often very little attention is given to increasing the level of interaction among participants. Interactivity design is a separate phase in the ID-OD model to highlight the importance of planning for a variety of learning activities and discussion formats to increase the level of interactivity in online learning. Four types of interaction that a learner can experience during formal online learning need to be considered. These are learner-learner, learner-instructor, learner-content, and learner-interface interactions. It is essentially learner-learner and learner-instructor interactions that are increased when instructional events incorporate activities that encourage dialogue and engage learners with questions and discussions (Schreiber, 1998). Learner-content interaction occurs when the learner processes the content of the course and incorporates that new learning into existing cognitive schema. Finally, learner-interface interaction is the learner's adjustment to the technology.

With regard to online discussions, Rohfeld and Hiemstra (1995) recommend that instructors plan for varied communication opportunities that allow students to share views, critique the views of others and reflect on their learning. Instructional designers and instructors can choose from a variety of discussion formats and learning activities identified in the literature, including dyadic discussions, small group discussions, critique, debates, role plays, polling, brainstorming, cooperative learning projects, group reports, synchronous discussions, guest lecturer or discussant, interviews, twenty questions, Socratic dialogue, personal journal writing, and student moderated discussions. (e.g., Eisley, 1999; Paulsen, 1995a; Rohfeld and Hiemstra, 1995).

Development

In the development phase of the ID-OD model, the instructional designer carries out the plans made during the design phases by fully developing the instructional materials and discussion questions, the evaluation materials, and the technology training materials. The development of instructional materials is a broad subject beyond the scope of this chapter, except to mention that development has a lot to do with questioning techniques, and readers are referred to guides elsewhere (see for example, Dillon, 1982; Eisley, 1999; Hunkins, 1972; Hyman, 1979; Savage, 1998). In the space we have here, let us summarize by saying that you can plan the start of a discussion in at least four ways: ask a question, use common experience, introduce a controversial issue, or list specific concerns (Vacc, 1993).

Ask a question. The discussion method is one of the most commonly used pedagogical techniques in the online classroom and asking a question is the most commonly used method to start a discussion. Questioning is a significant instructional design element for effective discussion. (Muilenburg & Berge, 2000).

Use a common experience. Another strategy for initiating a discussion is to use an experience that is common to all students. For example, viewing the same video prepared to illustrate particular objects or processes can be discussed. Student's discussion of something in which they have the same experiential background has obvious advantage, but in addition it may be particularly helpful to students who are shy about discussing their own personal experiences.

Introduce a controversial issue. A third way to initiate discussion is to present a topic that has opposing points of view or is a controversial issue for the students in your course. For example, one student states that "the best way to learn is through taking notes at an expert's lecture." Asking, "what do the rest of you think," may well start a very active and engaging discussion on teaching methods. The discussion coming from the introduction of a controversial issue are often most effective in generating higher order thinking when students have to justify their own point of view to their peers.

Make a list of specific concerns. The final discussion generating technique mentioned here is to list the specific concerns or problems of the students. In discussions generated with lists of concerns, students share their reasoning about their problems, with others having an opportunity to evaluate their own perspective. Students can modify their thinking or be persuasive in helping others to modify theirs accordingly.

Implementation

When well-planned, online discussion fails due to poor implementation, it is usually because the person facilitating is unable to overcome the initial difficulty of transposing leadership skills acquired in in-person settings to the online setting. There are relatively few instructors who have participated in online discussion, let alone an online course, either as an instructor or as a student. Instructors need to learn a new set of skills to effectively moderate online discussions. Not only do they need to learn new skills, but the relative importance of factors common to in-person teaching change in the online learning environment. Instructional elements, such as feedback to students and the instructor modeling appropriate online discussion, need to be increased for online instruction (Vrasidas & McIsaac, 1999).

While not the focus of this chapter, undoubtedly there has been more written about teaching or facilitating than any other aspect of the instructional systems design process for online education (see for example, Mason, 1991; McGee & Boyd, 1995; Paulsen, 1995b; Rossman, 1999; Winiecki, 1999).

Evaluation

The final step in the ID-OD model is to implement the evaluation plan. Student learning should be assessed according to the criteria that were presented to the students at the beginning of the course or lesson. If a series of discussions is being conducted, a formative evaluation should be completed after the first and several subsequent discussions. Using the first discussion as a pilot test can alert the instructor to changes that may be needed before future lessons are implemented. Materials and procedures can be reworked at any point in the process.

Courses are usually evaluated once they have been completed and a lot of valuable course improvement information tends to be lost because students can't remember it well after the event or don't want to linger over an evaluation when the course is completed. By conducting formative evaluation periodically throughout the course, important data can be collected on what works well and what does not, both in terms of content and technology. It also means that problems can be rectified during the current delivery of the course rather than only in subsequent courses.

The evaluation of online discussion as described in the literature falls into three areas: participation requirements or participation tracking, evaluation or grading rubrics, and content analysis. Participation requirements is the most frequently used method of evaluation because they are the simplest, requiring only tracking the number of posts made by each student. Powers and Dutt (1995) recommend a requirement for one original post and one or two responses each week. This helps to ensure that students are reacting both to the content and to each other.

Grading rubrics. List specific criteria that will be used for evaluating student posts. Criteria for outstanding, above average, average and below average posts should be included. Students clearly know what is expected for them to receive each of these grades. The example below gives the criteria for an outstanding post (Burke, 1999):

- Answers all portions of the posted questions
- Clearly states the main idea of the point that is being made
- Includes supporting detail for the main idea
- Quotes/paraphrases portions of the text or lecture to support main idea and includes page number of the text or URL of the Web site

- Names the author of the literature by last name
- Relates material in unit to previous unit lecture, discussion, and literature
- Grammatically error free
- Spelling is correct

Content analysis. Analyzing the content is a more complicated and time-consuming method of evaluating a discussion and is utilized by researchers more than practitioners. A set of response types along with codes is developed to identify particular types of contributions or responses by participants. Then the transcripts for a discussion are reviewed, the messages are coded, and frequencies for each type of response are tallied. Content analysis can examine types and patterns of interactions that are occurring, the level of cognitive processing, and student and instructor behaviors.

Additionally, at the conclusion of the instructional program, the *summative evaluation* should be conducted. Take a realistic look at how well the technology performed, the adequacy of the instructor's skills and knowledge, the quality of the instructional materials and the level of student achievement. Working with new technology and using new instructional methods can be a bumpy road. The mistakes and problems that occurred this go-round should be used to inform and improve the process and quality of future efforts. But also acknowledge the successes, and strive to continue the practices that were most effective.

CONCLUSION

The Instructional Design for Online Discussion (ID-OD) model was developed to be a useful guide for the design, development, implementation and evaluation of courses or lessons that utilize online discussions. By focusing on critical issues, such as technology training, increasing the level of interaction, facilitation skills and online evaluation techniques, the ID-OD model can help instructional designers and instructors avoid some of the pitfalls while reaping the benefits of online discussion.

QUESTIONS FOR FURTHER CONSIDERATION

1) How is designing for discussion teaching different than designing for instruction that does not take place in an environment that depends upon effective discussion?

2)   What training might be needed for both students and instructors regarding discussion teaching online?

3) How do planning and evaluation work together for designing instruction for the online classroom?

REFERENCES

Agostinho, S., Lefoe, G. and Hedberg, J. (1997). Online collaboration for learning: A case study of a post graduate university course. *Proceedings of the AusWeb97 Third Australian World Wide Web Conference*, July 5-9. Available on the World Wide Web at: http://ausweb.scu.edu.au/proceedings/agostinho/paper.html.

Brookfield, S. D. and Preskill, S. (1999). *Discussion as a Way of Teaching: Tools and Techniques for Democratic Classrooms*. San Francisco, CA: Jossey-Bass Publishers.

Brown, A. and Thompson, H. (1997). Course design for the WWW: Keeping online students onside. Paper presented at the *ACILITE 1997 Conference*. December 7-10. Available on the World Wide Web at: http://www.curtin.edu.au/conference/ASCILITE97/papers/Brown/Brown.html.

Burke, A. N. (1999). *Helpful Files for Online Teaching*. Available on the World Wide Web at: http://www.delta.edu/~anburke/mentor.

Center for Teaching and Learning. (2000). Discussion teaching. Chicago, IL: The University of Chicago, Center for Teaching and Learning. Available on the World Wide Web at: http://teaching.uchicago.edu/tac/tac09.html.

Collins, M. and Berge, Z. L. (1996). Facilitating interaction in computer-mediated online courses. Background paper for presentation at *FSU/AECT Distance Education Conference*. Tallahassee, FL. June.

Collins, M.P. and Berge, Z.L. (2000). *Technological minimalism. The Technology Source*, November-December. Available on the World WIde Web at: http://horizon.unc.edu/TS/commentary/2000-11.asp.

Dillon, J. T. (1982). The multi-disciplinary study of questioning. *Journal of Educational Psychology*, 74(2), 147-65.

Eisley, M. E. (1999). Guidelines for conducting instructional discussions on a computer conference. *DEOSNEWS*, 2(1). Available on the World Wide Web at: http://www.ed.psu.edu/ACSDE/deosnews2.1.htm.

Heinich, R., Molenda, M., Russell, J. D. and Smaldino, S. E. (1996). *Instructional Media and Technologies for Learning*. Englewood Cliffs, New Jersey. Prentice Hall, Inc.

Heming, D. (1996). Discussion teaching in college education. *College Quarterly*, Spring. Available on the World Wide Web at: http://www.senecac.on.ca/quarterly/CQ.html/D.000.ContentDate.html.

Hunkins, F. P. (1972). *Questioning Strategies and Techniques*. Boston, MA: Allyn & Bacon, Inc.

Hyman, R. T. (1979). *Strategic Questioning*. Englewood Cliffs, NJ: Prentice-Hall, Inc.

Keegan, D. (1990). *Foundations of Distance Education*. New York: Routledge.

Mason, R. (1991). Moderating educational computer conferencing. *DEOSNEWS*, 1(19). Available on the World Wide Web at: http://Webster.hibo.no/trond/deosWeb/vol1/nr19.html.

McGee, P. A. and Boyd, V. (1995). *Computer-Mediated Communication: Facilitating Dialogues*. Available on the World Wide Web at: http://www.coe.uh.edu/insite/elec_pub/html1995/173.htm.

Moore, M. G. (1989). Three types of interaction. *The American Journal of Distance Education*, 3(2) 1-6.

Muilenburg, L. and Berge, Z.L. (2000). A framework for designing questions for online learning. *DEOSNEWS*, 10(2). Available on the World Wide Web at: http://www.emoderators.com/moderators/muilenburg.html.

Paulsen, M. F. (1995a). *The Online Report on Pedagogical Techniques for Computer-Mediated Communication*. Available on the World Wide Web at: http://www.hs.nki.no/~morten/cmcped.htm.

Paulsen, M. F. (1995b). Moderating educational computer conferences. In Berge, Z. L. and Collins, M. P. (Eds.), *Computer-Mediated Communication and the Online Classroom in Distance Education*, 81-90. Cresskill, NJ: Hampton Press. Available on the World Wide Web at: http://www.emoderators.com/moderators/morten.html.

Powers, S. M. and Dutt, K. M. (1995). *Expanding Class Discussion Beyond the Classroom Walls*. Available on the World Wide Web at: http://Web.indstate.edu/cimt/powers.html.

Rohfeld, R. W. and Hiemstra, R. (1995). Moderating discussions in the electronic classroom. In Berge, Z. L. and Collins, M. P. (Eds.), *Computer-Mediated Communication and the Online Classroom in Distance Education*, 91-104. Cresskill, NJ: Hampton Press.

Rossman, M. H. (1999). Successful online teaching using an asynchronous forum discussion. *JALN*, 3(2), 91-97. Available on the World Wide Web at: http://www.aln.org/alnWeb/journal/Vol3_issue2/Rossman.pdf.

Santoro, G. (1995). What is computer-mediated communication? In Berge, Z. L. and Collins, M. P. (Eds.), *Computer-Mediated Communication and the Online Classroom. Volume 1–Overview and Perspectives*, 11-28. Cresskill, NJ: Hampton Press.

Savage, L. B. (1998). Eliciting critical thinking skills through questioning. *The Clearing House*, 71(5), 291-293.

Schreiber, D. A. (1998). Instructional design of distance training. In Schreiber, D. A. and Berge, Z. L. (Eds.), *Distance Training*, 37-70. Jossey-Bass: San Francisco, CA.

Thompson, G. (1990). How can correspondence-based distance education be improved? A survey of attitudes of students who are not well disposed toward correspondence study. *Journal of Distance Education*, 5(1). Available on the World Wide Web at: http://cade.athabascau.ca/vol5.1/11_thompson.html.

Vacc, N. N. (1993). Implementing the professional standards for teaching mathematics: Teaching and learning mathematics through classroom discussion. *Arithmetic Teacher*, December, 41(4) 225-27.

Vrasidas, C. and McIsaac, M. S. (1999). Principles of pedagogy and evaluation for Web-based learning. Paper presented at the *ICEM Conference*. Slovenia. Available on the World Wide Web at: http://seamonkey.ed.asu.edu/~mcisaac/ICEM99/pedagogymss.html.

Winiecki, D. J. (1999). Keeping the thread: Adapting conversational practice to help distance students and instructors manage discussions in an asynchronous learning network. *DEOSNEWS*, 9(2). Available on the World Wide Web at: http://www.ed.psu.edu/ACSDE/deosnews9.2.htm.

Chapter VII

Nothing but the Blues: A Case Study in the Use of Technology to Enrich a University Course

Tracy Chao and Bruce Stovel
University of Alberta, Canada

INTRODUCTION

Too often, computers become the focus of a technological integration endeavor in education. Instructors may well be excited about the potential uses of computer-assisted education, but at the same time feel lost in a high-tech jungle. However, computer technology is just a means to an end. The real question for instructors and course designers is how to understand a course holistically, including its goals, content, structure, teaching methods, and even the underlying theories of learning. This holistic analysis helps determine the best way to incorporate technology, or a variety of technologies, to deliver a course effectively. This chapter describes, through a case study, this holistic approach towards course design and presents the implications for using educational technologies in a conventional classroom setting.

The case study is an undergraduate course at the University of Alberta. English 483, Studies in the Literature of Popular Culture: Blues Lyrics as Lyric Poetry was a one-term course offered for advanced undergraduates. Given the subject matter, the advanced level of the students, and the instructional goals for this course, a traditional, lecture-centered teaching method was considered inappropriate. The instructor believed that students must experience the music and the lyrics for themselves and form their own interpretations from that experience. Thus, the design of the course and the use of technology were based upon two considerations: (1) how to expose students to an authentic learning environment where they could experience blues music as an artistic form; and (2) how to guide students to interpretations of blues songs that take account of their contexts in social history and blues traditions as well as their intrinsic literary value. The two considerations called for constructivist philosophy and principles. This course serves as an excellent example of the marriage between constructivist design principles and the actual practices in a classroom.

A variety of activities and technologies were implemented to materialize the design principles and to accomplish the aforementioned goals. As in traditional English courses, the students were asked to buy textbooks, to complete readings from them, to submit—on paper—a long essay, and to write a final examination. However, the instructor played selected blues recordings in each class and then invited analysis of them, assigned CDs of blues music and invited the students to explore other blues recordings, asked the students to submit assignments to a course Web site and to critique other students' work on the Web site. In addition, the instructor conducted both face-to-face and online asynchronous discussion, arranged an interview with a blues musician (via a Web-based chatroom but later by telephone), held live concerts in class, encouraged the students to consult a set of videos that were placed on reserve, and required an oral presentation from each student at the end of the term—and many of these presentations involved the student presenter showing a video or playing a recording to the class. This multi-faceted instruction allowed the students to understand the subject of the course and to interact with the instructor, musicians, and each other through face-to-face contact and computer-mediated communication.

This section of the chapter will discuss in detail the constructivist principles applied to the design of English 483, the way this course was conducted, and the outcomes as a result of the technology integration. The story and the reflection are meant to provide instructors in higher education with insights into designing courses that incorporate technology into classroom teaching.

Objectives for This Section of the Chapter

Upon reading this section of the chapter,

- you will learn to take a holistic approach towards course design and to anlayze a course in terms of its instructional goals, content, structure and teaching methods;
- you will understand and be able to apply some of the constructivist design principles to classroom practices;
- you will be able to incorporate appropriate instructional technologies to meet the goals that you have defined; and
- you will become aware of some essential issues concerning course design and the implementation of technology in classroom teaching.

CONSTRUCTIVIST DESIGN PRINCIPLES

Constructivism is central to the design of English 483. Students were not expected to memorize the lyrics to blues songs nor to learn to interpret them objectively. On the contrary, students were to experience the performed art in order to understand the poetic nature of the songs. Personal experience and immersion in an authentic environment were required to meet the instructional goals. It seemed that constructivism offers a strong theoretical foundation for this course.

Constructivist philosophy is founded on the premise that we each construct our own understanding and that learning occurs through the association of previous experience with newly acquired knowledge. It is up to the learners to make sense of a concept and to express their own perspectives. There is no one correct meaning, since individuals differ in their sense-making and viewpoints (Duffy & Jonassen, 1992).

Many theorists have articulated this philosophy in terms of its application in education. Dewey and Vygotsky are two of the theorists who offered insights on this matter. For Dewey (1944), education depends on action. Knowledge and ideas emerge only from a situation in which learners are induced to draw them out of experiences which have meaning and importance to them. These situations have to occur in a social context, such as a classroom where students join in manipulating materials and thus create a community of learners who build knowledge individually and collectively. Vygotsky (1978) further states that learning is a social process. Learners acquire knowledge by interacting with peers and with a subject expert. The zone of proximal development provides a clear application of Vygotsky's principle. Learners can learn from others who possess the desired knowledge, thereby acquiring and constructing their own knowledge.

Dewey and Vygotsky's views can be expanded into an argument for an authentic learning environment. It is believed that learning improves when it occurs in a meaningful and authentic context. In other words, the context must be an integral part of the content to be learned (Spiro, Feltovish, Jacobson, & Coulson, 1992). Constructivism promotes the idea that a learning activity must be situated and authentic (Brown, Collins & Duguid, 1989). The authenticity contextualizes learning; authenticity therefore helps learners see the usefulness of the knowledge and helps them transfer what they have learned to a real world situation.

Another principle that is at the heart of constructivism is active learning. Von Glaserfeld (1995) argues that constructivism requires self-regulation and the building of conceptual structures through reflection and abstraction. The emphasis is on an individual's autonomy in the learning process, as well as on knowledge construction instead of reproduction. It is more effective for learners to build their own knowledge from their experiences than to receive it passively (Perkins, 1992). By constructing knowledge the learners are actively trying to create meaning. They are more likely to retain it because they have interpreted and assimilated it into their previous knowledge. Cunningham (1992) suggests that a constructivist learning environment should promote active learning and facilitate the knowledge construction process, in other words, should help learners construct their own plausible interpretations.

In short, from a constructivist standpoint, learning is viewed as a social function and the focus is on knowledge construction. An individual must be an active agent in the learning process, and learning should occur in an authentic context. Later in this section of the chapter, we will describe the ways these constructivist principles have been applied to the design of the course.

THE CASE STUDY

The Course

English 483 was taught over a 13 week term; the class contained 22 students, most of them third or fourth year Honors English students or English majors. The course is one of some twenty variable-content 400-level English courses offered each year that are meant to provide sophisticated and specialized instruction to advanced students. The class met once a week, at night, for three hours.

The course explored the poetic art in the lyrics of selected blues songs, taking as its point of departure a claim made by Brooks, Lewis, and Warren

(1973): "The blues was one of the few unique contributions—perhaps the only unique contribution—that America has made to the world of art. . . . Waiving their value as musical art, blues songs represent a body of poetic art unique and powerful" (pp. 2753, 2759). The course aimed at allowing students to experience and understand blues lyrics, not as poems in the usual sense (words on a page), but as performed poetry—in other words, as elements in the songs in which they appear. Another goal was to help students understand the social context in which the blues developed, namely, the life of the black population of the United States in the twentieth century, a life that changed dramatically during the century as the majority of blacks moved from the country to the city and from the deep south to the north. The course surveyed the development of blues music by studying a different period or style each week, beginning with "Women Blues Singers of the 1920s" and continuing to the present; at the end of eight weeks of such a chronological survey, one week was devoted to studying the work of each of two immensely influential blues artists, Muddy Waters and B. B. King. The second-to-last meeting of the class consisted of student presentations, and the last week's class, according to University practice for night classes, was the final exam.

The students were asked to buy three textbooks and two anthologies of recordings of a wide variety of blues songs. Some thirty additional books and articles bearing on the course were placed on reserve in the university library, and an additional CD anthology was an optional purchase and available in the campus bookstore. The students also proved able to make excellent use of the thousands of blues LPs and CDs in the university's Music Library and in the city's library system. In addition, students were invited to consult ten videos of blues performances placed on reserve in the Audio Visual Center.

In-Class Activities

Each three hour class fell into three parts. The first hour was presided over by the instructor, who gave a lecture accompanied by question and answer discussion on the phase of blues studied that week. The second hour of each class focussed on four blues songs in the style of music under study that week: the students were divided at the start of the term into four groups, each containing five or six students; each group would listen to its assigned song, consult about its striking features and its significance, and then report back to the class, playing the song on the CD player and presenting their conclusions. The final hour of each class was allotted to "fun." Eight of these one hour sessions were devoted to live performances by blues artists living in Alberta; a video on blues music was shown in one final hour segment; a panel discussion by local figures in the blues business (such as DJs, booking agents, and in one case head of a recording label) was held one week, and once a prominent blues artist (Ann Rabson, founder of the acoustic trio Saffire) was to be interviewed through a Web-based chatroom facility in WebCT (WebCT, 1998).

The eight concerts were especially important. Each lasted for one hour and coincided in style with the kind of music under study that week; they were held in a separate classroom that is an amphitheatre, and members of the public were invited to attend. The series was advertised as "Blues in the Academy," and since the performers were all well-known, the audience at several of these concerts contained many people who were not students in the class. The performers spoke between songs about the music they were performing, and many of these comments made a deep impression on the students. The blues artists all performed for free out of love for their music; this donation by the musicians was itself something that the students appreciated.

At the end of the term, each student submitted a term paper of 2,500 words (eight to ten typed pages) on a topic of his or her choice: the only requirements were that the essay had to deal with the issues of the course and to discuss in some detail at least one blues song. Each student had a scheduled interview with the instructor about one month before the due date; this allowed students a chance to air their ideas and receive suggestions. Then, in the second-to-last class meeting, each student gave a brief oral presentation (ten minutes maximum) outlining his or her essay and invited responses from the class and the instructor. Finally, the essay was submitted two weeks later, one week after the final exam was written. The term papers were arresting and original in conception and execution. Most of the students used recordings on CDs or segments from videos in making their presentations.

The final exam was an important part of the learning experience. It covered the course as a whole and asked the students to synthesize the knowledge and insights that they had been accumulating all term; whereas the focus all term had been on the study of individual artists and songs, now the students were asked to step back and try to fit things together and see what it all meant. The exam was 2 ½ hours long, and the most important question—to be completed in 1 ½ hours and so worth 60% of the exam mark—was one in which the students were asked to choose one of six large topics and write an essay on it, referring to a variety of artists, styles, and periods (see Table 1). The exam also asked the students to apply their knowledge to new material that had not been studied in class: two shorter exam questions were given to them in advance, to be done in 30 minutes each, dealing with contemporary blues music. The questions asked each student to define the qualities that a blues song must have to become a blues standard and to identify the qualities that distinguish songs by the best blues songwriters from most blues songs.

Course Web Site

The course Web site was designed as an integral part of the course. WebCT was the delivery platform. Many of the students were already veteran Internet users, but some were novices who did not have access to a computer. The first hour of the second class meeting was devoted to an orientation session, conducted in a university computer lab, showing students how to access and use the course Web site and also how to make use of the university's computer labs. This session was to help students understand the role of the course Web site and provide them with necessary instruction so they would not feel too frustrated when they encountered problems. The Web components included (see Figure 1 for an overview of the course Web site):

Table 1: The allotment of grades in English 483

Term work	Percentage
Eight Weekly assignments	40%
Term paper	
Finished essay	10%
Oral presentation	10%
Class participation	
In-class contributions	5%
Contributions to online forums	5%
Final exam	
60% for an essay question; 40% for two short questions on contemporary blues music	30%
Total	100%

Course outline and syllabus. The outline and syllabus, which contains a weekly schedule, were handed out in class and posted on the course Web site. They provided overall guidance to the students and spelled out the course requirements.

Weekly assignments. Weekly assignments formed the core element in the course. Every week for nine weeks, each student was asked to choose a blues song, transcribe it, and write a brief commentary. Students had to report on songs they had actually heard; the songs had to be chosen from given chronological periods (for instance, for the first four weeks, the songs chosen had to have been recorded before 1945). Students found these songs on the assigned CDs or on CDs and LPs they discovered on their own. Each assignment was to consist of two pages, one page of transcription and one page of commentary. Each commentary had to have at least one factual paragraph, identifying the performer, the songwriter, the accompaniment, the place and date of the original recording, and the like, and at least one paragraph of interpretation. A sample weekly asignment is given in Table 2.

Figure 1: Homepage of the course Web site

Table 2: A sample student contribution to "Nothing But the Blues"

Lyrics of "Fine and Mellow" can be found on Blues Classics (Various Artists, 1996)

Commentary

"Fine and Mellow" is written by Billie Holiday and performed by Alberta Hunter. She is accompanied by Charlie Shavers on trumpet, Buster Bailey on clarinet, Lil Armstrong on piano, and Wellman Braud on string bass. It was recorded in New York on August 15th, 1939. This recording and recording information can be found on *Blues Classics.*

This song centers on a troubled relationship, a common theme in blues music. It is similar to some of the other songs that we discussed in class because of its inherent contradictions. On the one hand, the female speaker tells her listener about how mean her lover is to her. But this negative impression of the lover is contrasted with the fond lines "but when he starts in to love me/ he is so fine and mellow" (l. 10-11). The fact that "Fine and Mellow" is actually the title of the song emphasizes this contrast. These conflicting impressions of the speaker's lover are reinforced throughout the piece. The dysfunction of the relationship is reiterated by the references to drinking and gambling, for example. Yet the speaker's promise that if he only treats her right she will "stay home every day" suggests that the speaker still feels love for this man despite the way he has been treating her. This speaker is thus developed as a very interesting character who is torn between her love and what she knows is a bad situation. There is much reluctance and regret expressed as she sings "but if you treat me wrong baby/ you're going to drive me away" (l. 23-24).

What is particularly interesting about this song is the argument that such contradiction is inherent to love in general. This opinion is made clear in the second stanza, with the lines "love will make you do things/ that you know are wrong" (l. 17-18). Thus the speaker does not blame herself or her lover for their problems, but rather blames Love itself, almost as a personified character. This further develops the character and creates a tone of helplessness and frustration. By merely blaming the abstract force of Love for her problems she gives the listener the sense that she herself can do little to solve those problems.

The apparent contradiction between the man's mistreatment of the speaker and the love that they still seem to share is resolved by the final stanza. Here the speaker describes the fickleness of love by comparing it to a faucet, which explains the love-hate, off-and-on relationship that the two characters have. This stanza shows once again the speaker's lack of agency in her own relationship with the lines "sometimes when you think it's on babe/ it has turned off and gone" (l. 35-36). The faucet seems to have a mind of its own. The song is thus structurally effective because it builds up toward the final stanza in which the character and tone are reinforced, and the previous stanzas are explained and tied together.

These assignments were posted to the course Web site and gradually formed an anthology called "Nothing but the Blues." In fact, the students were allowed to hand in these assignments on paper and by e-mail to the course Web site; students were urged to post their work to the Web site, so that their ideas could be shared, but there was no penalty for those who handed in the assigment on paper only. The students quickly found it fascinating to read each other's work on the Web site, so that by the end of the course more than 90% of the assignments had been placed on the Web site.

The vehicle by which the students submitted their assignments was the e-mail function in WebCT. E-mail allowed students to send their assignments as private submissions to the instructor. The instructor could then provide feedback to the students, mark the assignments, and post them in "Nothing but the Blues." This process allowed the instructor to make minor editing changes to ensure that the assignments were all in the same format and to index each assignment. The students were to indicate each week whether or not they wanted their submission to the Web site to be identified as theirs; as a result, about 80% of the assigments found in "Nothing but the Blues" identify the student authors; the remainder are anonymous. The great advantage of the Web page anthology is that the students could read each other's work, week by week, and the assignments thus not only built up a store of songs known to all, but also a body of thought that could be built upon. Often students in their weekly assign- ments alluded in their commentary to points made in previous assign- ments by other students. The students also made frequent use of the ideas advanced by other students in "Nothing but the Blues" when they pro- duced their presentations, term papers, and final exams.

Nothing but the Blues. Every week, the instructor collected the students' e-mailed assignments, added the song titles to an index, and posted the assignments in "Nothing but the Blues" on the course Web site (see Figure 2). The anthology thus became a core repository of the course materials. This anthology served a variety of purposes. The primary benefit was the intellectual one noted above: a body of songs and a body of thought were defined as the course's primary concern. Another benefit was that students were actively engaged in publishing their work. This allowed the students to regard their work as a public contribution to an ongoing project and encouraged professionalism.

Students were also forced to consult "Nothing but the Blues" before completing each assignment, if for no other reason than to be sure of not writing on a song already in the collection. In fact, it occasionally happened that two or three students would write on the same song in the same week; it then became very interesting to compare the differences in the transcriptions and the different perspectives taken in the commentaries. In general, students not only learned by completing their own assignments, but also benefited from the multiple perspectives reflected in the anthology.

The instructor used a Web Authoring tool–DreamWeaver (1999)–to edit the Web pages for "Nothing but the Blues." Because submissions were done through email, the instructor was able to index the song titles and then cut and paste the submissions onto the course Web site. The instructor thus served as the editor of the emerging anthology, guaranteeing that it had consistency and clarity and also allowing the submissions to be identified by author or to remain anonymous, depending on each author's preference.

Figure 2: Nothing but the Blues: An anthology of blues lyrics from English 483. It can also be accessed at: http://www.arts.ualberta.ca/ENGL679A1/ nbb/lyricindex.htm

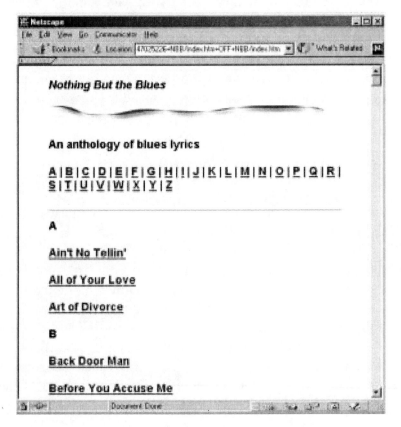

Conferencing. In addition to the discussions in class, the instructor introduced an on-line conferencing environment which allowed students to discuss issues from the course informally and on their own time. Unlike the email submissions for the weekly assignments, the submissions to the conferences on the Web site were public. The conferencing environment was organized into four forums. They were: (a) Talkin' the Blues, (b) The Checkerboard, (c) What Is Blues?, and (d) A Blues Timeline.

"Talkin' the Blues" was the title given to a conference in which anyone, students as well as the instructor, could post provocative or intriguing quotations that they had come across while reading about or listening to blues music. The instructor posted a few quotations to stir up conversation at the start of the course and added several other striking quotations periodically during the course. The students soon followed, and many of the submissions to this conference provoked several replies.

"The Checkerboard" was a conference from which the instructor was excluded: the students in the course could raise questions and voice opinions on issues that came up during their work in the course. The Checkerboard, by the way, is a famous blues club in the far south side of Chicago, deep in the black ghetto. According to students, the submissions to this conference were lively and helpful.

Participation in "Talkin' the Blues" and "The Checkerboard" was voluntary and played no part in the grades assigned to students. The other two forums, "What Is Blues?" and "A Blues Timeline," were marked, though each counted for relatively little (see Table 1). In each case, students were asked to submit a brief assignment to the forum (in the first, a brief definition of blues the student had found useful; in the second, a timeline of at least eight dates the student felt to be essential for an understanding of blues music). The two assignments were due on the days of the fourth and of the eighth class meeting, respectively, and then in each case within the next seven days each student was asked to respond to the assignments of at least two other students.

The marking of these assignments was based on the quality of the students' work both in their initial assignments and in their responses to other students' assignments, and the marks for these assignments were emailed to the students. These two conferences proved to be extremely productive: not only did they produce a wealth of valuable facts and ideas, they also forced the students to respond to—develop, qualify, connect—each other's thinking and to become able to post their thoughts to the Web site. They resulted in students realizing the value of on-line conversation and Internet civility.

Interview with Anne Rabson. On one occasion, the class was to interview, via a live chatroom facility on WebCT, an important blues musician, Ann

Rabson (founder of the all-female acoustic trio Saffire), at her home in Virginia. The chatroom is text-based, which means students must posses moderate keyboarding skills to maintain a dynamic conversation. On the day of the interview, students met in a computer lab and began conversing on the computers with each other. Anne Rabson had been enrolled in the course by the instructor and thus was able to log in to the course Web site prior to the interview. Unfortunately, disaster struck on the night of the interview: in the days before the scheduled interview, Ann Rabson had bought a new computer and discarded her old one—and for some reason the new computer was not able to access the conference function of the Web site. After some minutes of frustration for all involved, the instructor and Ann Rabson spoke on the phone and arranged to conduct the interview by telephone. Each student spoke with Ann Rabson for two or three minutes, and then after the twenty or so separate phone conversations the class assembled for fifteen or twenty minutes of debriefing: each student summarized for the others what he or she had discovered. The interview proved valuable and was carried out by technology, but, alas, was not the higher-tech triumph that was planned.

Learning resources. Learning resources was a section on the course Web site that offered students additional material that could be used to develop their thinking, to assist them in research, and to help them to make the best use of the course. For example, there were instruction on how to use the course Web site, interesting Internet links, and blues performances in and around the city.

Announcements. Announcements were posted on the Web site on an ongoing and as-needed basis. The home page of the course was a natural place to post announcements about upcoming classes, performances, and deadlines. This announcement function was especially important since the class met only once a week. The students soon learned they had to log on to the course Web site regularly to keep up-to-date with developments in the course.

ANALYZING THE COURSE

The design of the course took into account both the face-to-face contact and the characteristics of the Web as an educational tool. In fact the course Web site was integral to the teaching and learning in this course. It provided core content and communication channels to supplement the class activities.

Figure 3 is a map that delineates the entire structure of the course and the technologies used to support the constructivist design principles and various learning activities.

Figure 3: Various technologies used to support the learning process

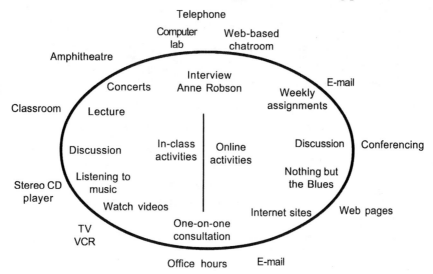

Constructivism in Action

So how were the constructivist principles applied to the design of English 483? The method employed can be described as an approach to build a rich, authentic environment for active learning (Grabinger & Dunlap, 1995).

The live concerts were probably the most authentic experiences students had in this class. The instructor also made an effort to invite a well-known musician to meet the class online; although the plan for the on-line interview fell through, the interview was conducted by telephone and the students were still able to ask Ann Rabson questions. The emphasis was authentic interaction between the students and blues music and musicians. In addition to firsthand encounters with musicians in the live concerts, listening to music recordings was an activity for every class. Discussions were all based on these experiences the students had. The instructor also provided information about blues performances around the city and on the radio. It is important to note that the authenticity varies in degree in different situations. Listening to music recordings in class may be less authentic than attending a live concert. Given the constraints and the resources available for classroom teaching, music recordings seemed to be a reasonable solution for exposing students to many blues songs from the past to the present. Cronin (1993) argued that authenticity exists on a continuum. The way authenticity was accomplished in this course was through the arrangement of various events in class and encouragement for students to explore blues music outside class.

Throughout the course, students were engaged in the listening and interpreting process. Weekly assignments were the outcome of this active learning process. Later in the course, the students worked on an essay and the accompanying oral presentation to externalize their learning. This promoted ownership of learning and turned students from passive recipients of instruction into active agents of learning. In addition to each individual's knowledge construction through writing weekly assignments and preparing his or her presentation and essay, the students were led by the instructor to explore course issues in in-class discussions. The topics in the on-line forums broadened the range of discussion and helped students learn from one another. With all of these working together, students were exposed to multiple perspectives on the subject of the course. Alternative perspectives are viewed by most constructivists as an effective approach to knowledge construction and as a way to deepen one's understanding of a subject (Spiro et al., 1992).

OUTCOMES

The outcomes of the course can be described under two headings: (1) students' evaluation of the course; (2) the instructor's reflections on the new course format.

Students' Perspective

The University of Alberta requires instructors to administer anonymous computer-marked evaluation forms in each course. In addition, the Department of English has designed a handwritten form, also anonymous, that students are to fill in at the same time. These evaluation forms, designed to assess classroom teaching, were filled out by the students in the third-to-last class meeting. The instructor also requested the instructional designer to implement a survey that dealt exclusively with the Web components of the course. The survey was done in the second-to-last class meeting.

Overall, the feedback from these evaluation forms indicated that students found the course valuable and thought that the combination of classroom teaching and on-line activities was a success.

On the key question on the university-wide computer-marked evaluation forms, "Overall, the instructor was excellent," the instructor received an average rating of 4.7 out of 5 (Strongly Agree =5 to Strongly Disagree =1). Another question, "Overall, the quality of the course content was excellent," drew a response of 4.6. The handwritten Department forms provided a similar picture. Two sample comments were the following: "The professor instigated discussion better than any previous instructor I've had in three years as an English major at this university"; "For the first time in an English class I actually felt like doing the assigned reading." Many students said they were grateful to the course for having taught them to appreciate blues music.

The one shared criticism came from six students who wanted more class time devoted to lectures. The comments were sometimes mild suggestions for improvement (e.g., "A little more lecture, less group work"); in two cases the students wanted more discussion of the assigned reading; two other students felt the lectures were deficient ("quite sketchy and not very helpful," according to one; "difficult to follow" and not clearly laid out, according to another).

On the survey regarding the Web components of the course, most students responded favorably. Weekly assignments, "Nothing but the Blues," and conferencing forums were accessed most frequently. Ninety-five percent of the students thought the Web site was well integrated into the course; 72% believed that the Web site helped them learn the course content. On a more qualitative note, many students thought "Nothing but the Blues" was a very valuable resource on the course Web site. They also liked the enhanced communication, the sharing of assignments, the extra exploration through the Internet links, and the interactivity the Web site offered.

Two students had technical difficulties and did not have computers or easy access to the Internet. They responded more negatively to the questions. They complained about the issue of access. This seemed to affect their overall perception about the use of computer technology in this course. They did not see its relevance and thought spending time on learning how to post assignments was not worthwhile.

Instructor's Perspective

The instructor believes the students advanced further in both knowledge and in sophistication than they would have had the course been taught in a more conventional manner. It seemed that the students came to know each other unusually well and to rely on each other's insights to an unusual degree as a result of reading each other's work on the Web site as well as from face-to-face interaction in class. The atmosphere in class was relaxed, friendly, and mutually supportive. The students also became very adroit at using Internet research (in addition to the course textbooks and other reference books) to support their ideas in the weekly assignments and in the end-of-term presentations and term papers. One bonus of having so much of the course work completed on the Web site was that the hour of class time devoted to lectures each week could be used to tackle interesting issues that emerged from the weekly assignments—subtleties, qualifications, complications, implications, historical explanations, and the like—since the students had already displayed a grasp of the elementary issues at stake.

LESSONS LEARNED

The case study and the description of the outcomes provide a clear picture of what was planned: the holistic design approach and the integration of technology into the course on constructivist principles. To offer instructors and course designers in higher education insights into the integration process, this section gives practical suggestions for those who are in a position and are interested in applying constructivism in university courses.

First of all, it is very important to consider pedagogical issues as primary, even though an instructor's immediate goal is to integrate technology into teaching. Without clear instructional goals, technology may not help at all. Tony Bates observes: "Good teaching may overcome a poor choice in the use of technology, but technology will never save bad teaching; usually it makes it worse" (1995, p. 12). Some key questions about the instructional goals must be considered, such as: what do we expect students to learn from this course? What learning activities will help students acquire the essential skills? How can technology help to achieve the instructional goals? These questions established the foundation for the course design and provide directions for decisions on the selection of course materials, learning activities, and the use of Web components.

Constructivism is the underlying philosophy for English 483. However, it is worth mentioning that constructivism was integrated into a conventional classroom teaching model. This partial implementation might be optimal for the majority of students (Bostock, 1998). As the student evaluations revealed, a small number of students resented the open-ended, student-directed kind of learning they were asked to do and wanted to have more lectures, more guidance from above as to what they should think and do. Also, those who responded negatively to the Web components of the course may have seen technology as restricting and daunting because they were not used to learning in this fashion. It is, though, quite encouraging to find that most students embraced the opportunity to explore and appreciated the chance to pursue active learning in an authentic environment. It seemed that an effective strategy is to apply constructivist principles to a course while maintaining a certain degree of instructor presence and guidance.

Student resistance may be an issue in a course like this. The instructor was very adaptive and allowed flexibility. For instance, the students could opt out of the on-line submisstion of weekly assignments. However, students realized that their own contributions were valued and that they could all benefit from sharing their work. By the end of the course, almost all of the students' assignments had been submitted online. It is true that individuals have different learning styles, and some simply will not like the openness in a constructivist environment. However, this course suggests that once students come to understand the benefits of such an environment, they will seize the opportunity, and resistance will dwindle to a relatively insignificant level.

Providing a rich and constructivist learning environment is also to increase the equality of learning opportunities among students. Since students respond differently to different types of media, a mix of in-class and on-line activities simply gives students more options. But we must be aware that the issue of access must be addressed. In the student evaluations, it was apparent that the lack of easy access to a computer and the Internet imposed a great constraint on a very few students' ability to adapt to this new course format. The instructor tried to address the access issue by booking several hours each week in university computer labs for use by his students. This solution may not be completely satisfactory, though it did guarantee that students without their own computers had access to computers on campus.

Providing support to students is another critical issue, and one related to the issue of access. This support encompasses the orientation students received in the beginning of the course and the ongoing troubleshooting for both technical and pedagogical issues. This burden of support can be quite challenging for an instructor, especially one who was in this case learning how to use the technology just a step ahead of the students. In the case of English 483, the support unit—the Faculty of Arts Technologies for Learning Center—was aware of the issue. Thus, the instructional designer along with the technical support staff supported the course throughout the implementation phase by being available for consultation by both the instructor and students.

CONCLUSION

More and more instructors in higher education are begining to see the potential of using technology in their courses. The mixed-modes model in which technology and classroom teaching are integrated will become an increasingly common practice in higher education. Through English 483, we learned that the key to successful integraton lies in solid design principles and adequate support for instructors and for students. What technology to use and how to use it are, at the same time, only a part of the whole picture for the instructor. The most challenging task is to be creative and imaginative when applying constructivism to classroom teaching and to find a balance between an open learning situation and instructor's guidance. Another challenge is the mindset and attitudes students have toward the new paradigm of learning. An instructor must communicate clearly—and then demonstrate—the purposes that the technology serves. The more students understand this, the more likely they are to flourish in the new environment and the less likely they are to resist and resent the change.

QUESTIONS FOR FURTHER CONSIDERATION

What are the advantages and the drawbacks of implementing constructivist principles in a course? What are some foreseeable problems if you were to follow the same principles in your course?

What are the benefits and challenges in integrating technology into a conventional course in higher education? How can you ensure that students have a valuable learning experience?

REFERENCES

Bates, T. (1995). *Technology, Open Learning and Distance Education.* London; New York: Routledge.

Bostock, S. (1998). Constructivism in mass higher education: A case study. *British Journal of Educational Technology*, 29(3), 225-240.

Brooks, C., Lewis, R. W. B. and Warren, R. P. (Eds.). (1973). *American Literature: The Makers and the Making.* New York: St. Martin's Press.

Brown, J. S., Collins, A. and Duguid, P. (1989). Situated cognition and the culture of learning. *Educational Researcher*, 18, 32-42.

Cronin, J. (1993). Four misconceptions about authentic learning. *Educational Leadership*, 50(7), 78-80.

Cunningham, D. J. (1992). Assessing constructivism and constructing assessments: A dialogue. In Duffy, T. M. and Jonassen, D. H. (Eds.), *Constructivism and the Technology of Instruction: A Conversation*, 35-44. New Jersey: Lawrence Erlbaum.

Dewey, J. (1944). *Democracy and Education.* New York: Free Press.

DreamWeaver. (Version 3) [Computer software]. (1999). CA: Macromedia.

Duffy, T. M. and Jonassen, D. H. (1992). *Constructivism and the Technology of Instruction: A Conversation.* NJ: Lawrence Erlbaum.

Grabinger, R. S. and Dunlap, J. C. (1995). Rich environments for active learning. *ALT-Journal*, 3(2), 5-34.

Perkins, D. N. (1992). Technology meets constructivism: Do they make a marriage? In Duffy, T. M. and Jonassen, D. H. (Eds.), *Constructivism and the Technology of Instruction*, 45-55. New Jersey: Lawrence Erlbaum.

Spiro, R. J., Feltovish, P. J., Jacobson, M. J. and Coulson, R. L. (1992). Cognitive flexibility, constructivism and hypertext: Random access instruction for advanced knowledge acquisition in ill-structured domains. In Duffy, T. M. and Jonassen, D. H. (Eds.), *Constructivism and the Technology of Instruction: A Conversation*, 57-75. New Jersey: Lawrence Erlbaum.

Various Artists. (1996). Blues Classics [3 CDs]. Los Angeles: MCA.

Von Glaserfeld, E. (1995). *Radical Constructivism: A Way of Knowing and Learning. London.* Watchington, DC: Falmer Press.

Vygotsky, L. S. (1978). *Mind in Society.* Cambridge, MA: The MIT Press.

WebCT. [Computer software]. (1998). Vancouver, BC: University of British Columbia.

Chapter VIII

Designing and Evaluating Instruction for e-Learning

Som Naidu
University of Melbourne, Australia

The focus of this chapter of the section is on designing and evaluating e-learning environments and directions for research in technology enhanced learning generally. Its particular emphasis is on models and approaches to learning and teaching that stand to take greatest advantage of the unique attributes of online learning technologies. These include the flexibility that they afford because of their time and place independence and the possibility of access to a variety of electronic and multimedia-based materials.

OBJECTIVES FOR THIS CHAPTER OF THE SECTION

The specific objectives of this chapter of the section are to:
1. Explore attributes and capabilities of online learning technologies and opportunities for e-learning that they afford
2. Explore limitations of contemporary practices in e-learning and examine innovative pedagogical designs for optimizing e-learning;
3. Discuss approaches to the evaluation of the impacts of technology enhanced learning and
4. Consider also some directions for further research in technology enhanced learning

ATTRIBUTES AND CAPABILITIES OF ONLINE EDUCATIONAL TECHNOLOGIES

Online educational technologies are information and communications technologies that enable the delivery and use of information and support communication in electronic formats. This section of the chapter will not attempt to describe the form and functions of these technologies as there is an abundance of literature in print as well as in electronic form on these technologies (see Collis, 1996; Rapaport, 1991; http://osf1.gmu.edu/~montecin/platforms.htm). Instead, it will briefly recount the critical and unique attributes of these technologies. These attributes are as follows: a) the flexibility that online educational technologies affords; and b) electronic access to a variety of multimedia-based material that these technologies enable.

The Flexibility that Online Educational Technology Affords

Flexible access to information and resources is the key attribute of online educational technologies, and learner choice is at the heart of the concept of flexible access. This incorporates the facility to access subject matter content and support at a time, place and pace that is suitable and convenient for the individual learner, rather than the teacher and/or the educational organization. Flexible access to content and learning activities orchestrated via online educational technologies across conventional classrooms, workplaces, homes, and community centers is the defining characteristic of what has come to be known as distributed learning (Dede, 1996; 2000). Online educational technologies such as various forms of "groupware" and computer conferencing technologies can support collaborative inquiry among students who are in different locations and often not available at the same time (Edelson, Gordin, & Pea, 1999; Edelson, & O'Neill, 1994). Through a range of online learning technologies, learners and teachers can engage in synchronous as well as asynchronous interaction across space, time, and pace (Gomez, Gordin, & Carlson, 1995). With the help of these technologies and tele-mentors, students from different locations can create, share, and master knowledge about authentic real world problems (Edelson, Pea, & Gomez, 1996; Gordin, Polman, & Pea, 1994).

Electronic Access To Hyper-Media And Multimedia-Based Resources

Online educational technologies also enable the delivery of subject matter content in a variety of media formats that is not possible within the spatial and temporal constraints of conventional educational settings such as the classroom or print materials (Dede, 2000). This means that learners in distributed educational settings can have access to a wide variety of educational resources in a format that is amenable to individual approaches to learning (Spiro, Feltovich, Jacobson, & Coulson, 1991) and accessible at a time, place and pace that is convenient to them (Pea, 1994). Typically these educational resources may include any combination of things like:

- Hyper-linked textual material, incorporating pictures, graphics and animation
- Videotaped elaboration of subject matter, including interviews and panel discussions
- Hyper-linked multimedia elements such as QTVs, simulations, graphics and animations
- Just-in-time access to a range of electronic databases, search engines and online libraries
- Just-in-time access to coaching and assistance via tele-mentors, e-communities and peers

However, the one limitation to this for many at the moment is the capability of their networks and bandwidth to deliver this information (Dede, 1991). But this situation is sure to change and for some, very rapidly indeed.

OPPORTUNITIES FOR e-LEARNING THAT ONLINE TECHNOLOGIES AFFORD

Research in learning and instruction suggests that people learn most effectively by pursuing realistic goals which are also intrinsically motivating (Schank, Fano, Jona, & Bell, 1994). Learning is greatly enhanced when it is anchored or situated in meaningful and authentic problem-solving contexts (Barron, Schwartz, Vye, Moore, Petrosino, Zech, Bransford, & The Cognition and Technology Group at Vanderbuilt, 1998; Brown, Collins, & Duguid, 1989; The Cognition and Technology Group at Vanderbilt [CTGV], 1990). While "goal-based learning" is not constrained by any particular media type, certain delivery technologies can impede anchored instruction or situated learning. Conventional classroom-based instruction for instance, while it may be cost-effective is constrained to a large extent by its fixed time and space in being able to situate learning in realistic contexts. Printed text as well, while it affords transportability, is limited by its inability to incorporate anything other than text, pictures and illustrations.

Contemporary online educational technologies, with its temporal and spatial flexibility and its ability to support resource rich multimedia content, afford us the opportunity to develop educational opportunities that are known as "generative learning environments" (CTGV, 1991). These are learning environments that are based on a theoretical framework that emphasizes the importance of anchoring or situating instruction in meaningful, problem-solving contexts. A major goal of this approach is to create shared learning environments that permit sustained exploration by students and teachers to enable them to understand the kinds of problems and opportunities that experts in various areas encounter and the knowledge that these experts use as tools.

Experts are known to be very familiar with the endemic nature of their disciplines or domains of practice. In order for novices to approximate this level of familiarity with the discipline, they need to become immersed in the culture of that discipline. This necessitates access to a range of resources and experiences, including multimedia-based simulation of components that are not readily accessible in real time, such as certain aspects of biological and medical science, engineering and educational practice. Online educational technologies afford the capability to house and deliver this kind of material.

CONTEMPORARY PRACTICES IN e-LEARNING

The use of the term *elearning* is growing rapidly and frequently being used interchangeably with terms such as *online education, virtual learning, distributed learning, networked learning, Web-based learning*, and *also open* and *distance learning*. Despite their unique attributes, each of these terms fundamentally refers to educational processes that utilize information and communications technology (ICT) to mediate asynchronous as well as synchronous learning and teaching activities. Indeed, with the exception of conventional print-based open and distance education, it can be argued that the emergence of elearning is directly linked to the development of and access to information and communications technology infrastructure. Without access to this kind of infrastructure support, the viability of such educational activities is undermined and those without access to such support are increasingly disadvantaged from accessing the educational opportunities they afford.

Elearning appears to be growing out of three distinct directions:
1. From within educational institutions, which have historically offered open and distance learning opportunities either in a single, dual or mixed mode.

2. From conventional educational institutions that have never been involved in open and/or distance learning. Such institutions are applying information and communications technology to support and enrich their campus-based face-to-face learning and teaching experience. Their goal, in most cases, is to increase flexibility and efficiency in the belief that doing so will enable them to tap into niche markets and student populations, which were previously out of their reach.
3. From the corporate sector, many of which are favoring elearning over residential workshop-based approaches to staff training and development. The corporate world is increasingly finding elearning to be an attractive model as it searches for flexible and "just-in-time" learning opportunities.

Forces driving the growth and development of elearning include:

1. The increasing accessibility of information and communications technologies and also their decreasing cost.
2. The capacity of information and communications technology to support and enrich conventional educational practices through resource-based learning and synchronous and asynchronous communication.
3. The need for flexible access to learning opportunities from distributed venues such as the home, workplace, community center, and the conventional educational institution.
4. The demand from isolated and independent learners for more equitable access to educational opportunities and services.
5. The belief among many educational institutions that the application of information and communications technology will enable them to increase their share in an increasingly competitive educational market.
6. The need, among educational institutions, to be seen to be "keeping up with the times" in order to attract the attention of parents, students and other funding donors.
7. The belief and the expectation that online learning will reduce costs and increase productivity and institutional efficiency (for a detailed discussion of e-learning trends, see Rogers, In Press).

Surveys by the United States Department of Education's National Center for Education Statistics (2000) have found that the number of distance education programs in the United States of America has been increasing exponentially, and many more institutions plan to establish distance education programs within the next few years. The United States National Survey of Information Technology in Higher Education, as part of its Campus Computing Project, carries out surveys annually on the use of information and communications technology in higher education. One of its recent surveys (1999) reveals that:

- Major challenges confronting colleges and universities in their use of information and communications technology include: a) getting faculty to integrate such technology into their teaching, b) providing adequate user support, and c) financial planning for information technology.
- An increasing number of college courses are incorporating ICT, including use of email, as part of their teaching and learning transactions, Internet resources as part of the syllabus, and the WWW for presenting course materials.
- Students and faculty alike are spending an increasing amount of their study time on the Internet and both student and faculty percentages in this regard are highest in research universities.
- Across all sectors of higher education, a growing number of institutions are using the WWW to provide students access to admission forms, financial aid applications, course catalogs, and other related material.

Quality of e-Learning Practices

In the midst of all this interest in and the proliferation of elearning, there is a great deal of variability in the quality of elearning and teaching. This shouldn't be any surprise, as there are just as many instances of poor and reckless face-to-face teaching as there are instances of excellence in that regard as well. A few years back, a group of adult educators from the University of British Columbia in Canada carried out an investigation of Web-based courses (Boshier, Mohapi, Moulton, Qayyaum, Sadownik, & Wilson, 1997). This is a somewhat dated study, and this snapshot of Web-based courses will be undoubtedly replaced by the fast pace of change in this area, but it does shed some interesting light on online learning and teaching practices, which are probably, on the whole, not very different at the moment. The focus of this investigation was on the attractiveness and face validity of 'stand alone' Web-based courses. These researchers defined a 'stand alone' course as one that "might include supplemental material but can be completed entirely without face-to-face interaction with an instructor" (Boshier et al., 1997, p. 327).

Of the 127 subjects they reviewed, the investigators classed 19 of them as 'not enjoyable' to walk through, 42 were considered as 'mildly enjoyable,' 43 as 'moderately enjoyable,' 19 as 'very enjoyable,' and 4 as a 'complete blast.' They also found that very few of the courses surveyed offered much interactive capability for the learner or opportunity for collaborative learning. They found that many of the courses seemed to have been overly driven by an obsession with statement of objectives, assessment outcomes, and a hierarchical ordering of subject matter content, as opposed to a focus on building rich resource-based learning environments around enduring themes. The researchers concluded from this study that the biggest challenge for Web-based course developers seemed to be conceptual and not technological. They suggest that course developers ought to be focusing more on how to make their courses "attractive, accessible and interactive" (Boshier et al., 1997, p. 348).

Despite the growing recognition of the important role and function of instructional design in teaching and learning, educators have on the whole, failed to make the best use of the opportunities that alternative delivery technologies can provide. Evidence of this is all around us in the form of innumerable university course Web sites which contain little more than the schedule, a brief outline of the course content, PowerPoint slides of lecturer's notes, and sometimes, sample examination papers. Instead of exploiting the unique attributes of information and communications technologies, such practices replicate the "education is equal to the transmission of information" model of teaching that is so common in conventional classroom practice. Regardless of the capabilities of the delivery medium, the nature of the subject matter content and learner needs, much of educational practice continues to be teacher directed and delivery centered. Rarely have we paused to think about why we are teaching the way we do teach and support learning and if our instructional approaches are based on sound educational principles of cognition and learning.

This kind of instructional practice has led to a great deal of frustration for learners and teachers, many of whom have grown increasingly skeptical about the benefits of the newer delivery technologies such as e-learning and distance education generally (Kirkwood, 2000; Rumble, 2000). This is a classic instructional design problem. It has to do with the failure of instructional designers and subject matter experts to come up with instructional and learning designs that best match the type of the subject matter and the needs of their learners within the constraints of particular learning environments. Notwithstanding this, there are in the midst of it all, examples of good instructional practice. These are instances when the educational experience has been carefully modeled to support the development of clearly identified learning outcomes, and in light of learner needs, learner readiness and the nature of the educational context.

RECONSIDERING CONTEMPORARY APPROACHES TO e-LEARNING

There is no doubt that information and communications technologies offer tremendous opportunities for building rich and resource-based learning environments. However, these technologies are simply vehicles of the educational transaction, and their impacts on learning outcomes are the subject of much contention (Clark, 1983; Kozma, 1991). In the rush to embrace online learning and teaching, many educators do little more than post the course syllabus and Powerpoint slides of their lectures on a course Web site which is not very different from making photocopies of such material and distributing them in class. Don't get me wrong—posting the course syllabus and one's lecture notes on the Web is worthwhile use of online educational technology. But there is a whole lot more that information and communications technology can enable by way of supporting learning and teaching. To make the most of the opportunities that these technologies offer, careful attention needs to be paid foremost to the pedagogy of the learning and teaching transaction. This refers to the design architecture of the learning and teaching environment, which incorporates, *inter alia*, consideration of how subject matter content is presented, what the learners will do, how learning will be supported, what would comprise formative and summative assessment, and how feedback will be provided.

There is in fact no shortage of advice on how to design rich and resourceful online learning environments and reconsider our approaches to teaching and learning to ensure that we are making the most of the delivery technology we are employing (Burgess & Robertson, 1999; French, Hale, Johnson, & Farr, 1999). Indeed, we do not have a choice in this regard. The changing needs of education and training in both business and higher education are forcing a reconsideration of our conventional approaches to teaching and learning. This incorporates, among other things, the changing role of the classroom teacher from one of being a "sage on the stage" to a "guide on the side." It also includes the changing nature of student learning from one of being "teacher-directed" to being "student-directed" or "self-directed." Information and communications technology has a significant role to play in supporting these foreshadowed changes in the nature of teaching and learning.

French et al. (1999) suggest three ways in which information and communications technology can be used to effectively support a self-directed and student-centered learning environment. These are 1) augmenting teaching; 2) virtual learning; and 3) progressive application. *Augmenting teaching* is based on the premise that educators can enrich their current teaching practices by supporting their classes with one or more aspects of ICT-based activities. Augmented classes may use anything from making use of the Web for distributing information about the course, to email communication for discussion between students and teachers and among students, and collaborative computer conferencing among students for group work. *Virtual learning* refers to the process of learning and teaching on the Internet without any face-to-face contact between or among the participants. In this mode, the Internet replaces conventional lecture formats, creating new opportunities for self-directed and flexible learning. Finally, *progressive application* refers to the process of applying ICT-based technologies to teaching and learning progressively as one develops his/her confidence in the use of the technology and its imperatives. The concept of progressive application of the technology is based on the notion of "just-in-time" learning, which is the process of having educational access at the time when one needs to learn something.

PEDAGOGICAL APPROACHES FOR OPTIMIZING e-LEARNING

This section of the chapter discusses a selection of pedagogical approaches that may reflect one or the other of the approaches to learning and teaching that stand to make the most of the opportunities afforded by information and communications technology. The focus here is on the "design architecture" of these approaches. A generic approach to the evaluation of these instructional designs follows the discussion of these models.

Goal-Based Learning

These are educational environments in which goal-based scenarios are used to anchor learning. The intent of these environments is to place learners in a contrived but an authentic situation within which they have the opportunity to learn by doing and by making mistakes in a safe environment (Naidu, Oliver, & Koronios, 1999). Goal-based scenarios (GBS) are essentially simulations in which there is a problem to resolve or a mission to complete. They require learners to assume the main role in the resolution of the problem or the pursuit of their mission (Schank, 1990; 1997). Hence goals in this context refer to the successful completion of the task at hand and not the achievement of grades. In order to achieve this goal the learner needs to acquire particular skills and knowledge and make informed decisions. Much of the information and knowledge that is required to achieve this goal is available in the form of stories of practitioners (Schank & Cleary, 1995). A GBS serves both to motivate learners and also to provide them with the opportunity to learn by doing, by making mistakes, and receiving feedback. A workable GBS is a situation where the goal is of inherent interest to learners, and the skills needed to accomplish those goals are the targeted learning outcomes (see Figure 1).

Figure 1 outlines the generic architecture of goal-based learning. Upon exposure to a goal-based scenario, learners are presented with their goal. This is best described as a mission or task that the learner is responsible for in the scenario, and it is presented in the context of a crisis or conflict which comprises the "precipitating event," i.e., the event that will launch the simulation. To ensure that the learner clearly understands his/her mission, the goal needs to be interpreted and clarified. This may include the identification of any sub-goals. The learner is then asked to proceed through the simulation, which requires making decisions at various points in the simulation. The making of these decisions will require learners to access content knowledge and engage in field research to gather relevant data and information. Learners will have access to this information as well as to a very rich repertoire of the experiences of practitioners in the form of stories indexed as video clips in the simulation database.

Figure 1: Goal-based learning (based on case-based reasoning)

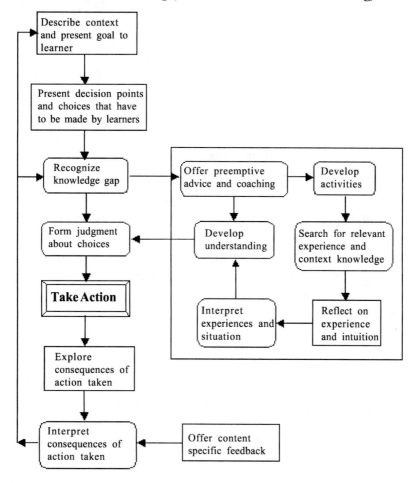

Learner's ability to make decisions at critical points in the simulation will be determined by the success or failure of his/her decisions. In the event of inappropriate or ineffective decision making, learners will be offered preemptive advice and coaching. This would comprise the formulation of new questions and enabling tasks that will require searching for additional relevant experience base and content knowledge to answer. It will also require critical reflection on these experiences, opportunity to interpret these thoughts and, hopefully, as a result of this, new understandings would emerge that would help bridge the knowledge gap that was initially identified. Learners then return to the point in the simulation where an action was required. Before taking action, they explore the consequences of taking this action, and interpret the consequences of taking that action in view of the goals they are seeking to achieve. Feedback is offered to learners on the line of action that they propose to take.

After all decision points in the simulation have been dealt with, learners are in a position to depict the outcome, which may be in the form of a recommendation or report. This is evaluated for its adequacy and alignment with the requirements implied in their goal in the simulation. It must be noted however that the level of success or failure to measure up to the standards set in the goal is not the main indication of the achievement of the intended learning outcomes. The more critical indication of the achievement of learning outcomes is the engagement of learners in the pursuit of the set goals, the learning that takes place from listening to the stories of practitioners, and using this experience base to make right or wrong decisions, all within the confines of a safe learning environment.

Learning by Designing

This is an educational context in which the core learning activity is the design of an artifact. Designing as a means for acquiring content knowledge is commonly used in practice-based disciplines such as engineering and architecture (Hmelo, Holton, & Kolodner, 2000; Newstetter, 2000). The obvious benefit of a design task is its inherent situatedness or authenticity. In design-based learning activities, students' understanding is "enacted" through the physical process of conceptualizing and producing something. The structures created, functions sought, and the behaviors exhibited by the design solution also offer a means to assess knowledge of the subject matter. As such, a student's conceptual understanding or misunderstanding of domain knowledge can be ascertained from that artifact. The failure of that artifact or attempt to achieve the goals set, for example, may suggest an incomplete understanding of the subject matter (Naidu, Anderson, & Riddle, 2000).

Designing a "Virtual Print Exhibition"
The National Gallery is planning a major exhibition to celebrate the re-opening of its print room, for which they have received a grant of $100, 000. You and your colleagues have been asked to put together a *virtual print exhibition* from the newly developed electronic database of Old Master Print Collection in the Library. To accomplish this task, you will need to prepare a proposal, in which you design, install and curate an exhibition online, focusing on an appropriate theme of your choice. The Director of the Gallery would like to see you put together a detailed plan with timelines and a budget with a detailed rationale before it can release the funds for you to begin work. The group with which you will work will have access to an asynchronous computer conferencing facility, to which you and your colleagues will be subscribed. You must conduct all your planning activity using this medium. You should complete the concept of the proposal in five weeks, submit it for discussion and feedback from other curators in the gallery as well as the exhibition committee. You will also be required to present your team's proposal in a seminar to the director of the museum. (p. 112)

A big advantage of setting a design task as the basis for the study of the subject matter is the variety of cognitive tasks required to move from a conceptual idea to a product. These include *information gathering, problem identification, constraint setting, idea generation, modeling and prototyping,* and *evaluating.* These tasks represent complex learning activities in their own right, and when they become the environment in which knowledge of the subject matter is constructed, students have the opportunity to explore that content in the different phases and through different representations (Naidu et al., 2000). The complexity of design activities such as these makes the act of designing excellent vehicles for knowledge acquisition. Design complexity requires iterative activity toward, as well as a need for, collaboration. A workable team possessing different kinds of knowledge and skills can tackle complexity more successfully than an individual. On student teams, one student might have good research skills, another complex domain knowledge, another refined drawing and representation skills, and another great construction skills.

Web-Based Role Play Simulation

Role play simulations are situations in which learners take on the role profiles of specific characters in a contrived educational game. As a result of playing out these roles, learners are expected to acquire the intended learning outcomes as well as make learning enjoyable. While role play is a commonly used strategy in conventional educational settings, it is less widely used in distributed Web-based learning environments. The technology is available now to support the conduct of role play simulations on the Web (Naidu, Ip, & Linser, 2000). The essential ingredients of a Web-based role play simulation are: a) goal-based learning; b) role play simulation; and c) online Web-based communication and collaboration. Let us consider each one of these in turn.

First, goal-based learning is acknowledged as a strong motivator of learning. Typically, goal-based learning comprises a scenario or context, which includes a trigger or a precipitating event. This event may be presented as a critical event and usually requires an immediate response from students. The *second* critical ingredient of this learning architecture is role play, both in the sense of playing a role, playing with possibilities and alternative worlds, and playing to "have fun." Students are organized into teams to play out particular roles within the context of a given crisis or situation. In order to play out their roles effectively they need to investigate and carry out research. The *third* critical ingredient of this learning architecture is the Web. The Web houses the virtual space for the role play and enables communication and collaboration among students and between the students and the facilitators. The role play simulation generator enables the creator of the simulation to specify the roles that are central to the operation and the success of the role play simulation. This generator also enables the simulation creator to define tasks, create conferences, assign rights to participants in these conferences, as well as provide specific information and scaffolds to support the simulation.

Distributed Problem-Based Learning

Problem-based learning (PBL) is a widely used approach to learning and teaching that uses an instructional problem as the principle vehicle for learning and teaching. The analysis and study of this problem comprises several phases that are spread over periods of group work and individual study (Barrows, & Tamblyn, 1980; Evensen, & Hmelo, 2000; Schmidt, 1983).

Distributed problem-based learning refers to the use of this strategy in a networked computer-supported collaborative learning environment where face-to-face communication among participants is not essential. The process starts with the presentation of a problem via a case or vignette that could be presented to learners via the network. Next, learners work individually to engage in problem analysis. During this phase they attempt to generate explanations for the occurrence of the problem in this case. Based on this exercise they identify what they know and do not know about the problem and make decisions about undertaking individual research. This activity may be carried out individually and its results reported to the group via the collaborative learning network. Following this, a reevaluation of the problem takes place and the first perceptions of participants are probably revised. All of this may be followed up with the preparation and presentation of a critical reflection, which is a personal synthesis of the discussion and engagement over the network.

The bulk of the learning task in this model takes place in an electronic environment which is supported by computer-mediated communications technology (Naidu, & Oliver, 1996). For each one of the topics addressed in the course, the learning experience in this electronic environment may unfold in stages over a defined period, such as four weeks. In the first week students are required to articulate their first perceptions of the problem as presented to them. They develop some hypotheses which are their conjectures regarding the problem, including its causes, effects, and possible solutions, outline how they were going to go about searching for evidence to support their hypotheses, and then collect that evidence. They "post" these comments on the electronic environment so that everyone can read other's approach is to the understanding and resolution of the same problem. In the second week, after reading the initial reactions and comments of others on their own thoughts, students re-examine their first perceptions of the problem. They expand and refocus their conjectures regarding the problem and if necessary revise their hypotheses and data gathering strategies and post these on the electronic environment. In the third week, as a result of the online discussions, students would be able to identify new or related issues, revise their conjectures regarding the problem and perhaps make modifications to their problem resolution strategies. In the fourth week they prepare and present their own "critical reflection record" on the electronic environment. This comprises their final comment on the problem situation and how they sought to resolve it.

Critical Incident-Based Computer Supported Learning

There has been growing interest in building learning environments that focus on supporting groups of learners engaged in reflection on critical incidents from their workplace (Wilson, 1996). A model of learning and instruction that embodies the essence of this focus is the "critical incident-based computer supported collaborative learning" (Naidu & Oliver, 1999, p. 329). It is so called because the model integrates reflection *on* and *in* action collaborative learning and computer mediated communication into a model of learning and instruction. It is inspired, *inter alia,* by knowledge of the fact that practitioners regularly encounter in the workplace critical incidences, which present them with learning opportunities. It serves to teach learners to recognize these critical incidences as learning opportunities, reflect on them critically while in action, and then finally share these reflections in a computer supported collaborative learning environment.

A critical incident (from the workplace) presents a learner with a learning opportunity to reflect *in* and *on* action. Learners can do this by keeping *learning log*, which is a record of learning opportunities presented. The log records how one approaches the incident, their successes and failures with it, and any issues that need to be resolved (e.g., things not fully understood or concepts that didn't make sense). The critical attribute of the learning log is that it concentrates on the process of learning. It is not a diary of events nor is it a record of work undertaken; rather, it is a personal record of the occasions when learning occurred or could have occurred. The learning log also relates prior learning to current practice and is retrospective and reactive in action.

Learners engage in this process of critical incident-based learning in a phased manner. Phase One in the process comprises identifying a critical incident. Learners do this by identifying an incident, from their workplace, which they consider as being significant to their roles. They describe the "what, when, where and how" of this critical incident including its special attributes and more importantly the learning gain they derived from this incident. Phase Two comprises the presentation of the learning log via the computer mediated communication system. This log outlines to the group the critical nature of the incident and the reasons for the actions taken by the practitioner during the encounter with the incident. It includes reference to what should or shouldn't have been done and the learning gain derived from the incident. Phase Three comprises the discussion of the learning logs posted on the systems by all students. Learners attempt to make insightful comments and observations about other's learning logs with the explicit intention of learning from the pool of experience that lies there in front of them in this shared electronic space.

Finally, Phase Four is about the coalescence of theory and practice, that is, bringing theory to bear upon practice and practice to inform theory. This last phase in the process has to do with learners making the connection between what they are being presented as part of their formal education and what they are being confronted with as a part of their daily work. This process leads to a summary reflection, which seeks to identify the extent to which learners feel that the theory enabled them to cope with the critical incident they encountered at their workplace. It also reflects the adequacies and inadequacies of their theoretical knowledge and any enlightenment they may have gained from reflecting on the learning logs of their peers and from the reflections of others on their own learning logs.

EVALUATING TECHNOLOGY-ENHANCED TEACHING AND LEARNING

The foregoing designs are by no means an exhaustive list of the pedagogical approaches to technology-enhanced learning and teaching that stand to make the most of the opportunities afforded by information and communications technology. They are most certainly a start in the right direction. For one thing, they are based on sound educational theory, and they also represent tried and tested models. Will they work for you, your subject matter and your learning and instructional context? How could you ascertain that? Answers to these questions lie in a commitment by instructional designers and educators to a systematic approach to the formative, summative, and monitoring (i.e., ongoing) evaluation of technology-enhanced learning environments. Unfortunately, however, systematic evaluation of these learning environments is one thing that is rarely carried out, and it is poorly conducted if it is carried out at all. In the following section of this chapter we engage in a brief discussion of approaches to the evaluation of learning and instructional designs for technology-enhanced learning environments.

Approaches to Formative, Summative, and Monitoring Evaluation

Evaluation of technology-enhanced learning comprises the systematic acquisition and assessment of information to provide useful feedback on the use, worth and impact of learning and instructional designs on intended or projected outcomes. This comprises formative, summative, and monitoring evaluation processes. The generic goal of such evaluations is to provide "useful feedback" to a variety of audiences including teachers, students/users, administrators and other relevant constituencies. Evaluation is perceived as "useful" if it aids in decision making or policy formulation through the provision of such feedback.

Evaluation Strategies/Approaches. Strategies or approaches to evaluation refer to broad, overarching perspectives on the data gathering process. Four major approaches to evaluation discussed here are the scientific-experimental approach, management-oriented systems approach, qualitative/anthropological approach, and participant-oriented approach. Most experienced evaluators are familiar with all the major approaches and adopt elements from each one as the need arises. It needs to be stressed here that each one of the approaches has its unique strengths and brings to the evaluation process a unique set of data and consequent enlightenment.

Scientific-experimental models are probably the most historically dominant evaluation strategies in use. Deriving their values and methods from the pure sciences, they focus on the need for objectivity in their methods, reliability and validity of the information and data that is generated. Most prominent examples of the scientific-experimental models of evaluation are the various types of experimental and quasi-experimental approaches to data gathering (Campbell & Stanley, 1963).

The second class of evaluation strategies is management-oriented systems models. The most common of these are the Program Evaluation and Review Technique (PERT), the Critical Path Method (CPM), and the CIPP model where the C stands for Context, the I for Input, the first P for Process and the second P for Product (Flagg, 1990). These management-oriented systems models emphasize comprehensiveness in evaluation and placing evaluation within a larger framework of organizational activities.

The third class of strategies is the qualitative/anthropological models. They emphasize the importance of observation, the need to retain the phenomenological quality of the evaluation context, and the value of subjective human interpretation in the evaluation process. Included in this category are the approaches known in evaluation as naturalistic inquiry, which is based on the grounded theory approach (Lincoln & Guba, 1985).

Finally, a fourth class of strategies is the participant-oriented models. As the term suggests, these emphasize the importance of the participants in the process, especially the clients and users of the program or technology. User and utilization-focused, client-centered and stakeholder-based approaches are examples of participant-oriented models of evaluation (Patton, 1978).

Types of Evaluation

Type of evaluation refers to the form and function of the process, which is identifiable by the object being evaluated, and the purpose of the evaluation. The most basic distinctions between types of evaluation are often drawn between formative, summative, and monitoring or ongoing evaluation.

Formative evaluation. This refers to the process of gathering data as part of the design and development process. The goal of this activity is to ensure checks and balances and to enable improvements to be made as the project unfolds. The term *formative* indicates that data is gathered during the formation of the project so that revisions to it can be made cost-effective. The formative evaluation process may also include, as part of what is also known as front-end analysis, a needs assessment, which seeks to determine who needs the program, how great the need is, and what might work to meet that need. A thorough formative evaluation activity comprises *design-based, expert-based*, and *user-based* evaluation processes.

The *design-based* evaluation involves a designer or evaluator ascertaining the match between the "learning task" or "user model" and the system design specifications; for example, an architect evaluating the match between functionality of a building and its design specifications. No real target users are involved in this theory-based evaluation approach. The typical methods for *theory-based* evaluation are *formal modeling* (conceptual, learning and instructional design).

The *expert-based* evaluation has the evaluator using the system or the educational innovation to determine whether the innovation matches pre-defined design criteria; for example, a building inspector assessing a building against the architect's plan of the building. This is sometimes referred to as "construct" or "content" evaluation and is carried out by design and/or content experts. The typical methods for the *expert-based* approach are w*alk through* (with think aloud), *observation* (combined with structured responses), *interview* (structured and/or semi-structured).

The *user-based* evaluation involves a representative sample of users completing one or more tasks in an appropriate environment. The typical methods for *user-based* evaluation are *observation, video-based recall of user interactions* (e.g., querying, think aloud), *user's self-reporting* (e.g., critical reflections, student diaries, learning logs), *structured* and *semi-structured questionnaires*, and *audit trail/user log data* (automatic collection of details on user login/use).

Summative evaluation. In contrast to formative, summative evaluation examines the impacts, effects and/or outcomes of the object or process. The term *summative* indicates that data is collected at the end of the process or project. Data that is collected as part of this process in many ways summarizes the project by describing what happened subsequent to the delivery of the program or technology. It would focus on whether the object can be said to have caused the outcome or determine the overall impact of the causal factor beyond only the immediate target outcomes and also estimate the relative costs associated with the object.

Summative evaluation comprises *outcome evaluations*, which investigate whether the program or technology caused demonstrable effects on specifically defined target outcomes. These can be ascertained through *formal assessment tasks* (i.e., marks attained in tests and examinations), *direct observation* (combined with think aloud and structured responses), and *protocol analysis based on learners' interactions* with the exercises. Summative evaluation also includes *impact evaluation*, which is broader and assesses the overall or net effects (intended or unintended) of the program or technology as a whole. These can be ascertained with *user's self-reporting*, which includes post-hoc comments gained through querying, think aloud, and interviews. Other strategies include the use of *semi-structured* and *open-ended questionnaires* for ascertaining user satisfaction with the materials, as well as *audit trail* of their interactions. Summative evaluation may also include *cost-effectiveness,* which addresses questions of efficiency by standardizing outcomes in terms of their dollar costs and values.

Monitoring or ongoing evaluation. This attempts to keep abreast with the extent to which the innovations, processes and products are being integrated into teaching and learning and what are their ongoing implications. As the name suggests, this is an ongoing process and is carried out as part of the post-implementation phase. Data gathered as part of this process is used for making improvements to the next iteration of the innovation.

Monitoring and ongoing evaluation may comprise *secondary analysis,* which seeks to reexamine existing data to address new questions or utilize methods (such as *analysis of user interactions*) that have not been previously employed. It could seek to assess the *integration of the innovation*, which tries to ascertain the extent to which the exercises and activities are forming an integral part of the teaching and learning process. It could also include an assessment of *time on task*, which is an estimation of the time spent by teachers and students on the required tasks. It may also comprise *meta-analysis*, which seeks to integrate the outcome estimates from multiple studies to arrive at an overall or summary judgement on an evaluation question.

DIRECTIONS FOR FURTHER RESEARCH

While interest in building generative technology-enhanced learning environments has been growing (see for instance CTGV, 1990; 1991), insufficient attention is being paid to supporting students in the cognitive tasks involved in these rich and resourceful educational settings. These new learning opportunities immerse students in complex learning environments with large amounts of data and provide them with all sorts of interesting tasks that create demands for new skills. Being successful in such learning environments requires the ability to organize, evaluate, and monitor the progress of one's learning activities. There is some evidence that not all learners are sufficiently equipped with the learning tools and strategies to function effectively in these complex and sometimes open-ended learning environments (see for example Schellens & Valcke, 2000).

A great deal of work has been done in supporting students' learning with various types of technologies in flexible educational settings (see for example Bates, 1990; Collis, 1996; and Khan, 1997). These studies survey several technologies, including print, radio, audio-cassettes, telephone, computer-based applications such as electronic databases and CD-ROMs, computer-mediated communication technologies including email, computer conferencing, bulletin boards, electronic document exchange and transfer, audio and video conferencing, broadcast television, and the Internet. Many of these technologies are ideal vehicles for content delivery and supporting communication, but in themselves, they are lacking in the capability to support or "scaffold" student learning activity.

A "learning scaffold" is best described as a "transitional support strategy or mechanism" which is put in place to guide student learning in desirable directions, or to enable the development of desirable cognitive skills in students. The expectation is that when the scaffold is removed from the learning context, the targeted skills become part of a learner's repertoire of learning skills. Parents or human teachers are excellent examples of learning scaffolds. Among other things of course, they are there to provide advice and support when these are most needed. At some point in the development of the child these types of supports are progressively removed and as such are no longer accessible or are accessible to them only in limited ways. Children go on to live and function in society independently of the supports and advisement previously provided by their parents and teachers.

Similarly, learners in flexible learning environments who often work independently with self-instructional study materials need help with the organization and management of resources as well as the skills to critically reflect on information they may have gathered. Some work has gone on in supporting student learning with various types of cognitive tools and strategies in classroom-based technology-enhanced learning environments (see for example Gordin, Edelson, & Gomez, 1996; Scardamalia & Bereiter, 1994). Very little exists in the form of support tools for e-learning and flexible technology-enhanced learning environments. Existing software-based cognitive tools provide support to students for learning in *face-to-face educational settings* where other forms of advisement and support are also available (Scardamalia, & Bereiter, 1991; Schauble, Raghaven, & Glaser, 1993). These support tools help learners organize their arguments for presentation and also guide them in their cognitive processes. They are less effective in more flexible educational settings where learners do not have access to additional advisement and support.

Work on developing scaffolds for student learning activity in such flexible learning environments is sorely lacking. Existing work on supporting student learning with various types of learning and study strategies (see for instance the works of Candy, 1991; Schon, 1987; Schmeck, 1988; Weinstein & Mayer, 1986) suggest that the development of learning strategies (for example *learning how to learn*) can influence learner characteristics. These authors argue that employing these strategies and methods can help with the cognitive process, which in turn affects learning outcomes. They have identified several categories of learning strategies, namely *rehearsal, elaboration, organizational, self-monitoring, and motivational* strategies. These strategies provide a pedagogically sound framework for supporting *"learning how to learn,"* and it is suggested here that they can be used to guide work on scaffolding student learning in e-learning contexts and other flexible learning arrangements.

QUESTIONS FOR FURTHER CONSIDERATION

1. What are the critical opportunities for learning and teaching that online learning technologies afford?
2. How can we design learning environments to take greatest advantage of these unique capabilities of online learning technologies?
3. How can we ascertain that the learning designs we develop are achieving their intended learning outcomes?
4. What are some of the ways of scaffolding student learning in technology-enhanced learning environments?

ACKNOWLEDGEMENTS

The pedagogical approaches for optimizing e-learning that are presented in this chapter are being applied in several courses with the collaboration and enthusiastic support of the following colleagues: Mary Oliver <oliver@usq.edu.au> (Distributed problem-based learning; Critical incident-based computer-supported collaborative learning); Jaynie Anderson <j.anderson@finearts.unimelb.edu.au> (Learning by designing); Albert Ip <albert@DLS.au.com>; and Roni Linser <ronilins@ariel.ucs.unimelb.edu.au> (Web-based role-play).

REFERENCES

Barron, B. L., Schwartz, D. L., Vye, N. J., Moore, A., Petrosino, A., Zech, L. and Bransford, J. D. (1998). The cognition and technology group at Vanderbilt. Doing with understanding: Lessons from research on problem and project-based learning. *Journal of the Learning Sciences*, 3/4, 271-312.

Barrows, H. S. and Tamblyn, R. (1980). *Problem-Based Learning: An Approach to Medical Education*. New York: Springer.

Bates, A. W. (Ed.). (1990). Media and technology in European distance education. *Proceedings of the EADTU Workshop on Media, Methods and Technology*. European Association of Distance Teaching Universities, Milton Keynes, The UKOU.

Boshier, R., Mohapi, M., Moulton, G., Qayyaum, A., Sadownik, L. and Wilson, M. (1997). Best and worst dressed Web courses: Strutting into the 21st century in comfort and style. *Distance Education*, 18(2), 327-349.

Brown, J. S., Collins, A. and Duguid, P. (1989). Situated cognition and the culture of learning. *Educational Researcher*, 18(1), 32-42.

Burgess, B. and Robertson, P. (1999). Collaboration: How to find, design and implement collaborative Internet projects. Available on the World Wide Web at: http://www.bonuspoint.com/learnres.html#Anchor-Learning-49575. Saratoga, CA: BonusPoint, Inc.

Campbell, D. T. and Stanley, J. C. (1963). *Experimental and Quasi-Experimental Designs for Research*. Boston: Houghton Mifflin Company.

Candy, P. C. (1991). *Self-Direction for Life-Long Learning*. San Francisco: Jossey-Bass.

Clark, R. E. (1983). Reconsidering research on learning from media. *Review of Educational Research*, 53(4), 445-460.

Cognition and Technology Group at Vanderbilt. (1990). Anchored instruction and its relationship to situated cognition. *Educational Researcher*, 19(6), 2-10.

Cognition and Technology Group at Vanderbilt. (1991). Technology and the design of generative learning environments. *Educational Technology*, 31(5), 34-40.

Collis, B. (1996). *Tele-Learning in Digital World: The Future of Distance Learning*. London: International Thompson Computer Press.

Dede, C. (1991). The evolution of constructivist learning environments: Immersion in distributed, virtual worlds. In Wilson, B. G. (Ed.), *Constructivist Learning Environments: Case Studies in Instructional Design*, 165-175. Englewood Cliffs, New Jersey: Educational Technology Publications.

Dede, C. (1996). Emerging technologies and distributed learning. *American Journal of Distance Education, 10*(2), 4-36.

Dede, C. (2000). Emerging technologies and distributed learning in higher education. In Hanna, D. (Ed.), *Higher Education in an Era of Digital Competition: Choices and Challenges*. New York: Atwood.

Edelson, D. C., Gordin, D. N. and Pea, R. D. (1999). Addressing the challenges of inquiry-based learning through technology and curriculum design. *The Journal of the Learning Sciences*, 8(3-4), 391-450.

Edelson, D. C. and O'Neill, D. K. (1994). The CoVis collaboratory notebook: Supporting collaborative scientific inquiry. In *Recreating the Revolution: Proceedings of the National Educational Computing Conference*, 146-152. Eugene, OR: International Society of Technology in Education.

Edelson, D. C., Pea, R. D. and Gomez, L. (1996). The collaboratory notebook: Support for collaborative inquiry. *Communications of the ACM*, 39, 32-33.

Evensen, D. H. and Hmelo, C. E. (Eds.). (2000). *Problem-Based Learning: A Research Perspective on Learning Interactions*. Mawah, New Jersey: Lawrence Erlbaum Associates, Inc.

Flagg, B. N. (1990). *Formative Evaluation for Educational Technologies*. Hillsdale, NJ: Lawrence Erlbaum Associates, Inc.

French, D., Hale, C, Johnson, C. and Farr, G. (1999). *Internet-Based Learning: An Introduction and Framework for Higher Education and Business*. Pentoville Road, London: Kogan Page.

Gomez, L. M., Gordin, D. N. and Carlson, P. (1995). A case study of open-ended scientific inquiry in a technology supported classroom. In Greer, J. (Ed.), *Proceedings of AI-Ed '95, Seventh World Conference on Artificial Intelligence in Education*, 17-24. Charlottesville, Virginia: Association for the Advancement of Computing in Education.

Gordin, D. N., Edelson, D. C. and Gomez, L. M. (1996). Scientific visualization as an interpretive and expressive medium. In Edelson, D. C. and Domeshek, E. A. (Eds.), *Proceedings of the International Conference on the Learning Sciences*, July, 409-414. Evanston, IL. Charlottesville, VA: AACE.

Gordin, D. N., Polman, J. L. and Pea, R. D. (1994). The climate visualizer: Sense-making through scientific visualization. *Journal of Science Education and Technology*, 3, 203-226.

Hmelo, C. E., Holton, D. L. and Kolodner, J. L. (2000). Designing to learn about complex tasks. *The Journal of the Learning Sciences*, 9(3), 243-246.

Khan, B. (1997). *Web-Based Instruction*. Englewood Cliffs, NJ: Educational Technology Publications, Inc.

Kirkwood, A. (2000). Learning at home with information and communications technologies. *Distance Education*, 21(2), 248-259.

Kozma, R. B. (1991). Learning with media. *Review of Educational Research*, 61(2), 179-211.

Lincoln, Y. S. and Guba, E. G. (1985). *Naturalistic Inquiry*. Beverly Hills, CA: Sage Publications, Inc.

Naidu, S., Anderson, J. and Riddle, M. (2000). The virtual print exhibition: A case of learning by designing. In Sims, R., O'Reilly, M. and Sawkins, S. (Eds.), *Learning to Choose—Choosing to Learn*, 109-114. Coffs Harbor: Southern Cross University.

Naidu, S., Ip, A. and Linser, R. (2000). Dynamic goal-based role-play simulation on the Web: A case study. *Educational Technology & Society,* 3(3), 2000.

Naidu, S. and Oliver, M. (1996). Computer supported collaborative problem-based learning (CSC-PBL): An instructional design architecture for virtual learning in nursing education. *Journal of Distance Education,* 11(2), 1-22.

Naidu, S. and Oliver, M. (1999). Critical incident-based computer supported collaborative learning. *Instructional Science: An International Journal of Learning and Cognition*, 27(5), 329-354.

Naidu, S., Oliver, M. and Koronios. (1999). Approaching clinical decision-making in nursing practice with interactive multimedia and case-based reasoning. *The Interactive Multimedia Electronic Journal of Computer Enhanced Learning* (http://imej.wfu.edu/).

National Survey of Information Technology in Higher Education. (1999). *Distance Learning in Higher Education*. The Campus Computing Project, Ecino, CA: The Institute for Higher Education Policy for the Council for Higher Education Accreditation.

Newstetter, W. C. (2000). Guest editor's introduction. *The Journal of the Learning Sciences,* 9(3), 247-298.

Patton, M. Q. (1978). *Utilization-Focused Evaluation*. Beverly Hills, CA: Sage, Inc.

Pea, R. D. (1994). Seeing what we build together: Distributed multimedia learning environments for transformative communications. *The Journal of the Learning Sciences*, 3(3), 285-299.

Pea, R. D. and Gomez, L. (1992). Distributed multimedia learning environments: Why and how? *Interactive Learning Environments*, 2(2), 73-109.

Rapaport, M. (1991). *Computer Mediated Communication*. New York: John Wiley & Sons, Inc.

Rogers, P.L. (In Press). Traditions to transformations: The forced evolution of higher education. *Educational Technology Review*.

Rumble, G. (2000). Student support in distance education in the 21st century: learning from service management. *Distance Education*, 21(2), 216-235.

Scardamalia, M. and Bereiter, C. (1991). Higher levels of agency for children in knowledge building: A challenge for the design of new knowledge media. *The Journal of the Learning Sciences*, 1, 37-68.

Scardamalia, M. and Bereiter, C. (1994). Computer support for knowledge-building communities. *The Journal of the Learning Sciences*, 3, 265-283.

Schank, R. C. (1982). *Dynamic Memory: A Theory of Reminding and Learning in Computers and People*. New York: Cambridge University Press.

Schank, R. C. (1986). *Explanation Patterns: Understanding Mechanically and Creatively*. Hillsdale, New Jersey: Lawrence Erlbaum Associates.

Schank, R. C. (1990). *Tell Me a Story*. Evanston, Illinois: Northwestern University Press.

Schank, R. C. (1997). *Virtual Learning: A Revolutionary Approach to Building a Highly Skilled Workforce*. New York: McGraw-Hill.

Schank, R. C. and Cleary, C., (1995). *Engines for Education*. Available on the World Wide Web at: http://www.ils.nwu.edu/~e_for_e/, Hillsdale, New Jersey: Lawrence Erlbaum Associates.

Schank, R. C., Fano, A., Jona, M. and Bell, B. (1994). The design of goal-based scenarios. *The Journal of the Learning Sciences*, 3(4), 305-345.

Schauble, L., Raghaven, K. and Glaser, R. (1993). The discovery and reflection notation: A graphical trace for supporting self-regulation in computer-based laboratories. In Lajoie, S. P. and Derry, S. J. (Eds.), *Computers as Cognitive Tools*, 319-337. Hillsdale, NJ: Lawrence Erlbaum Associates.

Schellens, T. and Valcke, M. (2000). Re-engineering conventional University education—Implications for students' learning styles. *Distance Education*, 21(2), 361-384.

Schmeck, R. R. (Ed.). (1988). *Learning Strategies and Learning Styles*. New York: Plenum Press.

Schmidt, H. G. (1983). Foundations of problem-based learning: Some explanatory notes. *Medical Education*, 27, 11-16.

Schon, D. A. (1983). *The Reflective Practitioner*. New York: Basic Books.

Schon, D. A. (1987). *Educating the Reflective Practitioner*. San Francisco: Jossey-Bass.

Spiro, R. J., Feltovich, P. J. Jacobson, M. J. and Coulson, R. L. (1991). Cognitive flexibility, constructivism, and hypertext: Random access instruction for advanced knowledge acquisition in ill-structured domains. *Educational Technology*, 31(5), 24-33).

United States Department of Education's National Center for Education Statistics. (2000). *Quality on the Line: Benchmarks for Success in Internet-Based Distance Education*. Prepared by the Institute for Higher Education Policy.

Weinstein, C. E. and Mayer, R. E. (1986). The teaching of learning strategies. In Wittrock, M. (Ed.), *Handbook of Research on Teaching*, 315-327. New York: Macmillan.

Wilson, B. G. (Ed.). (1996). *Constructivist Learning Environments: Case Studies in Instructional Design*. Englewood Cliffs, New Jersey: Educational Technology Publications.

Section V

Designing for Learning Environments

Chapter IX

Designing Hypermedia Instruction

Lorna Uden
Staffordshire University, United Kingdom

INTRODUCTION

Hypermedia technology is increasingly being used as a vehicle to deliver instruction. All hypermedia involves the integration of hypertext with images, video, sounds, animation and simulations, i.e., multimedia. Hypermedia offers many potential benefits to teachers for delivering instruction. However, to develop effective instruction that facilitates learning is not trivial. It must be based on sound instructional design principles, research from hypermedia development and multimedia interface design from cognitive psychology.

This chapter of the section describes a method that can be used by teachers to develop hypermedia instruction. The most important criterion for the development of a hypermedia application is to consider the type of learning outcome required. There are different types of learning requiring different instructional strategies (Gagné, Briggs, & Wager, 1988). Hypermedia supports the design of both objectivist and constructivist learning.

The chapter of the section begins with guidelines for the design of these two types of instruction using hypermedia. As hypermedia instruction involves the use of multimedia to enhance communication and enrich its presentation, it is important that we have effective methods of utilizing the most appropriate medium for the type of information presented. To address the issue of multimedia interface design, we need principles that can guide us in the selection of correct medium for use. The principles derived must be based upon sound cognitive psychology. To cope with this issue, the multimedia interface presentation design is based on the method of Sutcliffe and Faraday (1994). A case study is used to illustrate how multimedia interface design is performed using the method. There then follows a discussion on future trends and a conclusion.

Objectives for This Chapter of the Section

In summary, the main objectives of this chapter of the section are:

- To cite the benefits of using hypermedia technology to deliver instruction
- To describe the types of learning that can be supported using hypermedia
- To point out the problems of multimedia interface design
- To describe modality theory and its implications for multimedia interface design
- To describe a method for guiding designers to develop effective multimedia instruction
- To provide guidelines for the selection of appropriate medium to use for the information chosen
- To discuss future trends in hypermedia development

BACKGROUND

Hypermedia is an application that uses associative relationships among information contained within multiple media data for the purpose of facilitating access to, and manipulation of, the information encapsulated by the data (Lowe & Hall, 1999). Hypermedia systems offer the user free access to all information units represented in the hypertext base by means of two information retrieval modes, browsing and searching. Probably the most well-known hypermedia system is the World Wide Web (WWW), which offers a range of significant benefits for the delivery and content of curriculum in education. Among these are that it is virtually free, it can be used for both local and distance learning, and it operates irrespective of borders of nations or of disciplines.

The use of hypermedia technologies for learning and teaching activities has been widely discussed (Allinson & Hammond, 1989; DeRose, Durand, Mylonas, & Renear, 1997). The apparent match of structural and functional features of hypermedia technology with constructivist principles of learning and knowledge representation has nourished expectations that hypertext-based technologies may overcome difficulties inherent in the communication and information processing approach to teaching and learning. What is distinct about hypermedia is its ability to represent, in its own structure and presentation, the structure of the knowledge it is attempting to convey.

Problems with Hypermedia

Although hypermedia promises great potential for instruction, there are significant problems plaguing both designers and users of hypermedia. According to Conklin (1987), disorientation and cognitive overload are the two most challenging problems related to hypertext. The hypermedia systems currently in existence deal with the problem of disorientation by using navigational instruments like browsers and overview diagrams or question/search mechanisms (Nielsen, 1990). However, these do not always provide an effective solution because of the high number of nodes and/or connections and the lack of orientation by many users toward visual processing (Conklin, 1987).

Cognitive overload is the additional mental overload on authors to create, name and keep track of nodes and links. For readers, it is the overload due to making decisions as to which links to follow and which to abandon, given a large number of choices. The process of pausing (either to jot down required information or to decide which way to go) can be very distracting. It can become a serious problem if there are a large number of nodes and links.

Multimedia

The terms "hypermedia" and "multimedia" are often used inter-changeably. However, a distinction is sometimes made. Not all multimedia applications are necessarily hypermedia. A network representation of information is one of the defining characteristics of hypermedia. An instance of hypermedia consists of pieces of information connected in an arbitrary manner to form a network of references (Begoray, 1990). In this paper the terms will be used synonymously.

BENEFITS OF MULTIMEDIA FOR LEARNING

Studies have shown that computer-based multimedia can help people learn more information better than traditional classroom lectures (Bagui, 1998). Several factors have been attributed to the success of multimedia in helping people to learn. First, there is a parallel between multimedia and the 'natural' way people learn, as explained by the Information Processing

Theory (Gagné et al., 1988). The similarities between the structure of multimedia and the information processing theory account for a large part of the success of learning with multimedia. This is due mainly to the dual coding aspect of the Information Processing Theory. Dual coding refers to using more than one code in the learning process. According to Najjar (1996), dual coding contributed much to the increase in learning through multimedia. Several studies have shown that two media improve learning better than one medium (Parlangeli, Marchigiani, & Bagnara, 1999; Shih & Alessi, 1996). Dual coding not only helps in terms of allowing a person to absorb information from the environment using two channels, it also helps in reducing cognitive load in a person's working memory.

Second, information in computer-based multimedia is presented in a non-linear hypermedia format. The nature of hypermedia allows learners to view things from different perspectives. Hypermedia systems also allow users to choose information freely. Third, computer-based multimedia is more interactive than traditional classroom lectures. Interacting appears to have a strong positive effect on learning (Najjar, 1996). Fourth, another feature of multimedia-based learning is flexibility. Multimedia programs are flexible in terms of how they may be used in classrooms, by individuals or small groups. There is empirical evidence (Najjar, 1996) that interactive multimedia information helps people learn. Multimedia information is most effective when (a) it encourages dual coding of information, (b) when the media support one another, and (c) when the media are presented to learners with low prior knowledge or aptitude in the domain being learned.

DESIGNING HYPERMEDIA LEARNING APPLICATIONS

Both objectivist and constructivist design approaches are supported by hypermedia instructional applications. The goal of objectivist design is to affect learners' processing of information "in order to map that predetermined conception of reality onto the learner's knowledge" (Jonassen, 1991, p. 9). Traditional instruction is typically objectivist in its approach. Objectivist design emphasizes controlling the nature, sequence and frequency of learning activities in such a way as to replicate the knowledge of an expert performer in the most efficient manner possible. A constructivist approach to design is based on the belief that all people create their own understanding of a body of knowledge based upon their perceptions of stimuli in an environment. Constructivist design seeks to create supportive learning environments in which learners can interpret information to develop a better understanding of that information.

Designing Hypermedia Instruction

Objectivist conceptions of learning assume that knowledge can be transferred from teachers or transmitted by technologies and acquired by learners. Elaboration Theory (ET) can be used to design objectivist instruction (Reigeluth, 1983). Two important issues need to be considered when designing hypermedia instruction. The first is concerned with how structured the information in the hypermedia knowledge base should be. The second issue is what type of structure is most appropriate for the application and how that structure should be designed. According to Reigeluth (1983), one of the major aspects of instruction is how to organize instruction effectively. In order to structure instruction effectively using hypermedia, it is essential that a macro strategy be used. Elaboration Theory (ET) emphasizes the relationships among content subtopics, thus making this sequence appropriate for hypermedia instruction focusing on (or dependent upon) those relationships. The interrelatedness of knowledge is fundamental to ET and hypermedia allows designers to make the appropriate links on the applications level. In essence, ET provides the prescriptions that determine the framework for building structures to model knowledge, while hypermedia provides the tool for putting them into action (Rezabek & Ragan, 1989).

The position taken here, that ET and hypermedia are compatible, appears to be well-supported by the following quotation from Rezabek and Ragan (1989):

As its name implies, Elaboration Theory is concerned with designing levels of instructional information that will link in an 'elaborated' relationship. Thus, hypermedia and Elaboration Theory utilize the same basic concept as a basis for organization. Elaboration Theory provides us with the prescription of what to do in the organization content and hypermedia provides us with the means for how to deliver it. In other words, hypermedia would appear to be an ideal vehicle for the delivery of instruction and Elaboration Theory can spell out the design specifications that are necessary to make instruction on masses of information effective and efficient. (p. 5)

The simple-to-complex sequencing of ET facilitates execution of a simple version of the terminal behavior at the initial stage of instruction. In addition, the ability to zoom in for detail and zoom out for review and synthesis that is possible with hypermedia significantly influences potential retention and transfer of learning. Finally, the epitomes and elaboration levels of ET serve as a kind of map or wayfinding mechanism that mirrors the interrelatedness of the knowledge components, which deals with the problem of getting lost in a hypermedia environment. Figure 1 shows an ET approach to hypermedia instruction structure.

Guidelines for Designing Hypermedia Instruction

Elaboration Theory is a model for sequencing and organizing courses of instruction. The basic ET strategies are summarized below:

Organizing structure. It is important to determine a single organizing course structure that reflects the course's primary focus. This organizing structure may be one of three types: conceptual, procedural or theoretical. According to Reigeluth (1983), every course holds one of these features to be of more importance than the other two. The other types of content, plus rote facts, are only introduced when they are highly relevant to the particular organizing content ideas that are being presented at each point in the course.

Simple-to-complex sequence. Design the course proceeding through the identified structure in a simple-to-complex fashion, with supporting content added within the lesson. This method is known as Simplifying Conditions Method (SCM). It begins with a lesson containing a very simple kind of case that is as representative as possible of the task as a whole. This kind of case constitutes the "epitome" of the task. Next, the ways in which the simple version of the task differ from the most complex versions are identified and listed as "simplifying conditions"–real world conditions that distinguish the epitome version from more complex versions of the task. The simplifying

Figure 1: An Elaboration Theory approach to linking

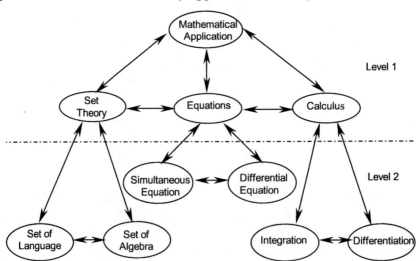

conditions are then relaxed, usually one at a time, in the order that introduces the most important and most representative remaining versions of the task first. When such a primary simplifying condition is relaxed, then and only then are secondary simplifying conditions identified and inserted.

Constructivist learning. The constructivists take on instructional design differently. Constructivism offers different perspectives on the learning process, from which we can make inferences about how we ought to engender learning. According to Jacobson (1994), two theoretical perspectives can be linked to the development of hypermedia constructivist learning environments. These are Cognitive Flexibility Theory and Situated Cognition Theory. Only Cognitive Flexibility Theory (CFT) will be discussed here.

CFT is a case-based theory of learning that was originally proposed to help address difficulties many advanced students experienced in acquiring complex knowledge (Feltovitch, Spiro, & Coulson, 1989). A central assertion of the theory is that advanced learning involves the development of flexible representations of knowledge that will help promote deep conceptual understanding and the ability to use knowledge adaptively in new situations. While Cognitive Flexibility Theory is a general theory of advanced stage learning, it has also been articulated as a theoretical perspective for the design of hypertext and hypermedia (Jacobson & Spiro, 1995).

The instructional medium itself should model the cognitive flexibility desired for the learner. Hypermedia, because of its hypertext capabilities, is well-suited to modeling this flexibility due to its multidimensionality and non-linearity. Hypermedia programs can be seen as "intellectual erector sets" that permit "open-ended exploration in the context of some background structure" (Feltovich, Spiro, & Coulson, 1989).

Guidelines for designing constructivist learning using CFT. Five principles of CFT can be used to design hypermedia learning environments (Jacobson, 1994). These are:

1. Use multiple conceptual representation of knowledge.

The use of monolithic or unidirectional depiction of complex and ill-structured knowledge often misrepresents important conceptual facts of the domain. Multiple ways must be used to represent knowledge in instructional activities (e.g., multiple theme, multiple schemas, multiple analogies and multiple intellectual points of view) to reflect accurately the multifaceted nature of complex knowledge.

2. Link and tailor abstract concepts to different case examples.

Rather than presenting decontextualized conceptual knowledge, illustrate abstract concepts using multiple case examples to demonstrate to the learner the nuances of abstract conceptual variability associated with ill-structured domains.

3. Reduce domain complexity early.

It is important to introduce complexity in a cognitively manageable manner that reflects some of the multifaceted interactions of various conceptual elements.

4. Stress the interrelated and Web-like nature of knowledge.

Demonstrate conceptual interrelationships in multiple contexts to help learners to cultivate a rich and flexible understanding of a complex content area. Do not teach isolated and abstracted knowledge.

5. Encourage knowledge assembly.

Rather than requiring learners to retrieve from memory a single, monolithic knowledge schema that may not be appropriate to a new situation, suggest that learners assemble relevant abstract conceptual and case-specific knowledge components for a given application or problem-solving task.

Multimedia Design

A large number of presentation guidelines have been reported for educational multimedia (Kozma, 1991; Park & Hannafin, 1994) that advise selecting certain media for different types of content and learning goals. Investigation by Schaife and Rogers (1996) revealed that many of these products exhibit poor usability and are ineffective in learning. Although there are guidelines available to help designers, they give little understanding about why multimedia may be effective in psychological terms.

Multimedia design is currently created by intuition (Sutcliffe, 1997). Given the complexity of multimedia interaction, it is unlikely that a craft-style approach will produce effective interfaces. A methodical approach to multimedia interface design is needed. Guidelines are required to cover selection of media resources for representing different types of information and presentation design. These guidelines must address the key issues of selective attention, persistence of information, concurrency and preventing information overloading. Multimedia provides designers with many opportunities to increase the richness of learner interface, but with richness comes the penalty that interfaces can become overcrowded with too much information. Using multimedia does not ensure that information is conveyed in a comprehensive manner. Careful design is required to ensure that the medium matches the message and that important information is delivered effectively. To date, there are few methods available that give detailed guidelines to help designers choose the most appropriate medium based on the information types required. Subsequent sections below describe a method known as Multimedia Instructional Design Method (MIDM) that can be used by novice designers to develop multimedia instruction based on recent multimedia research.

MULTIMEDIA INSTRUCTIONAL DESIGN METHOD

The method developed is based on the work of Sutcliffe and Faraday (1994). It consists of four main stages: a task analysis stage, an information analysis stage, a media selection stage and a presentation stage, as shown in Figure 2. The method is illustrated with a case study using a university fire emergency system.

The first step is the creation of a task model incorporating specification of the content information requirements. A resource model describing the information media available to the designer then follows this. The method advises on selecting appropriate media for the information needs and scripting a coherent presentation for a task context.

The next design step is to direct the learner's attention to extract the required information from a given presentation and focus on the correct level of detail. This forces designers to be aware of the cognitive issues underlying a multimedia presentation, such as selective attention, persistence of information, concurrency and limited cognitive resources such as working memory.

Task analysis. The method starts with a standard task analysis using one of the instructional task analysis methods. Both hierarchical task analysis and information passing task analysis methods can be used. A learner analysis

Figure 2: Overview of the method

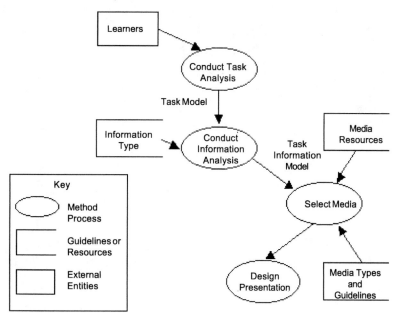

should also be conducted. The task analysis would have produced a hierarchy of goals, composed of sub-goals, which in turn contain procedures, actions and objects. A sample of the overall task model, the procedure for dealing with the outbreak of fire in a chemistry laboratory in a university would consist of:

- To fight fire
- To contain fire and
- To evacuate people

Information analysis. The main objective of information analysis is to specify what type of information is required during a task. The outcome of the information analysis is to produce the task information model. To form the task information model, the initial goal hierarchy from the task analysis model is elaborated by attaching information types, which specify the content to be communicated to the learner. The resulting model should allow the designer to answer the question, "What information content does the learner need for this task sub-goal or input/output interaction?" A set of amodal information types is required to characterize lesson needs.

Information types. Information types are used to specify the message to be delivered in a multimedia application and are operated on by mapping rules that select the appropriate media types. The information types are similar to those found in many tasks or data models (e.g., actions, objects, procedures). Task actions may require operational information (the nature of the action to be performed), temporal information (the time course of the action to be performed), or spatial information (the physical nature of the action). Task objects may require descriptive information (details of the object) or spatial information (the location of the object). Information types are amodal or conceptual descriptions of information components that elaborate the content definition. Table 1 describes some of the information types that can be used.

Information types are also used to help refine descriptions of the necessary content. The motivation is to provide informal categories, which help assessment of what type of information is required to support user and system tasks.

Information can be broadly divided into static data about objects and dynamic data describing actions, events, and changes in the environment. Information types are based on the schema of Task Knowledge Structures (TKS) (Johnson, 1992), which makes the distinction between Dynamic Task Knowledge and Static Domain Knowledge Structures (DKS), composed of object hierarchies. The information types used here are based on Sutcliffe (1997), which is an extended version of the DKS/TKS definitions. The list is based on approximate ascending order of complexity. For example, to show

Table 1: Types of information

Abstract information	Facts or objects which do not have a physical existence; e.g., human knowledge, facts, concepts, plans.
Causation	Description of the cause and effect of an event, including a sequence of events that describe causation; e.g., heat causing water to boil, behavior of an algorithm that results in a desired goal.
Composition	The aggregation or assembly of an object, whole-part relationships; e.g., components of a car engine, parts of a computer processor, memory, motherboard.
Description	Facts that describe an object, entity or agent; e.g., red apples, texture of stone.
States	Descriptions that remain constant for part of the world, objects or agent world, during a period of time; e.g., a person is sleeping.
Physical	Objects or agents that have a physical existence; e.g., chair, table.
Visio-spatial	Visual attributes of objects, structures, pathways, spatial distribution, location, size, shape; e.g., layout of furniture in a room, direction to bus station, shape of a mountain.

the concept of a person running a 100-meter race, we would need information–types of spatial (appearance) and temporal (time) requirements. Figure 3 shows a task model for the case study example of managing a university fire system. In this figure, the "Move Team" procedure requires descriptive information on team composition, spatial information on team location and operational details of team movement.

Media resources. A media resource analysis is also carried out in this stage. This section describes the media resources available to the application for presentation. The media resources considered here are linguistic (text and speech), still image (photographs, drawings) and moving image (animated diagrams, video). The classification is based on the psychological properties of the representation rather than the physical nature of the medium (e.g., digital or analog encoding in video). Table 2 lists the media type definitions and examples. These definitions are combined to describe any specific medium, so speech is classed as an audio, linguistic medium, while a cartoon is classified as a non-realistic (designed) moving image. Each media resource will contain one or more information types: temporal information, spatial information, operational information or descriptive information.

Resources within the case study. A sample of the media selection and associated information types for the fire emergency case study is given in Table 3. Several media may be able to present each form of application data, e.g., a text or still image for fire extinguisher locations.

Figure 3: Task model for fire emergency

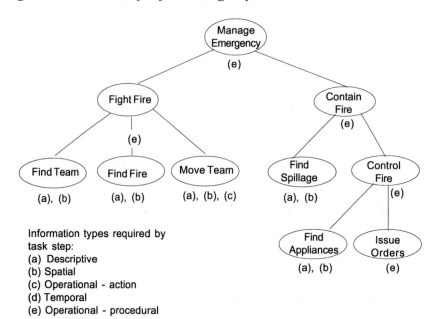

Information types required by
task step:
(a) Descriptive
(b) Spatial
(c) Operational - action
(d) Temporal
(e) Operational - procedural

Table 2: Media type definitions and examples

Media Type	Description	Example
Non-realistic	Content created by human action rather than being captured from the real world.	Diagrams, graphs, cartoons.
Realistic	Content perceived by users to have been captured from the natural world rather than being explicitly designed.	Natural sounds, photographic images, film showing people and natural scenes.
Audio	Any medium received by the audio channel (hearing), sounds.	Dog barking, music, traffic noise, speech.
Linguistic	Text, spoken language and symbols interpreted in linguistic terms.	Alphanumeric text, symbols and signs.
Moving image	Visual media delivered at a continuous rate.	Video, film, animated diagrams and simulations.
Still image	Visual media that are not presented continuously.	Photographs, drawings, graphs.

Table 3: Sample media selection and other information

Application Data	Information Type	Media Type
Fire Location	Spatial, descriptive, temporal, operational Spatial, descriptive	Moving Image. Text.
Class Location	Spatial, descriptive, temporal, operational Spatial, descriptive	Moving image. Text.
Appliance Location	Spatial, descriptive	Still image, Text.
Chemical Descriptions	Descriptive	Text.
Fire Control Procedure	Operational, Descriptive, Spatial, Temporal	Text, Still image, Moving image.

Mapping from task to dialogue act. Having defined the resources available for presentation, the information task model and the information requirements for the task, we now have to decide which media types to use for the task's information needs. To do this, the task model is first elaborated by attaching dialogue acts to specify the desired effect of presenting the information. Dialogue acts are added to the task model to designate the communicative effect to be achieved, answering the questions: "What information does the user need for the goal?" and "How should the user's attention be drawn to important information?" These questions can be answered by splitting the dialogue acts into subject and presentation-based acts (see Table 4).

Subject-based acts elaborate the information types according to the procedure and the action level detail in the task model. The subject acts are subdivided into subject-informative acts, which define information needs according to stages of task procedure and subject-organizing acts, which control the sequence of presentation and hence organize the subject-informative acts.

Presentational acts are used on media resources to draw the user's attention to particular information type(s), thereby supporting the subject act. The dialogue acts are linked to the task model by "walkthrough," asking, "What information or explanation is required at this step?"

At the start of each task procedure, describe its order (sequence), the goal (summary) and any preconditions upon it being performed (conditions). Information may be necessary as input for task actions (enable), followed by display of results of action (result). The users' needs could be to "Foreground" the information type (e.g., draw attention to a property of an object associated with a particular task action), or to present an information type at a higher, more general level such as may be necessary

Table 4: Dialogue acts and their communicative effects

Act Type	Act Name	Communicative Effect
Subject-informative	Enable Result Cause Inform	Communicate actions to achieve a task sub-goal. Give information about the outcome of a task sub-goal. Give information concerning the causality of a task sub-goal. Display information as-is.
Subject-organizing	Sequence Summary Condition	Specify a succession of linked steps. Provide overview of task sub-goal(s). A particular task sub-goal is a precondition.
Presentational	Locate Foreground Background Emphasize	Draw attention to an information type. Give further detail of an information type. Give content information. Make an information type prominent.

at the start of a task (summary), or to draw attention explicitly to important information (emphasize).

Example. In the case study scenario, a fire breaks out in the university's chemistry laboratories. The first sub-goal, as illustrated in Figure 4, is to "Fight Fire" and this is assigned a sequence organizing act (as the sub-goals follow a sequence), followed by a summary act to give an overview of the procedure. The learner will then need to "Find Fire Team" to extinguish the fire. This step is assigned an inform act to give spatial and descriptive information of the department layout and the fire team's location within it, followed by a background act to allow the learners to orientate themselves within the department and a locate act to draw the learners' attention to the fire team's location. The "Find Fire" task step is then performed. This is assigned an inform act to give spatial and descriptive information of the fire location. The "Move Team" step is assigned a result act, showing information of the team movement toward the fire; locate, drawing attention to the fire team and emphasize giving spatial information of the team's path through the department.

Media selection. Several issues need to be addressed when designing multimedia applications. When selecting a medium for use, we should select one that is specifically suited/adapted to represent the information requirements of the concept, i.e., to describe the appearance of a person, a photograph

Figure 4: Task analysis initiated with dialogue acts and information types

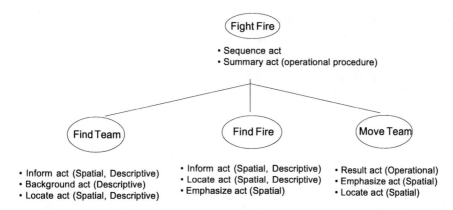

should be used in preference to a text extract as it provides a clearer description. This involves the use of theory on media usage, because the aim is to select a medium that best addresses the information requirements of the concept to be represented. The way to do this is to use media selection rules derived from Modality Theory. Modality is the medium used, hence it is the mode of representation to present the required message. Another issue to be considered is how can optimal media or combinations be selected? These issues highlight the need for theoretical methods. Combining methods with Media Theory enables us to derive principles that can guide us toward making optimal media and combination decisions.

There are thousands of modalities in existence, both input and output, that can be incorporated into interface designs (Bernsen, 1994). To select an optimal unimodal modality from this vast array of alternatives is difficult, due to each modality having a set of information representation characteristics, making it good for the representation of certain information types and bad for others. The combination of two or more of these modalities exacerbates the problem, as when several modalities (both input and/or output) are involved, media interference needs to be taken into consideration.

According to Bernsen (1994), Modality Theory addresses the following general information mapping problem: "Given any particular set of information which needs to be exchanged between the user and system during task performance in context, identify the input/output modalities which constitute an optimal solution to the representation and exchange of the information" (p. 348).

There are a few methods that are available for the design of multimedia systems. Each of these methods provides a positive foundation contributing to the steps, tasks, tools and techniques in multimedia design. Current multimedia research attempts to address modality design by creating methods that remove the ad hoc nature of solutions by providing theoretical frameworks for developers to follow. The problem these methods must solve, if viewed in the most basic terms, can be regarded as the information mapping problem. This problem requires that a mapping exist between task requirements and a set of usable modalities.

Media selection guidelines. When different media resources are available, we need to choose the medium to deliver the information needed. Task and user characteristics influence media choice. For instance, verbal media are more appropriate to language-based and logical reasoning tasks. Conversely, visual media are suitable for spatial tasks, including moving, positioning and orienting objects. The selection guidelines are based on the information types required for the subject dialogue act and the task step type. The information types used with the media selection guidelines are shown in Table 5.

The guidelines may be used in multiple passes. For example, when a procedure for explaining a physical task is required, we can first call realistic image media, then a series of images and text. Guidelines that differentiate physical from abstract information are used first, followed by other guidelines.

Having designed the presentation, a set of validation guidelines is applied to the presentation design. The guidelines are derived from the psychological and instructional design literature. The following guidelines are adopted from Sutcliffe and Faraday (1994).

Table 5: Overview of media selection preferences and examples

Information types	Preferred Media Selection	Example
Physical	Still or moving image	Building diagram
Abstract	Text or speech	Explain sales policy
Descriptive	Text or speech	Chemical properties
Visio-spatial	Realistic media - photograph	Person's face
Value	Text/tables/numeric lists	Pressure reading
Relationships (values)	Design images - graphs - charts	Histogram of rainfall per month
Procedural	Images, text	Evacuation instruction
Discrete action	Still image	Make of coffee
Continuous action	Moving image	Maneuvers while skiing
Events	Sound, speech	Fire alarm
States	Still image, text	Photo of weather conditions
Composition	Still image, moving image	Exploded part diagrams
Causal	Moving image, text, speech	Video of rainstorm causing flash flood

1. If visual and verbal modalities are used concurrently, ensure congruent presentation by checking the information on each modality is semantically related.
2. Use text or still images for key messages.
3. Use verbal channel for warning.
4. Multiple attention-gaining devices should be avoided within a single task sub-goal presentation.
5. Do not present different subject matter on separate channels.
6. Use only visual-verbal channels concurrently.
7. Present only one animation or changing still image resource at a time.
8. Beware: visual media tend to dominate over verbal - place important messages in visual channel in concurrent visual-verbal presentations.
9. If several information types need to be semantically integrated, then use a common modality as associations are formed more effectively within, rather than between, single semantic systems.

Presentation Design

Sutcliffe (1999) states that presentation design is primarily concerned with visual media, as the user's viewing sequence is unpredictable. The design should make important information salient in speech and sound. It is important that a designer in multimedia links the thread of a message across several different media. Presentation techniques are used to help to direct the learner's attention to important information and to specify the desired order of reading or viewing. While the information model defines the high level presentation order, presentation bar charts are used to plan the sequence and duration of media delivery.

First, the information types are ordered in a "first cut" sequence. The selected media are then added to the bar chart to show which media stream will be played over time. Decisions on timing depend on the content of the media resource, e.g., length of a video clip, frame display rate, etc.

It is important to add focus-control actions to the first cut presentation script to either make specific information within a medium more salient or to draw the learners' attention to message links between media. The need for focus shifts between information components is identified. Attention marker techniques are selected to implement the desired effect. The things to consider here are:

1. Plan the overall thematic thread of the message through the presentation or dialogue
2. Draw the learners' attention to important information
3. Establish a clear reading/viewing sequence
4. Provide clear links when the theme crosses from one medium to another

Direct Learner Attention Techniques

When the message is important and cross-referencing is critical, it is important to draw the learners' attention to both the source and destination medium. "Contact point" is used to describe a reference from one medium to another (Sutcliffe, 1999). There are two types of contact points: direct contact points and indirect contact points. With direct contact points, attention-directing effects are implemented in both source and destination media. Conversely, with indirect contact points, an attention-directing effect is implemented only in the source medium.

Guidelines for Contact Point Uses

Direct contact points for key thematic links. A direct contact point should be used if the connection between information in two different media is important. For example, speech is used to direct the learners to the object in the image while highlighting the object being spoken about; e.g., look at the map, the location of the laboratory is (*highlight*), or a text caption is revealed with an arrow pointing to the laboratory.

Direct contact points for linked components. Direct contact points should be used if components in both source and destination medium are important and have to be perceived; e.g., locate fire team in the diagram (speech track), the team location is highlighted (with arrow).

Indirect contact points. Indirect contact points are used when the connection between information in two media is necessary, but perception of the destination component is less important; e.g., look at the diagram, speaking about object while displaying the image.

This concludes the method stages, which have now produced a detailed and thematically integrated presentation design. The guidelines can be applied either to the specification bar chart before implementation or interactively during a cycle of prototype implementation, evaluation and critiquing. Figure 5 shows a bar chart for sequencing presentation of the case study.

FUTURE TRENDS

Hypermedia development is currently at the stage that software development was thirty years ago. Most applications are developed using an ad hoc approach. There is little understanding of development methodologies, measurement and evaluation technologies, development processes, and application quality and project management. This current approach to developing hypermedia is, in many cases, failing to deliver applications that have

Figure 5: Bar chart for sequencing presentation

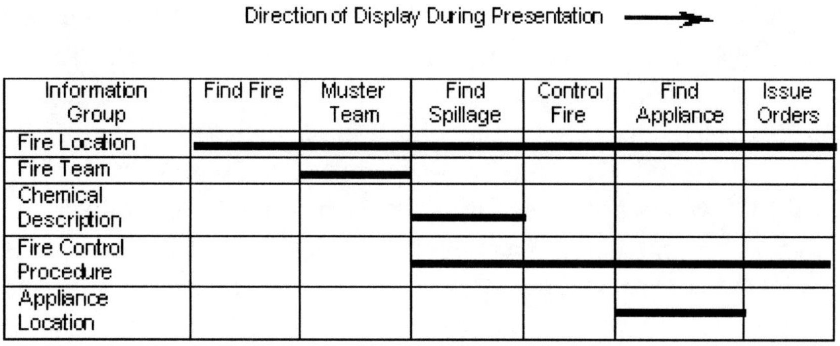

Direction of Display During Presentation ⟶

Information Group	Find Fire	Muster Team	Find Spillage	Control Fire	Find Appliance	Issue Orders
Fire Location	▇▇▇	▇▇▇	▇▇▇	▇▇▇	▇▇▇	▇▇▇
Fire Team		▇▇▇				
Chemical Description			▇▇▇			
Fire Control Procedure			▇▇▇	▇▇▇	▇▇▇	
Appliance Location					▇▇▇	

acceptance quality, especially in terms of information access and usability. According to researchers (Lowe & Hall, 1999), this failure is largely due to a lack of process. As hypermedia applications grow in scope and complexity, we need an evolution (or revolution) to occur, similar to that which occurred in software development. Just as the focus in software development shifted from programming to process, the focus with hypermedia must shift from the use of specific authoring tools in handcrafting applications to broader process issues which support the development of high quality, large scale applications. This includes aspects such as framework, tools and techniques, validation methods, metrics, etc.

Although hypermedia development tools are important, as with software tools, they must be used appropriately within an overall development process that gives them a suitable context. Small applications can still be readily handcrafted, but for large applications, and especially those which that evolve over the time, we need to adopt a more formal and thorough approach, i.e., a "hypermedia engineering" approach. Hypermedia engineering is the employment of a systematic, disciplined, quantifiable approach to the development, operation and maintenance of hypermedia applications. Applying an engineering approach to hypermedia development underlines two primary emphases. First, hypermedia development is a process. This process includes more than just media manipulation and presentation creation. It includes analysis of needs, design management, metrics, maintenance, etc. The second emphasis is the handling and management of information in order to achieve some desired goal. Hypermedia engineering is the combination of these two emphases–the use of suitable processes in creating hypermedia applications that are effective in managing and utilizing information.

CONCLUSION

The design and development of hypermedia instructional applications is not trivial. To produce effective hypermedia applications, it is necessary that guidelines used must be based on principles of cognitive psychology. The method proposed is, we believe, the first comprehensive multimedia presentation design method. Although there are many guidelines that have been proposed by researchers to direct designers in their multimedia development, none of these researchers have integrated their guidelines into a design method. One criticism that may be leveled against all of these guidelines is that they produce recommendations that expert designers would have come up with anyway. This misses the point that methods *are* produced and introduced to help novice designers improve their performance and ensure that they achieve at least an adequate standard.

Evidence produced by Sutcliffe (1997; 1999) has shown that the proposed method did help improve multimedia applications. Our own experience in using the method to develop multimedia instructional applications has been very encouraging. The above method has been used successfully by over sixty students from the multimedia degree course in our university to develop different multimedia applications. So far, the method has proved useful as a means of exploring the issues involved in multimedia design. The method provides a tool for thought about presentation issues concerning what information is required and when.

However, the guidelines within the method need further usability testing and evaluation of their effectiveness. Many of the guidelines will appear in the forthcoming multimedia user interface design standard, ISOI 14915. The method, while making no claim to have solved the multimedia interface design problem, has explored the issues that must be addressed in multimedia interface design. The guidelines and the method can, however, be used as sound design advice to help novice designers develop multimedia instruction.

QUESTIONS FOR FURTHER CONSIDERATION

1. Information can be understood as the interpretation of data within some context. It is therefore important that we can place data that is provided to users in some appropriate context (both a global context of the entire application or Web site and a local context of the specific concepts being presented and their immediate neighborhood). How can we address information contextualization?

2. It is likely that maintenance of hypermedia information applications will become increasingly important as the size and the scope of the

applications continues to evolve. How is the issue of application maintenance addressed?

3. Most hypermedia applications will involve complex information structures. How is the issue of cognitive management during browsing addressed?

REFERENCES

Allinson, L. and Hammond, D. 1989). A learning support environment: A hitchhiker's guide. In McAleese, J. R. (Ed.), *Hypertext: Theory into Practice*, 62-74. Norwood, NJ: Ablex Publishing.

Bagui, S. (1998). Reasons for increased learning using multimedia. *Journal of Educational Multimedia and Hypermedia*, 7(7), 3-18.

Begoray, J. A. (1990). An introduction to hypermedia issues, systems and application areas. *International Journal of Man-Machine Studies*, 33, 12-147.

Bernsen, N. O. (1994). Foundations of multimodal representations: A taxonomy of representational modalities. *Interacting with Computers*, 6, 347 - 371.

Conklin, J. (1987). Hypertext: An introduction and survey. *IEEE Computer*, 20(9), 17-41.

DeRose, S. J., Durand, D. G., Mylonas, E. and Renear, A. H. (1997). What is text really? *Computer Documentation*, 21(3), 1-24.

Feltovitch, P. J., Spiro, R. J. and Coulson, R. L. (1989). The nature of conceptual understanding in biomedicine: The deep structure of complex ideas and the development of misconceptions. In Evans, D. and Patel, V. (Eds.), *The Cognition Sciences in Medicine*, 113-172. Cambridge, MA: MIT Press.

Gagné, R. M., Briggs, L. J. and Wager, W. W. (1988). *Principles of Instructional Design* (3rd ed.). London: Holt, Rinehart & Winston.

Hoffman, S. (1997). Elaboration theory and hypermedia: Is there a link? *Educational Technology*, 37(1), 57-64.

Jacobson, M. J. (1994). Issues in hypertext research: Towards a framework for linking theory to design. *Journal of Educational Multimedia and Hypermedia*, 3(2), 141-154.

Jacobson, M. J. and Spiro, R. J. (1995). Hypertext learning environments, cognitive flexibility and the transfer of complex knowledge: An empirical investigation. *Journal of Educational Computing Research*, 12(5), 301-333.

Johnson, P. (1992). *Human Computer Interaction: Psychology, Task Analysis and Software Engineering*. England: McGraw-Hill.

Jonassen, D. H. (1991). Objectivism and constructivism: Do we need a new philosophical paradigm? *Educational Technology Research & Design*, 39(3), 5-14.

Kozma, R. B. (1991). *Learning with media. Review of Educational Research*, 61(2), 179-211.

Lowe, D. and Hall, W. (1999). *Hypermedia and the Web: An Engineering Approach*. New York: Wiley & Son.

Najjar, L. J. (1996). Multimedia information and learning. *Journal of Multimedia and Hypermedia*, 5(2), 129-150.

Nielsen, J. (1990). The art of navigation through hypertext. *Communications of the ACM*, 33(2), 296-309.

Park, I. and Hannafin, J. (1994). Empirically-based guidelines for the design of interactive multimedia. *Educational Technology Research & Development*, 4(3), 63-85.

Parlangeli, O., Marchigiani, E. and Bagnara, S. (1999). Multimedia systems in distance education: Effects of usability on learning. *Interacting with Computers*, 12, 37-49.

Reigeluth, C. M. (1983). Elaboration theory. In Reigeluth, C. M. (Ed.), *Instructional-Design Theories and Models: The Current State of the Art*. Hillsdale, NJ: Lawrence Erlbaum Associates.

Reigeluth, C. M. and Rogers, C. A. (1980). The elaboration theory of instruction: Prescriptions for task analysis and design. *NSPI Journal*, 19(1), 16-26.

Rezabek, R. H. and Ragan, T. J. (1989). Elaborating resources: An instructional design strategy for hypermedia. Paper presented at the annual meeting of the *Association of Educational Communication Technology*, Dallas, Texas, Feb 3, 5. (ERIC Doc # ED316175).

Robinson, C. P. and Eberts, R. E. (1987). Comparison of speech and pictorial displays in a cockpit environment. *Human Factors*, 29(1), 31-44.

Schaife, M. and Rogers, Y. (1996). External cognition: How do graphical representations work?. *International Journal of Human-Computer Studies*, 45, 185-213.

Shih, Y. F. and Alessi, S. M. (1996). Effects of text versus voice on learning in multimedia courseware. *Journal of Educational Multimedia and Hypermedia*, 5(2), 203-218.

Sutcliffe, A. G. (1997). Task related information analysis. *International Journal of Human Computer Studies*, 47, 223-255.

Sutcliffe, A. G. (1999). A design method for effective information delivery in multimedia presentation. *The New Review of Hypermedia and Multimedia, Applications & Research*, 5, 29-58. UK: Taylor Graham Publishing.

Sutcliffe, A. G. and Faraday, P. F. (1994). Designing presentation in multi media interfaces. In Adelson, B., Dumais, S. and Olson, J. (Eds.), *Proceedings of CHI-94*, 92-98. New York: ACM Press.

Chapter X

Applying Instructional Design Principles and Adult Learning Theory in the Development of Training for Business and Industry

Anne-Marie Armstrong
Lucent Technologies, USA

INTRODUCTION

Learning and instruction exist beyond secondary and post-secondary education. In business and industry, corporate universities and learning institutes are replacing the traditional human resource-based training departments. Learning communities such as Motorola University or SAS Institute Boot Camp are being studied and replicated throughout the world as the importance of knowledge as a resource and knowledge management as a strategic goal become indicators of a system's economic health (Newman & Smith, 1999). e-Learning, CBT, and WBT can also replace costly training systems and provide a wider dissemination of consistent and up-to-date knowledge and skills throughout an organization without huge impacts on the bottom line (Hyland, 2000).

But the old ideas of training for efficiency or productivity and old paradigms of learning as something that takes place in "schools" have to be retooled to meet these new needs. Training does not just consist of psycho-motor skills. Most jobs today have huge knowledge bases that continue to grow and, for the newer jobs, cognitive skills have surpassed perceptual and physical skills in importance. Training approaches in today's corporate world need to have more performance orientation as opposed to the learner perspective being taught in public schools and universities. Learning and regurgitating facts, skills, and content is not enough.

The idea of training for performance is as old as the apprenticeship systems used by craft guilds in the Middle Ages. Then a person learned a trade or craft by working under the guidance of an experienced workman or master craftsman (Cooper, 1978). The apprenticeship system of on-the-job learning was prevalent up until the Industrial Revolution when schools replaced it as the source for acquiring job-related skills. Pre-job training in special voca-tional schools augmented any skills that were not learned in the normal public school. World War II challenged this system and brought about formal training programs conducted in the work environment, i.e., on-the-job train-ing (Scales & Yang, 1993). Skills were parsed. Knowledge was specific and individualized to the company's needs. Sub-optimization was frowned upon. The system must be optimized.

On-the-job training is still a necessity, but the rapid changes taking place in the work environment call for both formal and informal work-place training. The information needs of even low-skill jobs such as fast food cashiers cry for the design of better machine-human interfaces, embedded training, and performance support programs in the form of help screens or task wizards that pop up with advice even before the worker calls for assistance.

Because instructional design uses a system approach to developing training, it is being used more and more by business and industry to improve their competitive edge. Business first saw the value of the system approach to training when it began working more and more with large-scale military projects and, more recently, with the space program.

Objectives for This Chapter

The purpose of this chapter of the section is to demonstrate how corporations can deliver efficient and effective learning to their in-house designed courses and demonstrate that they add value to the corporation. Using instructional design principles can shorten training cycles, improve retention, and empower learners. It can also provide companies with the knowledge edge needed to survive a high competence, high knowledge, high volume, and transaction intensive global economy.

At the end of this chapter of the section, the reader will be able to:

- Classify the instruction needed by cognitive domain (verbal information, intellectual skills, cognitive strategies, motor skills, attitude) for specified learning objectives
- Describe appropriate instructional events and accompanying evaluation strategies
- Describe the type of training you would propose for specific training/development needs

RATIONALES, PRINCIPLES, AND THEORY

In adult training, the purpose is change to improve or produce performance at an optimum level. It is an interaction between the instruction and the learner during which knowledge and skills are acquired or refined, diverse experiences are integrated, and the learner grows in competence and confidence. Today, training's goal is not just to make employees more efficient and productive but is to give them confidence in their ability to do their job (Olesen, 1999). It can be one of the most complex interactions between humans. (Even a behaviorist-oriented programmed course is ultimately an interaction between humans. It just mediates the interaction with printed text, audio, computer/video screens, or Web pages.) But it can also be very rewarding for both.

The art and science of helping adults learn is sometimes called andragogy. It is based on four crucial assumptions about adult learners (Knowles, 1975; 1984). As persons mature they:

- Become more independent and self-directing and they benefit from an active role in the process
- Use their own experiences as starting points and learning resources
- Are ready to learn that which is related to their present roles and responsibilities
- Want to immediately apply what they are learning to something real in their lives

The adult learning model requires that instruction include five conditions:

1. Letting learners know why something is important to learn
2. Showing learners how to get the information
3. Relating the learning to the learner's experience
4. Recognizing that the learner determines readiness to learn
5. Helping learners overcome old inhibitions, behaviors and beliefs about learning.

Traditional Instructional Design

The typical ID developmental model is a top-down "waterfall" method of courseware development. It had many advantages prior to the existence of the present authoring systems and the concept of rapid prototyping. Its form insists that each step be completed before the next step is begun. It served its purpose when programming languages and development tools were fixed and non-flexible and minimal changes were expected. However, it also had several disadvantages, including assumptions of closure on the part of the developers and customers and the completion of all previous stages. There was also a tendency to isolate designers from development specialists who would work in an assembly line atmosphere. For these reasons, more flexible instructional design models have been developed and have proved more adaptable to designing training in today's businesses and industries.

The Layers of Necessity Model

According to authors, Tessmer and Wedman (1990), "The essential perspective of the layers of necessity model is this: based upon the time and resources available to the developer, the developer chooses a layer of design and development activities to incorporate into an instructional product or project" (p. 79). In short, the layer is matched to the necessities of the project and each layer is a self-contained ISD model (see Figure 1). And though each ISD model differs in terms of the sophistication and detail used, it is still based on instructional and learning theories, on communication theory and on systems design and theory. Each layer of the model contains the components basic to good instructional design and development:

- Situational assessment
- Goal analysis
- Instructional Strategy development
- Materials development
- Evaluation and revision

But, depending on the amount of time and resources available, the designer can start working with the developers and the subject matter experts with one layer and can readily increase or decrease the amount of complexity involved. This results in a more timely and more relevant product without sacrificing quality. Further, the layers-of-necessity model contains all the elements of the ADDIE (Analysis, Design, Development, Implement, Evaluate) system. And, at the same time, it is more flexible, makes more use of the content and context of the subject matter, and is

Figure 1: The layers of necessity model

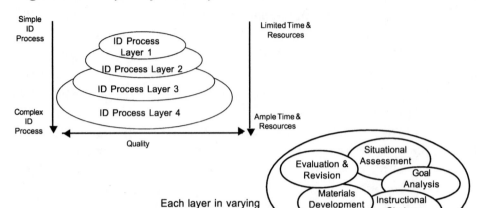

more customer and learner focused. The layers of necessity model differs from traditional ISD models in that it emphasizes:

- Task enhancement rather than task closure
- ISD **principles** rather than ISD **procedures**
- Merging and combining stages of design and development rather than discrete and separate stages
- Assessment by effectiveness and efficiency rather than just by efficiency

Working hand-in-hand with the layers of necessity model in designing instruction is the concept of rapid prototyping.

Rapid Prototyping

Rapid prototyping (see Figure 2) is an old technique borrowed from manufacturing that offers the means to test ideas and elaborate alternatives. It assumes that the final design will not be the first product. Instead, designers rapidly put together different concepts and possibilities for the final design in a product-like form. Prototypes may contain breadth or depth. That is, they might cover one particular part of the product in detail or generalize the entire product.

Examples might take the form of a few pages of a student handbook or a typical module or interface for the CBT. By using rapid prototyping insights are made, communication is clearer, and refinements and elaboration are made earlier in the process, thereby saving much rework. Rapid prototyping allows the subject matter experts and other members of the development team to:

- Concretely view the form, medium, and content of possible products
- Contribute their opinions and ideas about appropriateness of the various forms, and
- Predict the ultimate utility of those products and forms

Figure 2: A rapid prototyping model

The development and proliferation of authoring tools, graphical interfaces, graphics and multimedia programs, and page layout software made rapid prototyping possible for curriculum and course development.

ANALYSIS

The analysis stage of instructional design of training courses for business and industry serves more than one purpose (see Figure 3). First of all it becomes the basis for drafting the training objectives. Next, it provides a structure that the designer can use to uncover the unobtrusive and indirect effects of the particular company's culture and environment on job and task performance. Finally, it may also uncover the real reason and needs for the performance problems and then lead to non-training solutions.

Figure 3: Analysis and design: Situational assessment

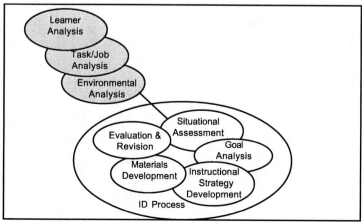

Learner Analysis—Who Will Receive the Instruction?

Trainees may already have a good understanding of the particular work and in many cases will benefit from instruction in which the context is based on their own work environment. This is in keeping with Knowles principles of adult learning.

Most learner analysis tools will first ask for demographic information.

- Department/grouping
- New or transferred
- Union or non
- Job classification(s)

Next it will ask for job or task specific information usually covering the following:

- Aptitudes
- Physical attributes
- Experience levels
- Cognitive and/or learning style assessment

Lastly, it needs to identify the Subject Matter Expert, the course sponsor, any power or expert users, and, if possible, the names of some novice users. Novices are helpful for quick assessments of the instruction during rapid prototyping. If you use experts for the tryouts, they may have the skills internalized so much that they can't verbalize some of the steps or may not notice that parts of the instruction are weak. Try to obtain contact numbers and schedules.

When Might a Detailed Learner Analysis Be Skipped?

In certain situations an in-depth learner analysis may not be necessary. Usually an industry or organization already has a good idea of the makeup of their workforce. Instructional designers in large corporations or the military may refer back to the recruitment requirements, to an employee skills list, or to the reports generated by their training management program to obtain at least some of the learner analysis information. And a quick double check with the course sponsors for confirmation of the documented information and to inquire about any other relevant variables, e.g., students' first languages, might suffice.

There might also be cases when additional analysis is required by the sponsor. For example, government and military agencies frequently ask for a mission and/or requirements analysis. A mission analysis determines the overall purposes or objectives and capabilities of the system and the environment in which the system must operate. The requirements analysis assesses the feasibility and internal compatibility of the system requirements and defines the measurements of performance for the mission, human and job/tasks.

Job/Task/Skills Analysis—What Is Needed to Get the Job Done?

The first step to developing training objectives is to identify performance objectives, gaps, and the criteria used for determining different levels of performance. What will the performer do when performing the goal? It is important to first get an overview of the job from more than one perspective. What is needed to get this job done according to: 1) the SME, 2) management or the course sponsor, and 3) the operator. In the case of the Job/Task/Skills Analysis, a summary or synopsis of the job can be developed. Appendix A is an example of a form used to obtain a Job/Task/Skills Analysis in a manufacturing facility.

At this stage, it can be extremely helpful to list the Knowledge, Skills, Abilities (KSAs) needed and to classify them according to type (see Table 1). Once the type is listed a format for later displaying or instructionally presenting, the skills can be chosen.

Elicit the complete description of the performance required and the acceptable result. A good methodology to use is forward or backward chaining. With this technique you can start at either the beginning (no end product exists) or at the end (product satisfactorily exists) and chain each event to each event.

The rest of the Job/Task/Skills Analysis should list:

- The job/task/skill sequence in a manner that is commonly and logically followed
- Decision points along with their criteria
- Possible hazards, safety requirements and personal safety equipment
- common errors or problems encountered along with any critical incidents, i.e., events which are unusual but which have happened and which would result in an alternative procedure
- Rating the complexity and criticality of each part of the recorded job/task/skill analysis.

Table 1: Sample of knowledge, skills and abilities

KSA Type	Display and Presentation Format
Procedural (cognitive or psychomotor)	Flow chart
Intellectual	Tables or columns of attributes, commonalities and distinctions
Verbal information	Outlines
Motor skills	Photos, pictures, diagrams, movies, animations
Attitudinal	Description of sampled overt behavior

Environmental or Situational Analysis—What Impacts the Job?

This analysis identifies any situational, sociological, or environmental variables that impact the development, delivery, or application of the job and/or the course. At the first level of analysis that would include:

- Location, times, temperature, air quality, etc.
- Frequencies
- Concurrent events
- Shifts
- Tool use

Table 2 is used to determine any further information needed for secondary or elaborated analysis.

Once the above three analyses have been completed to the level necessary, an instructional designer can determine if training is the suitable method for meeting the objectives, and if so, determine the course type and establish the timeline. Table 3 is a typical "checklist" for determining training needs.

If training is not the entire solution to the performance improvement, then ask:

1. Does discrepancy result from inadequate information, environmental constraints, improper reward and incentive plan, knowledge skill deficiency or other performance related factors?

Table 2: Determining further analysis

Environmental Variable		Examples
Developmental	Timelines	Earliest and latest dates, actual vs. desired
	Organization's culture	Union, nonunion, professional, technical, clerical, etc.
	Organization's rules	Time length of charges to production, training charge numbers, security requirements.
	Organization's structure	Shifts, supervision, work breaks
	Quality control	How will training affect 6σ?
Delivery	Pre-determined methods	Must be OJT? Or only classroom available?
	Communication flow	Who needs to know what, when?
	Instructor's experience needs	Has training or experience in delivery method or delivery equipment?
	Support/equipment needed	Availability of trainees, instructors, and equipment. Student-to-instructor ratio
Application	Time pressures and stress levels	On-the-job time criticality or piece work requirements, physical or cognitive overloads
	Variety of equipment and scheduled changes	Is new or updated equipment scheduled for installation?
	Work area layout	*Clean* areas, high bays, pits, etc.
	Ergonomics	Tools, settings, equipment, interfaces, noise levels, temperature requirements, etc.

Table 3: Sample checklist for determining training needs

	Action Taken	Date
No course needed–not a training problem		
Job aid or job knowledge delivered–no course needed		
Structural changes needed		
Other recommendations		
Course type needed (choose type below)		
Classroom		
OJT		
CBT		

2.   What environmental changes are needed?
3.   What motivational changes are needed?
4.   What information needs to be disseminated?

Goal Analysis

If it has been decided that training will be needed to enhance performance, the training objectives must be determined. Completing goal analysis (see Figure 4) will identify the training objectives.

Figure 4: Goal analysis

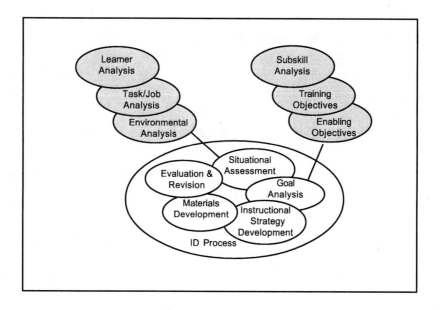

WRITING OBJECTIVES

Now the designer is ready to write the performance objectives. Objectives differ from goals in that goals are simply expressions of the general results desired. They may or may not be measurable. Performance objectives are tied to the work activities or linked to the work's subject matter and "need-to-know" information. Objectives describe the desired results in measurable terms. Objectives are a technical description of the desired performance, including task variability complexity and criticality levels. Performance objectives have three parts:

1. Performance—what the learner will be able to do at the end of instruction
2. Criterion —how well the learner will be able to do it
3. Conditions, if any, under which performance will occur

The performance objectives should make what the learner will know very tangible. The performance statement begins with a verb and that verb is linked to the type of task to be learned. To do this:

1. First classify the performance outcome according to the learning domain or type–cognitive, psychomotor, or affective.
2. Second, further classify the performance outcomes by level of complexity within the learning domain
3. Third, choose the verb which best describes the performance and which is suitable for measurement under the criteria (see Table 4).

Enabling objectives are developed in the same manner as performance objectives:

1. Begin with a verb
2. Describe how the learner will perform
3. Describe any conditions that must exist for the performance.
4. Check to make certain that objective is measurable (see Figure 5).

Writing objectives is more difficult than it first appears. Some mistakes that should be avoided are:

1. Avoid making them too long. Make them as concise as possible.
2. Do not use vague language. Words like "know" or "understand" are generally too vague.
3. Use the proper verb even if it has been used before. Objective writing is not creative literature. Repetition of verbs is frequently proper and necessary.

Figure 5: Formula for writing objectives

Table 4: Classifying

Cognitive Domain Level	Knowledge	Comprehension	Application	Analysis	Synthesis	Evaluation
Characteristics	Remembering, recalling, recognizing, things, terms, facts, etc.	Knowing what a message, concept, or fact means; interpreting information	Using what has been previously learned under actual conditions	Break down knowledge into parts and whole relationship	Bring together parts of knowledge to form a whole and build new relationships	Assessing the value of ideas, things, etc; make judgments on basis of criteria
Verbs associated with:	Arrange Define Duplicate Label List Match Memorize Name Order Recognize Recall Relate Repeat Reproduce	Classify Describe Explain Express Identify Indicate Locate Recognize Report Restate Review Select Sort Tell Translate	Apply Choose Demonstrate Dramatize Employ Illustrate Interpret Operate Practice Prepare Schedule Sketch Solve Use	Analyze Appraise Calculate Categorize Compare Contrast Criticize Diagram Differentiate Distinguish Examine Experiment Inventory Question Test	Arrange Assemble Collect Compose Construct Create Design Formulate Manage Organize Plan Prepare Propose Set up Synthesize Write	Appraise Argue Assess Attack Choose Compare Estimate Evaluate Judge Predict Rate Score Select Support Value

Psychomotor Domain Level	Reflexes	Fundamental Movement	Perception	Physical Abilities	Skilled Movement	Nondiscursive
Characteristics	Involuntary movement	Simple movements	Response to stimuli	Developed psychomotor movement	Advanced learned movement	Most advanced learned movement
Verbs associated with:	Stiffen Extend Flex Stretch	Crawl Walk Run Reach	Turn Bend Balance Catch	Move heavy objects Make quick motions Stop and restart movement	Play instrument Use a hand tool	Dance Change expression

Affective Domain Level	Receiving	Responding	Valuing	Organization	Characterization
Characteristics	Paying attention	Minimal participation	Internalizing preferences	Development into value system	Practicing as a total philosophy for life
Verbs associated with:	Listen to Perceive Be alert to Show tolerance of	Reply Answer Follow along Approve Obey	Attain Assume Support Participate Continue	Organize Select Judge Decide Identify with	Believe Practice Continue to Carry out

Adapted from: Rothwell, W.J. & Kazanas, H.C. (1992). Mastering the instructional design process. San Francisco, CA: Jossey Bass

Table 5: Sequencing objectives

Approaches to Sequencing

Chronological	Known-to-unknown
Topical	Unknown-to-known
Whole-to-part	Part-to-part-to-part
Part-to-whole	General to specific
Step-by-step	

4.   Avoid criteria that are linked to instructor or supervisor satisfaction or that may lead to arbitrary assessment of achievement.
5.   Avoid lengthy lists of required equipment or resources. List only that which would not be obvious to the reasonable person.

Sequencing Objectives

There are a variety of ways in which the objectives can be sequenced. However, usually only one of two ways would be appropriate to the expected outcomes (see Table 5). One rule of thumb is to notice that most learners fall into one of two learning style preferences: whole-to-part or part-to-whole. Use the sequence approach that is most applicable to the task, but if possible, provide an alternative presentation by including summaries, flow charts, or tables.

MATERIALS DEVELOPMENT AND DELIVERY SYSTEMS

Material development in the layers of necessity model is driven by the instructional strategy, time constraints, and resource constraints. In the case of the many businesses, material development is also governed by their present skills, needs, and resources. Figure 6 illustrates materials development.

Materials are usually developed and delivered in the most timely and economical manner. Any and all material that is developed should be subjected to the test of the nine events of instruction.

EVENTS OF INSTRUCTION

For instructional effectiveness there are nine events (see Table 6) that usually must take place (Gagne, Briggs, & Wager, 1992). The event need not take a lot of time or resources, but being aware of the events and checking your materials and the delivery system for their presence will ensure that they are present.

Figure 6: Materials development in the layers of necessity model

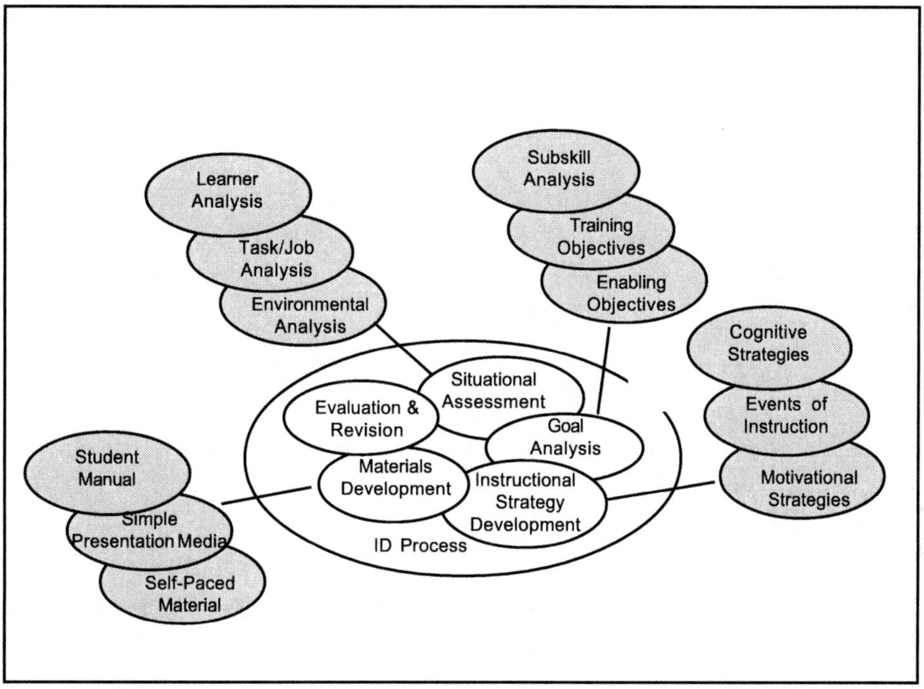

Table 6: The nine events of instruction

Events of Instruction	Examples, Explanations
1. Gain Attention	Lights, sound, color, pictures, dramatic examples, questioning, etc.
2. Inform learner of objective	State or list all objectives in student handbook, on presentation slide, at beginning of CBT, video, etc.
3. Stimulate recall of related learning	Give purpose of instruction and relate to job assignment and product being assembled
4. Present the material	Use appropriate instructional strategy, i.e., lecture, diagram, flow chart, modeled behavior, etc.
5. Provide learning guidance	Stop and point out important steps, elicit examples, use bulleted statements, show a variety of situations, summarize and repeat
6. Elicit the performance	Question on specifics, provide exercises, worksheets; Get volunteers to try it out; Have pairs critique each other
7. Provide feedback on performance	Be specific and note both positive and negative performances; Don't just generalize.
8. Assess the performance	Checklists, informal questioning, performance, products, short tests and reviews
9. Provide aid for retention and transfer	Summarize in different presentation. Provide real examples. Combine OJT with classroom and the reverse. Provide job aids and refreshers and updates. Elicit questions. Provide your own questions and answers, FAQs.

Table 7: Matching the nine events to learning objectives

Learning Objective	Instructional Event			
	Stimulate Recall	Present Material	Guide Learner	Elicit Performance
Name or Label	Show association with concrete object	Provide examples	Relate to previous experience or learning	Point and ask for identification
Abstract concept	List relevant features	Describe instances and non-instances	Draw Table of Attributes	Have identify from field of many
Rule use	Review needed concepts and steps	Present instance and non- instances of rule application	Demonstrate rule use and provide any needed memory aid	Request performance using rule
Problem solving	Review all subordinate rules	Present novel task or problem	Model rule usage or problem solving	Request performance in problem solving task

The specific instructional events may vary according to the learning domain and the objective. For examples see Table 7.

TRAINING DELIVERY MECHANISM AND TRAINING TECHNOLOGY

General Approach

The type of media used to deliver training will depend on the job skills, the amount of information, and the level of performance required. In some cases more than one type of media or a hybrid of more than one type will be used. Cost estimates are based on 1998 dollars and were averaged from various cost reports found on the Internet. Descriptions of the media type follow the Table 8.

Live instructor/facilitator training: Requires the presence of a trained instructor or facilitator in the same physical location as the learners or students. Live instruction/facilitation is usually accompanied by good presentation skills and equipment (real or simulated), reference material, and appropriate instructional and motivational strategies.

Small group/peer training: Designed so that all members of the group are active participants and initiators of instruction. Individual members may take turns in leadership roles. Emphasis is on consensus, cooperation, and developing group solutions to training and to problem solving. Usually results in synergistic learning.

Web-Based Training: Delivery is dependent on the server, the user's hardware, and the type and power of the connection. Some interactivity is possible and its use will continue to expand as the hardware and communication equipment improves. It is best for motivated, adult students who read well. Web-based

Table 8: Matching instructional media with learner outcomes

Training Delivery Media Capabilities

Type of Training Delivery Media	Est. Development Costs	Perceptual Skills			Mental Skills		Motor Skills		Communication Skills			Information Needs			Level of Conseq.			Level of Perform.		
		Visual	Auditory	Tactile	Verbal Info	High'rOrder Think'g	Discrete	Continuous	Listen	Inform	Instruct	High	Medium	Low	High	Medium	Low	Trained	Effective	Expert
Live Instructor /facilitator/equipment	$730 day plus eqpt costs				x		x		x						x					x
Small group/peer	$280 day per indiv.				x	x	x	x	x	x	x				x	x			x	
Web-Based	$3K hour				x							x	x		x	x		x		
Computer-Based	$2.5K - $4K hour	x			x								x	x						
Instruction		x	x																	
Interactive Multi-media	$8K /hour	x	x	x	x	x	x					x	x	x	x			x	x	
Electronic Performance Support	$????		x		x			x					x	x	x	x			x	
Simulation	$14K hour	x	x	x		x	x	x		x	x				x	x			x	x
Gaming Virtual Reality*	$14+K hour plus eqpt	x	x	x		x	x	x	x										x	x
Video	$15K hour	x	x			x										x				
Teleconference (2-way TV)		x														x				
Audio tape/CDs			x			x	x		x	x	x				x	x			x	
Searchable database			x		x		x												x	
Automated Aids					x	x						x	x		x	x			x	x
CBT/Mmedia Hardware	$4K																			
Internet Access T-1 line	$40K year																			
Satellite transmission	Original Signal + $4K + $650 per site																			
Mobile computer/HMD	$1K to $100K																			

　* Studies on the use of virtual reality show mixed results for the learning and practice of tactile or motor skills. New developments in VR equipment are expected and could clarify its use in motor skills training

instruction may also promote reflection. There are two types of Web-based instruction. Synchronous courses often involve the use of chat groups, or even face-to-face discussion, so the learning is synchronized with the instruction. Asynchronous courses are those that use the Web, e-mail, and discussion groups as a teaching medium, causing the learning to take place at a different time than the instruction. It can be augmented through e-mail, chat rooms, bulletin boards, and conferencing.

Computer Based Instruction (CBI): With CBI, training is provided through the use of a computer and software, which guides a learner through an instructional program.

Electronic Performance Support System (EPSS): The training is designed as part of the work environment and may include a Help program, Process Reviews, Advice and Feedback on performance, and online access to technicians. It is actually a hybrid technology including traditional CBT, Web-based training, links to electronic technical manuals, and databases.

Simulation: The technique of simulation is most often used when practicing a skill in its real context is too costly or dangerous. Simulation provides an opportunity for experimentation and allows students to test assumptions in a realistic context. Simulations are also used to model real-world situations that are not physically dangerous or costly, in order to build realism and relevance into the training situation.

Virtual Reality (VR): An artificial environment created with computer hardware and software and presented to the user in such a way that it appears and feels like a real environment. To "enter" a virtual reality, a user dons special gloves, earphones, and goggles, all of which receive their input from the computer system. In this way, at least three of the five senses are controlled by the computer. In addition to feeding sensory input to the user, the devices also monitor the user's actions. The goggles, for example, track how the eyes move and respond accordingly by sending new video input.

Gaming: Training games may supplement other instruction and be used to provide motivating and engaging opportunities for practice after a skill or new information is taught. Training games capitalize on the competitive interests of learners and add entertainment value to instruction.

Video: Two-way video is closest to traditional instruction, but its high cost should prohibit its being "wasted" on purely verbal knowledge content, unless some other factors, like learner characteristics, demand its use. Learning domains that demand the use of the physical senses and real objects, such as discriminations and concrete concepts, are taught well using some sort of video technology. The drawbacks to one-way video are its lack of interaction and immediate feedback from the instructor.

Teleconference: Conducting a conference between two or more participants at different sites by using computer networks to transmit audio and video data. For example, a point-to-point (two person) video conferencing system works much like a video telephone. Each participant has a video camera, microphone, and speakers mounted on his or her computer. As the two participants speak to one another, their voices are carried over the network and delivered to the other's speakers, and whatever images appear in front of the video camera appear in a window on the other participant's monitor. Multi-point video conferencing allows three or more participants to sit in a virtual conference room and communicate as if they were sitting right next to each other. Whiteboards are a principal component of teleconferencing applications because they enable visual as well as audio communication.

Audio Tape/CDs: Audiotapes and CDs are useful for one-on-one instruction of verbal or procedural information. Some learners can even make use of the tapes while engaged in other activities. The use of headphones makes the taped information somewhat unobtrusive. Foreign language learning has generally been a good use of this media. CDs can be used the same way as tapes but have the advantage of also being easily searched.

Searchable Databases: A database which is available in electronic form serves as a reference tool for activities which have high informational needs. Databases are also used in conjunction with other media to create simulations based on "real" information from the field. The information can be manipulated to create new decision-making scenarios from which predictions of results and probabilities of action can be generated.

Automated Aids: Decision trees, procedural maps, etc. in handheld electronic devices.

EVALUATION AND REVISION

Evaluation and revision are important parts of any instructional design model. Even at the top layer of necessity where resources are scarce, adequate attention must be made to evaluation (see Figure 7). In fact, instructional development is not complete until it has been demonstrated that trainees can indeed learn from the material. At the very least the following questions must be answered:

- Is the content accurate?

Figure 7: A model for evaluation and revision

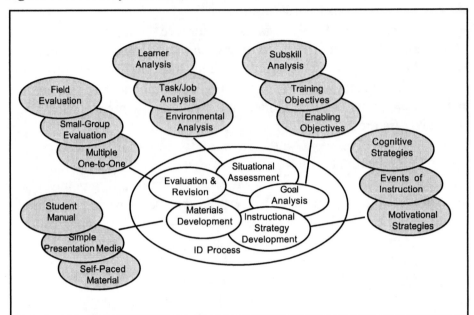

- Is the instructional strategy adequate?
- What revisions must be made before full-scale implementation?

There are two basic types of evaluation. Normative evaluation is a continuous process that takes place during the other design and development stages, that is, during assessment, goal analysis, strategy development and materials development. Summative evaluations are performed once the product is ready for delivery, after it has been delivered, and it may continue during the entire time period while the product is being used. The possibilities for evaluation are:

Normative Evaluation
Internal evaluation
Prototype results
Course materials
Presentation
OJT
SME evaluation of course
    1. Subject matter expert analysis
    2. One-to-one (power user and beginner) analysis
    3. Small group evaluation
    4. Field evaluation

Summative Evaluation

Student evaluations of course
Instructor evaluations of course
Percentage meeting objectives and criteria
Content validation and diagnostics
Skill and knowledge retention
Performance assessments

Under ideal circumstances all testing and evaluation is preceded by a test plan and a procedures manual. Those learners being tested must be informed of the test objectives and procedures. All tests developed will be subject to standards of:

- Usability
- Validity
- Reliability
- Predictability

Any test which is used as a condition of employment or advancement must be documented and the results verified and recorded.

Link Tests and Evaluations to Objectives and Strategies

Further tests and evaluation instruments should be linked to both the instructional objectives and the instructional strategies. At a minimum the evaluation procedures will consist of evaluations of the course materials, the OJT and the CBT by the instructors, the students, and the subject matter experts.

SUMMARY

Some things in training do not change. Training continues to be about context. Measurement or metrics are based on clearly defined objectives that are related to the strategic goals of the corporation. But the needs of today's work world are complex. Work takes place in teams or in clusters. Automation and human-machine interactions are part of everyone's job whether that person is the company courier or the CFO. Seeking and using information, working with others, and problem solving are top training issues in most organizations (Carnevale & Derochers, 1999).

The globalization of the workplace is also driving business and industry's training needs. English is now accepted as the language of business as French was once the language of diplomacy. However, delivering training to workers for whom English is their second language adds a new parameter to most needs assessments. Training and continuous improvement is also being used as a benefit for attracting and retaining employees (Olesen, 1999). Integrated skills such as those used in project management, product design, and marketing are heading the list of "must haves" by corporate HR departments in their employee searches. Catalogues of major corporations no longer only list courses but now define entire curriculums. Training will benefit in many ways from the use of instructional design in the development and delivery of training, training systems, and performance support systems.

QUESTIONS AND ACTIVITIES FOR FURTHER CONSIDERATION

Given the following learning objectives, classify the instruction needed by cognitive domain (verbal information, intellectual skills, cognitive strategies, motor skills, attitude) and then write appropriate instructional events and accompanying evaluation strategies.

- List procedures used by electronic specialists to augment the non-combat expenditure allowance.
- Describe the functions and support provided by a Type Commander.
- Explain the operations of the Shipboard Maintenance Material Management system.
- Interpret a machine's analysis of toxic materials and either clear or hold production within a factory.
- Match the graphic usages with the appropriate class of video cards.
- State the purpose of the verification report.
- Appreciate the benefits of the instructional design process
- Name the forms, points of contact, and lead times for ordering publications.
- Describe the process used in formatting a floppy disk.
- Differentiate between a bus network and a ring network.

Read the following descriptions from a task analysis summary and then describe the type of training you would propose to the software provider of a large multi-national telecommunications company:

Using a new software interface, the customer service representative must respond to new and existing orders and changes for telecommunications services. Median educational level of customer service reps is community college level. The representative is not technically trained in the software but will be responsible for entering the initial data that will then trigger the automated provisioning processes. The system is designed so that the entire process of providing the service will automatically interface with the many different features available and with multiple vendors of services while also providing accurate and timely billing for the different companies involved. In some cases, the representative will also be expected to activate the customer's mobile instrument.

Use the following description of learners and job requirements to write a training plan and course curriculum:

Organizational security systems are big business. The tools used in security systems include a large variety of electronic and non-electronic equipment. That equipment may be evasive or non-evasive and could potentially harm persons with whom contact is made. The systems themselves will vary in locale, physical settings, environmental variables, shifts, procedures and cognitive and physical workload. Security jobs also involve a great deal of stress created by the consequences of the decisions made and by the tedious and somewhat boring nature of the job. The individuals need to be able to make quick decisions with whatever information is at hand. They must also adapt to new technologies and continually learn new skills, operations, procedures and behaviors. But in reality the present civilian security job positions are entry level, have high turnover rate, low education requirements, and low compensation. The challenge of this system is to provide training, motivation, support and assistance to a highly mobile, somewhat ill-prepared, and at times technically illiterate population.

How does training add "value" to a company and it various components, i.e., sales, marketing, production, human resources, research and development? Explain your answer.

In what ways does using a systems approach to instructional design benefit a company's training program and in what ways might it be detrimental?

REFERENCES

Carnevale, A. P. and Derochers, D. (1999). *Training in the Dilbert economy. Training and Development*, 53(12), 32-36.

Cooper, K. S. (1978). Guilds. *The New Book of Knowledge*, 401-403. New York: Grolier, Inc.

Gagne, R. M., Briggs, L. J. and Wager, W. W. (1992). *Principles of Instructional Design*, 4th ed. Orlando, FL: Harcourt Brace Jovanovich.

Hyland, L. (2000). Banking the benefits of an eLearning strategy. *Learning Technology Newsletter*, 2(4), 3-7.

Knowles, M. (1975). *Self-Directed Learning*. Chicago, IL: Follet.

Knowles, M. (1984). *The Adult Learner: A Neglected Species*. (3rd Ed.). Houston, TX: Gulf Publishing.

Newman, A. and Smith M., (1999). How to create a virtual learning community. *Training and Development*, 53(7), 44-48.

Olesen, M. (1999). What makes employees stay. *Training and Development*, 53(10) 48-52.

Scales, G. R. and Yang, C. (1993). Perspectives on electronic performance support systems. Paper presented at the *16th Annual Meeting of the Eastern Education Research Association*. Clearwater Beach, FL, February 17-21. (ERIC document ED 354 883).

Tessmer, M. and Wedman, J. F. (1990). A layers-of-necessity instructional development model. *Educational Technology Research and Development*, 38(2), 77-85.

US Department of the Army. (1999). Systems approach to training management, processes, and products. *TRADOC* (U.S.A.T.A.D.C.) Fort Monroe.

West, C. K., Farmer, J. A. and Wolff, P. M. (1991). *Instructional Design Implications From Cognitive Science*. Needham, MA: Allyn and Bacon.

APPENDIX
JOB/TASK/SKILLS ANALYSIS

Operation: Actions essential to performing the task and subtasks.

- ❖   _Action 1_____
  - ➢   sub 1_____
  - ➢   sub 2_____

- ❖   _Action 2_____
  - ➢   sub 1_____
  - ➢   sub 2_____

- ❖   _Action 3_____
  - ➢   sub 1_____
  - ➢   sub 2_____

> Tasks observed performed on the floor:
>   ♦   _____
>   ♦   _____
>   ♦   _____

- ❖   Available technical manuals, manufacturer publications, position descriptions, job standards, etc. Note titles:

_____

Knowledge: Prerequisite learning necessary before one can perform any of the task elements.
1.   Completion of classroom instruction in

   _____
2.   Safety precautions to be enforced on the shop floor_____
3.   Required inventories, special activities, etc.

   _____
4.   Documentation and record keeping_____
5.   Safety violations and notification of proper authority_____
6.   Sequencing of task(s)

   _____

   _____

> Decision points in process:

_____

> Possible safety hazards or issues:

_____

> Common errors or problems, unintended errors, slips:

_____

> Critical incidents:

_____

Training need identified by subject matter expert:

_____

Training need identified by Management:

_____

Training need identified by operator:

_____

➢   Number of personnel requiring training approximately:_____

➢   The target audience _____

➢   Existing documentation or courseware:_____

✳ Certifications needed: _____

✳ Currencies required:_____

Chapter XI

A Blended Technologies Learning Community–From Theory to Practice

Barbara Rogers Bridges, Mary C. Baily, Michael Hiatt,
Deborah Timmerman and Sally Gibson
Bemidji State University, USA

INTRODUCTION

This chapter of the section will share the journey of a higher education faculty development team as they meet the challenge to modify a state accredited teacher licensure program to be delivered in a technology-enhanced learning environment. The Bemidji/Metro Urban Teacher Education Collaborative faculty for physical education, art, music, educational psychology and Foundations of American Education recently began to develop hybrid (blended technologies and face-to-face) courses which will meet the new K-8 Minnesota state licensure competencies. In this chapter of the section, we will also suggest a model for future blended technologies program development.

Objectives for This Chapter of the Section

This chapter of the section will briefly review existing technology-enhanced curriculum programs; describe meetings with funders, administrators and other potential supporters; describe program development pre-planning; and discuss strategies for faculty course development incentives. While not specifically applicable to individual course planning, readers will gain strategies and insights useful for creating change in their own education programs.

Next, this chapter of the section documents the reflective statements from participating faculty and administrators and an example of a Paradigm Shift Worksheet, intended for designing curriculum for "hi-touch" disciplines such as visual art, music and physical education/movement.

Finally, recommendations for future blended technologies program development is suggested.

WHAT DO WE KNOW TO DATE?

Turn of the millennium teachers are facing the most dramatic paradigm shift to emerge within the educational community in the last several centuries. Both teachers and students must become Webslingers, like Spiderman; enter a chaotic realm, anarchy; merge onto the super highway, the no speed limit Autobahn; and willingly embrace a new learning model that may prove to be exhilarating and frustrating, challenging and rewarding.

Current educators, by and large, were educated using an *instructivist* model. Instructivism is teacher centered: we lecture–the students learn. Johnson and Dupis (1999) discuss instructivism in terms of truth: "Truth is best when understood by the person with expertise who is the authority" (p. 388). The experts (teachers) "hold" the knowledge and "tell" the students, who in turn "hold" the knowledge.

In contrast, blended technology delivery methods are inherently embedded with *constructivist* possibilities. The students are actively involved in discovering the curriculum content: "the constructivist curriculum teacher invites the student to learn by shaping their own understandedness" (Johnson & Dupis, 1999, p. 404). The interactive nature of the blended technologies involves the student in constructing their own knowledge using several thinking and learning tools (see Chapter One of this book).

BLENDED TECHNOLOGY OPTIONS

We think of "blended technologies" as the merging or blending of a variety of different delivery technologies to distribute academic curriculum. Bemidji State University has a history of using a variety of technologies, including the Internet, CD-ROM, videotape, interactive television, satellite, and broadcast television to deliver course content regionally, nationally and internationally, though most courses do not use extensive multiple media as proposed by the new program. By blending multiple instructional technologies into course and program delivery, we can create a learning environment for teacher education students where technology enhances the learning process, as opposed to distracting from it.

A Review of Available Technologies

ITV (Interactive television). Use of this technology is expanding exponentially to meet the growing demand for greater access for rural and non-traditional students (Parkay, 2000). Many believe the ITV format removes dynamic interaction between professor and student, making it difficult to create a face-to-face style "community" where students become involved and contribute to learning in a thoughtful manner (Parkay, 2000). Thoms (1999) suggests appropriate training for instructors and students and Parkay (2000) recommends special attention to size and color of room and materials, furniture and its placement, microphone and its acoustics, lighting, heating, ventilation, monitor placement, and bandwidth potential. "The key concept with ITV is access, not real time replacement" (p. 86). Thoms (1999) has specific suggestions for curriculum construction strategies: using color, plenty of photographs, simple visuals elements and principles of design, consistent backgrounds, minimal use of capital letters, incorporation of whole space, horizontal format, and keywords.

In 1999, Crain Communications created its first domestic (in-home) broadband interactive television service for low-income people in Hong Kong. The usage fell well below the 1.6 million households targeted, with only 11,000 households signed up to date. There is some speculation that wiring the low-income apartment blocks was a sensible installation strategy but did not make sense as a marketing strategy. The low-income audience is less sophisticated technologically and less likely to have money for "frills." Crain is working with Bill Gates at Microsoft to develop a project, which will converge PC and TV creating a new era of multimedia (Madden, 1999).

Home-based or "domestic" ITV technology arrived in the United States in 2000 in San Diego, California. Cox Communications installed the option in 354,000 homes (Larson, 2000). Spyglass Inc. has installed similar systems in Illinois (Ascierto, 1999). However, long-term study results are not yet available. Domestic ITV might be an option for urban, non-traditional students but would not be cost effective for rural students.

In any case, campus-based ITV use in rural Minnesota has been a mainstay of most distance programs offered by colleges and universities. ITV is supported in Minnesota through a legislative mandate, thus providing all educational institutions essentially free access to the medium through six interconnected ITV regions. Universities, colleges, and schools need only build and fund their own studio spaces and train faculty in the use of the medium. Fortunately, every institution in the Minnesota State Colleges and Universities system, the University of Minnesota, several private higher education institutions, and many public schools have access to this medium.

Web-based curriculum. Mechanical problems are revealed when we review curriculum Web sites. The most common problem for the average viewer are issues of equipment capacity. Graphics-heavy sites are often slow to download (Borland, 1997). Site navigation designs are often confusing and become too time consuming for students to locate specific resources quickly, while others are too simple with unattractive, static HTML design. The designers appear to have a lack of understanding of the constituent's apprehension of the emergent technology learning models (Gailbraith, 1997).

More technical support (May, 1994) and Web page text written in accessible language is another necessary requirements for successful use of this medium. The use of "insider text" is a phenomena described as the often-intimidating "Unassailable Voice" by Walsh (1997).

Finding time to learn to use the technology is a major challenge for many teachers (Borland, 1997) There are positive trends in Web-based curriculum design including increased collaborative learning opportunities and improved computer skills (Thiele,1999), as well as increased access to the professor and possibilities for employing a constructivist Web-based model (Hernecker, 1999).

WebCT and Blackboard software programs are cost effective as long as technology training opportunities for both students and faculty can be justified and paid for in the department or through special grants (Clyatt, 1999). Web-based curriculum could also provide access for the physically challenged, including those with hearing loss.

Attention to the strengths and weaknesses in Web-based curriculum is particularly critical at this point in designing the new program. Beginning in 2001, Minnesota State Colleges and Universities is funding the adoption of instructional management software (IMS) for all fifty-three campuses in the state system. Each campus may choose from three different vendors: Blackboard, IntraKal, or WebCT and receive full funding for purchase of the site license and staff development needs.

While several professors on campus have been developing various types of Web-enabled courses, this is the first system-wide initiative to provide greater access to higher education throughout the state and beyond. Our teacher education program will benefit greatly from this initiative and from the lessons learned from Web pioneers.

VCR and CD-ROM technologies. Video cassette recorders (VCR) are everywhere, including the homes of the majority of those seeking access to higher education. The advantages of designing for VCR programming include low probability of equipment failure and reports of a high rate of learner usability and accessibility (Herron, 1999). The obvious disadvantage, both time-wise and financially, is the high expense of first time production.

Similarly, CD-ROMs may have a high initial production cost, but replication and updating are relatively cheap and easy to produce. Our team determined that video and CD-ROM would be an essential part of the new program. Since many textbooks currently in use at Bemidji State include a CD-ROM and Web site access, and since most students have created videos for course presentations, the issue of familiarizing students with these media is minimized.

The team approached Minnesota Satellite and Technologies, a group that manages the satellite and video production technology for the state of Minnesota, to discuss the use of their studios and editing equipment for VCR and CD-ROM production. After much discussion and two meetings it was estimated that a 20-minute "program" using live dialogue, graphics and music would cost a minimum of $10,000. Considering the high level of professionalism and the resources needed for high quality programming, this cost will likely be deemed very reasonable by anyone who has produced video and CD-ROM materials.

Other technologies. Certainly as access to other technologies becomes available or more feasible, such as Web casting, desktop video conferencing, full screen video and so on, we will refine and reconsider our teacher education program design. It is important to note that the blended technologies approach provides enough flexibility to adopt newer technologies as needed or desired.

CURRENT USE OF BLENDED TECHNOLOGIES

In February 1998, the Distance Education Council (Roberts, 2000) surveyed 61 accredited member institutions. The result was a broad-based look at the state of distance learning. Online communication was used 31% of the time, with 39% of communications focusing on email. Audiotapes were employed 21% of the time, and hardware kits 17%, with videotapes at a 14% use. Internet-based learning consumed 11% of the curriculum, with 10% using CD-ROM disks, and 7% multimedia disks.

Only a small number of programs, 6%, required mandatory resident training. It is interesting to note that 60% of the programs used pre-printed motivational letters and 22% fax letters with 14% offering motivational incentive awards to students entering the programs.

Use of systematic email and live/canned video production provides solid pedagogical applications that enhance student/teacher discourse and Web-based curriculum. Careful selection of blended technologies is supported by Gavin (1999). Hartley (2000) recommends developing an e-learning strategy early in planning: "Not having a strategy is like going to the supermarket without a shopping list. You end up buying things you don't need" (p. 37) As has been stated elsewhere in this book, curriculum developers must be kept focused on the lesson objectives and encouraged to select delivery methods to meet those specific objectives. In short, they must follow sound instructional design practices.

STAKEHOLDER TESTIMONIALS

It is time to let the faculty team and administrators tell the story and share their journey. It is important to note that the Bemidji State University DLiTE program, Distributed Learning in Teacher Education, is primarily a faculty initiative. Dr. Patricia Rogers started discussions and spent at least a month with me as I tried to prove the idea unworkable. I failed. She succeeded in convincing me that a hybrid (blended technologies/face-to-face) model could provide a wider range of different exciting learning opportunities which could/would meet the competencies outlined by the state of Minnesota for a K-8 teacher licensure.

DLiTE: Distributed Learning in Teacher Education. The phrase that always came to mind while thinking about designing an e-learning program for teacher education was "all of the stars are aligned."

At the time, I was working in our state system office as a system director for instructional technology, which meant I had access to statewide information on distance learning. I knew that the state system was funding a major initiative to purchase an information management system to allow faculty members to design and manage courses on-line. My university, Bemidji State, and indeed all six of the teacher education programs in the Minnesota State system, had just completed a revision of the teacher licensure programs. At Bemidji State, two major threads were woven through the core program: art and technology.

Bemidji State has a long history of distance learning experience. Every faculty member has taught using interactive television (ITV), and many have used Web sites to enhance their courses. Students in rural areas have long driving distances in often harsh weather, so ITV and other technologies are used to meet their need for access to education. Moving into a blended program that requires minimum "seat time" would not be a hard process for students or faculty members.

So, a teacher education program that combined all of these elements in a quality program seemed feasible. As the program grows under the direction and design of Dr. Bridges, we will continue to assess a variety of technologies such as satellite, Web casting, streaming video, and so on to provide multiple media and methods of teaching and learning. Based on research in the field, we know that solid, quality programs require some face-to-face contact to build a supportive community environment. The DLiTE program was designed with the assumption that "education" is a people business. Therefore, it must have a personal, people oriented approach. And, true to the art and technology threads, students in the program learn new technology skills while taking courses. Face-to-face meetings are held at an arts school and professional development center.

Dr. Patricia L. Rogers
Associate Professor
Bemidji State University

We called a meeting and proposed the idea to key collaborative faculty. They expressed reservations, but also a willingness to work on their own learning and technology adoption issues. Next, we scheduled a pontoon boat ride (typical for Northern Minnesota planning meetings!) with our Clinical Experiences Supervisor (the most "nuts and bolts" member of the faculty and in charge of the most problematic area of the program from a blended technologies delivery standpoint–student teaching) and our Professional Education Department Chair. Having both of these key individuals in a "captive" setting assured that we could present the entire idea without interruption. We invited them to prove our concept unworkable. They did not:

My first reaction to this distributed learning initiative was a deep sense of fatigue. As a partially seasoned department chair, I had already dealt with a mandated change from a quarter system to a semester system of curriculum delivery. I was in the midst of a complete program revision to meet a new state teaching licensure law, and I was preparing for a five-year program accreditation review. Coupling these responsibilities with oversight of twenty-one faculty and four off-campus program settings had already filled my professional plate beyond its capacity.

After my initial reaction and the day of discussion on the pontoon boat I became a believer. The potential for positive impacts of these learning opportunities on our students could not be denied.

I also have to admit that a significant part of my cautious approach to this effort stems from my own inadequacies relative to modern technology and twenty-first century opportunities for learning and professional growth. My colleagues have convinced me to leave my old paradigm.

Dr. Jack Reynolds
Chair Professional Studies
Bemidji State University

We attended several meetings with the Vice-President for Academic and Student Affairs, including a meeting with the Bemidji State accountants, and the Deans of the College of Professional Studies and the Center for Extended Learning where we discussed the financial details. After a great deal of conversation among all stakeholders and a few more meetings, the Vice President emerged as a strong supporter. These key administrators agreed to contribute initial development money.

As Dean of the Center for Extended Learning, I was excited to learn of the DLITE initiative. Having had previous experience developing Web-based programs, I was well aware of the commitment of resources that would be necessary to implement an effective virtual learning environment. Funding for course development, technical support and student services would need to be secured in order to create the infrastructure necessary to support the creation and delivery of a quality online program. Dr. Bridges and Dr. Rogers both worked diligently in this regard, contacting numerous state and private agencies in an effort to locate funding sources for course development. In addition, new staff positions were created on campus to assist faculty with the challenge of creating new technology-based teaching strategies. While much work remains to be completed, the necessary foundation for success has been laid through the collaborative efforts of the University administration, Department of Professional Education and a few key innovative, creative and resourceful faculty who realized the potential of utilizing various distributed learning technologies to better serve our students.

Dr Robert Griggs
Dean of the Center for Extended Learning
Bemidji State University

The teacher education program at Bemidji State University enjoys a long history of recognition as a high quality experience. I take considerable pride in that and my initial concern with the DLiTE proposal was that we do everything possible to enhance our positive reputation and that we do nothing to diminish it. My fear was that students enrolled in DLiTE courses would not be active participants in their own learning and that they would have few opportunities to interact with their instructors and with other students. Proponents of the technologies associated with DLiTE have convinced me that students will be active learners and that they will have ongoing opportunities for interaction and personal feedback. I have come to believe that DLiTE will deliver a high quality program of which we can be proud.

DLiTE will also enable us to reach out to talented people who would otherwise be excluded from teacher education at a time when gifted teachers are in great demand. My skepticism has been replaced with optimism and I now consider myself to be an advocate for this initiative.

> Dr. Dave Larkin
> Dean of Professional Studies
> Bemidji State University

Amy Kim advises that a virtual community must "Empower your leaders" and "Honor your elders"(2000, p. 144-145). Such advice is critical to a successful wholesale change as proposed in the DLiTE program. Without the support of key administrators, virtual communities cannot be maintained or provide another window of access to the campus.

After an initial analysis, a figure of $10,000 per course was advanced as a probable minimum number needed for blended technologies course development. This figure includes using a combination of Web-based software, ITV and VCR programming. The Minnesota initiative was fortunate to have several visionary leaders in the public and private sector. Several local arts organizations, The Perpich Center for Arts Education and The Walker Art Center, impressed with the work Bemidji State had done in the area of arts integration within the K-8 teacher preparation curriculum, agreed to pledge seed development money, meeting facilities and staff training:

This project is an exciting blend of knowledge power and technology power. Linked together they help us meet some of the key challenges of teaching and learning. The Perpich Center is pleased to work in partnership with Bemidji State University to support and develop this innovative approach which not only supports people learning the profession of teaching, but also deepens our knowledge and practice as learners. Both as individuals and as organizations we must keep learning—and creative, breakthrough work such as this challenges us to do just that, and makes it exciting as well. We will also be seeking future corporate sponsorship for student scholarships and hardware requirements.

Dr. David O'Fallon
Executive Director
The Perpich Center for Arts Education

In addition, the Minnesota Department of Children, Families and Learning (Minnesota's state education department) met with the Bemidji team and encouraged us to proceed. They suggested we offer incentives for those students interested in pursuing licensure in science and math. Our plan is to seek corporate support for full scholarships for students working towards licensure in these specialties.

What the Faculty Think

Program Director: *My first reaction to the suggestion that I should think about taking the Bemidji/Metro Collaborative into cyberspace was one of aversion. I was concerned about quality. I am a constructivist and I found it daunting to imagine how I could remain committed to this approach without frequent face-to-face meetings. I was concerned about admission standards and creating appropriate interaction between students and professor. How would we find funds to create a quality program? How much would we need to charge? Would I have time for this challenge? My experience with ArtsNetMN (Bridges, 1997) and the Bemidji Metro Collaborative (Bridges, 1999, 2000) had taught me that cyber bonding could replace some face-to-face interaction but I remained convinced that launch and final assessments/presentations still needed to be done in "real time."*

My initial reflections: Disadvantages–Technical failure, loss of face-to-face dynamics, higher attrition, time/financial intensive development, loss of personal power and connectedness/authenticity/interchange; Advantages–opportunities to use the community resources, more work on writing skills, accessing students when they are rested and ready to learn, access for underserved population, opportunities for more interaction for non-verbals, model transcends issues of personal appearance and physical disabilities.

Barbara Rogers Bridges, Ph.D.
Director, Bemidji/Metro Urban
Teacher Education Collaborative

Visual Art Faculty: Questions and Concerns
- Converting a "hands-on" classroom to a virtual community.
- How can I, or what can I, substitute for in-class experiences—maybe explore gamelike software; probably find some answers there.
- Ask students what is available in "fun" learning software; I can incorporate these ideas.
- Is there a related virtual model of some kind to look at?
- Licensing problems for videos used in class—can these be used in an online format?
- Time to create videos for studio production.
- Time to create virtual museums, create virtual connections for students to explore.
- Attached some Web addresses I found; how do I go about getting their permission to be part of program?
- Time to search for Web sites online—locate Web sites for enrichment.
- Setting up chat rooms for various subject matter. Finding colleagues willing to participate in online discussions.
- Contracts for students to appear online, Web sites? Legal parameters.
- How do I go online to explain materials—allowing for analysis, synthesis and encouraging the utmost creativity?
- How do I foster support for creative endeavors when I am miles away?
- That technology is available to my students?
- What software is available to students… concerns about Macs and PCs being compatible… so often can't download material sent to me.
- Resolution on the Internet—great sources of styles and technique, not very good on detail.
- Creating virtual slide shows and hyper studio programs will take time.
- Where is software being kept?
- How will supplies be disseminated to students?

Sally Gibson, Art Specialist
Pine Lake Elementary School
Brooklyn Center, MN
Adjunct, Bemidji State University

Music Faculty: *My initial reaction at the prospect of this type of instructional medium was one of real excitement about the possibilities. I must also admit to a great deal of uncertainty concerning the unknown factors of beginning this type of instruction without much, if any, previous experience. As we work our way through the development of the course, it becomes a challenge to know what is the correct order of process to follow. I have found it takes much more time in the development stages because you cannot assume anything to be a given. I felt we had to examine each piece of the curriculum not only for content but also for the appropriate method of presentation. This is very time consuming and hopefully will become easier as we become more fluid in the type of presentation. I look forward to expanding my teaching skills to fit into this type of presentation format. I think this will definitely cause me to carefully examine my teaching development process with a real open mind and know that much revision will need to take place as we proceed. It is with real spirit of adventure that I enter this course and process.*

Michael Hiatt
Director of the Professional Development
Institute, Perpich Center for Arts Education
Minnesota Music Education Coordinator
Adjunct, Bemidji State University

Physical Expression Faculty: *My initial reaction to this type of play activities was the primary component of my teaching, it seemed like a large challenge to figure out how to keep the integrity of participation in this kind of format. My current thinking is I will concentrate on the play activities when we are together and work with the cognitive piece through technology. It would be nice to have an introductory component online to establish some basic vocabulary and then meet with the students to experience play. The following distance lessons will focus on relating the concepts to the play experience and building activities that are developmentally appropriate for connecting movement to academic concepts.*

Deb Timmerman
Physical Education/Expression Specialist
Adjunct, Bemidji State University

Educational Psychology: *Some of us started this journey towards blended technology delivery as far back as the early 80s. We didn't know it at the time, and those visionaries that tried to tell us found themselves up against up against a lot of disbelief. Computers were new. In most places there was one in each school for student use that was donated by an up-and-coming computer company with fruit as the logo. Chances are that that one was kept under tight security and rolled from classroom to classroom on a sign out basis. We were told that in the future a computer would be built into every student's desk and every student would have one at home just like a TV In some scenarios we were told that students would be able to go to school without ever leaving home. The cost would be affordable...but we didn't believe.*

So here we are several decades later. I find myself reading what I can off the Internet for course design and ADA compliance. I'm digging and researching on my own...looking for workshops and conferences. Personally it has been quite a trip.

> Mary C. Bailey
> Assistant Director/Student Teaching Supervisor
> Bemidji/Metro Urban Teacher Education Collaborative

STRATEGIES FOR FACULTY INCENTIVES

As you might conclude from the testimonials, all stakeholders should be included in the decision making and design roles from the startup of any large scale design project. Stakeholder theory has its origins in law and strategic management initiatives. According to Dr. Marianne Jennings (1999) a stakeholder is "any identifiable group or individual who can affect the achievement of an organization's objectives or who is affected by the achievement of an organization's objectives" (p. 478.)

It is a somewhat daunting challenge for faculty to incorporate the new technological delivery opportunities for e-learning curriculum development. Hooper and Reiber (1995) outline a five level hierarchical model of technology adoption (see Chapter 1). The levels are: Familiarization, Utilization, Integration, Re-orientation and Evolution. The third level, Integration, "marks the beginning of appropriate uses for computer-based technologies particularly in delivering and developing instruction" (Rogers, 2000, p. 458). The early stage of the integration level is where many of the faculty team found themselves as we began the brainstorming our DLiTE program development.

At the *Integration level*, the educators need to start driving the technology, instead of allowing the technology to drive them. They need to *re-orient* their way of thinking. Keeping the learning objectives clearly at the forefront, the curriculum developers need to take advantage of the expanded delivery systems and learning opportunities that the new technologies provide.

This is an area fraught with conflict and emotion. Who will "own" the class? Will professors be required to develop these courses as part of their current assignments? Will they be paid some additional fee to teach the courses? Where will they find the time for all aspects of this model?

Course Development Stipends

The Center for Extended Learning agreed to pay each faculty member between $1,000-$1,500 for the development of each course. Stipends are considered in terms of work-for-hire contracts, which means all courses developed by the faculty team will belong to the department and are not the intellectual property of individual faculty members. In some institutions, this is a very controversial issue and it should be addressed early on in any similar program development projects. In fact, it is wise to have agreements documented and signed to avoid any possible misunderstanding over intellectual property.

Flexible Time Schedule

The most dramatic benefit to professors working in a blended technologies program will prove to be the option of flexible hours. Once development of the initial course materials is complete, the course can be structured to meet individual needs and possible disabilities when the course is offered. Flexible time is also advantageous from our non-traditional students' point of view who frequently have other demands on their time and require a flexible educational program.

Technology Training

The training for the Web-supported software, as well as other blended technology options, will be offered by the Center for Extended Learning. Lead faculty have agreed to spend time on training if they are compensated. Compensation may take the form of release time, small stipends for completing training, or other similar incentives with respect to union contracts.

STAKEHOLDER BRAINSTORMING

Early in the analysis phase of program and course designing, a brainstorming workshop session was held for the involved stakeholders. An additional meeting with the art, music, physical movement and educational psychology faculty and the Deans of Professional Studies, Center for Extended Learning, as well as the Executive Director of The Perpich Center for Arts Education was called for the purpose of *re-orienting* our thinking. The re-orienting proved to be a challenge. Re-orienting our thinking was tantamount to a paradigm shift!

So, a paradigm shift worksheet for the Foundations of American Education course was developed as an example (see Tables 1 and 2). Warning: It was very difficult for the dynamic, hands on faculty to avoid trying to duplicate what they presently do in the classroom. Using the Paradigm Shift Worksheet (see Tables 1 and 2), the faculty listed their course objectives and then they re-oriented their thinking as they planned how to meet the state mandated objectives with the new opportunities the technological delivery options provided.

Recommendations for Future Blended Technologies Program Development

Based on the literature and on our experiences to date, we feel confident in suggesting recommendations for successful blended technologies teacher education programs.

1. Involve all the stakeholders from the very beginning.
2. Provide "re-orientation" support (staff development) for all faculty members early on in the process.
3. Do not be seduced by the bells and whistles. Select your technology options using realistic criteria (your server and network capabilities, your constituents' equipment, your faculty's technology and design competencies, etc.) Avoid the use of technology for it's own sake (see the Muilenburg and Berge chapter elsewhere in this book).
4. Use a systematic method or model to rewrite the courses, making sure objectives are being met (see Tables 1 and 2).
5. Seek additional outside funding for development costs.
6. Hire a technology coordinator.
7. Seek funding for faculty stipends to cover curriculum development and release time.

The evolution of our learning environments, from place bound to virtual, is not a prediction for the future. It is here now. Students return to school because of the technology, not in spite of it. e-Learning extends way beyond the old correspondence course, a limited paradigm that provided no opportunity for immediate feedback. Blended technologies e-learning brings educational opportunities to place or situation bound students, as well as those with economic and physical challenges. In 1998, there were 1.6 million students taking courses online. By 2003, distance learning will be a ten billion dollar industry (Roberts, 2000).

We gravitate toward situations that enable us to communicate and form communities because that is a basic human need. The Bemidji DLiTE Virtual Community will provide the opportunity for geographically disconnected people to become "connected" by a shared interest in thinking and talking about education, creating curriculum, and becoming teachers.

Table 1: Paradigm shift worksheet for Foundations of American Education

Lesson Objectives	Current Activities	8 hours face-to-face	Web CT	VCR	ITV	Email	E-mentor visit	Web Research	Community Resources
Understand different lifestyles of various cultural and economic groups	Lecture/ Banks Model/ culture iconography "smart people" (variation of blue eyes/ brown eyes) Global awareness profile contract Video Stand and Deliver	1. Paradigm lecture 20 min. 2. Global awareness discussion 30 min.	Syn/ chat with guests Complete Global Awareness Profile Post GAP contract	10 min. lecture Culture paradigms Watch, Stand and Deliver Video analysis worksheet	G U E S T L E C T U R E R	Online discussions with diversity guests Cohort discussion on Stand and Deliver	Diversity guests: 30 minute conversaton Ethnic socio-economic/ mentally physically challenged Gay and lesbian'	Find 3 sites-- post URLs to group Discussion diversity issues	Interview someone from 3 of the following groups about their K-12 experience: immigrant, ethinic, low income, gay & lesbian, physically, mentally challenged.
Grad standards	Hand out standards Discussion					Discuss teacher interviews	Mentor gives Quiz 2	Go to CFL.org Download standards	Interview teacher. How are the grad standards working for them?
Assessments	3 Quizzes, 1 Final, 2 Papers, 1 Lesson Plan, Presentation, Critical Analysis, Ed. Philosophy	Final 60 mins.	Quiz 3 60 min			Quiz 1 and pass in papers Ed. Phil. lesson plan	Present lessons Critique		Critique from practitioner
Use technology to deliver instruction	Use powerPoint overheads, slides Face-to-face syllabus review Web site demonstration	Over-rheads Computer Lab Demo	Pre-review APA writing style Pre-review syllabus before launch event.	Watch the lecture tapes. Optimal: Tape your lesson for pre-review. Send to professor	IT V > 2000 mi.	Participate in one-on-one and group conversations MANDAT-ORY	Discussion before visit	APA review on their Web site Grad standards Diversity	Use library K12 resource room Community college video production
Support student learning in speaking / writing and other media	*Complete 2 formal APA papers *Plan and present one lesson *Use ttechnology for research and presentation	1. Intro-duction with nametags 45 min. 2. Present synthesized info.-60 min. 2. Les Pres 60	Deposit two papers Discuss-ions	Tape history lesson-send snail mail		Practice writing At least 30 emails during the course MANDA-TORY	History lesson presentations Mentor gives critique	View examples of good writing	Interview K-12 teachers Tape their lesson on VCR Practitioner review of lesson and plan

Table 2: Paradigm shift worksheet for Foundations of American Education

Lesson Objectives	Current Activities	8 hours face-to-face	Web CT	VCR	ITV	Email	E-mentor Visit	Web Research	Community Resources
Experience being a reflective practitioner and a critical thinking	* Reflective observation journal * Lesson presentation/ critique Paper clip strategy Newest thought	Synthesize and present chapters 14-15 Paper Clip	Paper clip for best reflection of the week.	• Tape history lesson, send to prof. with complete lesson plan		Pre-launch assignment: Write paper "What is biggest distance learning challenge for me?"	Lesson plan presentation Critique peer professor	Seek ou research teach Web sites	Seek advice on time management Feedback on lesson paper
Understand historical/ philosophical foundation of education	Paradigm lecture * Student research and history lesson presentation Trends Lecure	Paradigm lecture 1. Select theorist 5 min.	Create history lesson Peer critique Trends lecture	Look for tapes in library	G U E S T	Disucssion on paradigms Theorist discussion class will role play theirtheorist	Q and A with mentor 15 min. Discuss trends	Research-Position, History paper Diversity Research trends	One interview with community school administrator as a reference for position paper
Understand methods of inquiry, self-assessment problem-solving strategies	•Create quiz Chapters 14, 15 • Position psaper • Corn seeds (Task ttimeline)	Review and synthesize chapter 14-15 1. Create quiz question 30 min 1. Task timeline- 5 min.	Quiz 1, 2, 3 position paper Corn seeds Task Timeline	VCR lesson tape Conduct self-critique using critique rubric		Self-critiques using rubric Students will use Cohort Group as a resource	Individual counseling 5 min. each	Find three studies focused on educational research-- Read them	One interview with community school administrator as a reference for position paper
Know major areas of research on teaching	Read text Paradigm lecture	1. Paradigm lecture	Post three studies' URLs	Trends lecture		Discuss Trend lecture	Ask asvice	Use Web Pals	Ask PhD in community about their topic--Your response paragraph
Use professional literature, colleagues to support development of student and teacher	Guest speakers History paper Research	1. Admin. welcome 10 min.	Each student must bring an expert to our multi-cultural discussion	Watch educational channel		Email "experts for advice & to attend conver-sations at Mondays w/ Elliott	Bring guests and hard copy lesson to share with peers, mentor	Find experts for all topics	Bring guest speakers to Mondays with Elliot online chats
Drug use and abuse	1. Stat Lecture 10 min.		STAT sheet	Watch Trains-potting		Discuss Stats Trains-porting	Discuss STATs	Find 3 articles and review	Ask student from drug culture to Mondays with Elliot

REFERENCES

Ascierto, J. (1991). ITV to boom, firm says. *Electronic News*, 46(28), 58.

Barker, B.O. (2000). Anytime, anyplace learning. *Forum for Applied Research and Public Policy*, 15(2), 88.

Borland, C. (1997). ArtsEdNet: Assessing an arts education Website. In Bearman, D. and Trant, J. (Eds.), *Museums and the Web*, 315-321. Pittsburgh, PA: Archives & Museums Informatics.

Bridges, B. R. (1997). ArtsNetMn. Minneapolis Institute of Art. *Weisman Art Museum, and Walker Art Center*. Available on the World Wide Web at: http//: www.ArtsNetMN.org.

Bridges, B. R. (1999). Collaboration and student involvement on an art curriculum Web site: Study for the Perpich Center for Arts Education, Golden Valley, MN. Available on the World Wide Web at: http://www.pcae.k12.mn.us.

Bridges, B. R. (2000). If we build it, will they come? *Tech Trends*, 44 (4), 44-46.

Clyatt, B. (1999). Web-Based distance learning: A tool for change. *Journal of Instruction Delivery Systems*, 13(12), 13-15.

Farrell, G. M. (1999). The development of virtual education: A global perspective. Vancouver, British Columbia: Open Learning Agency. (ERIC Document Reproduction Service No. ED 432 668).

Gailbraith, L. (1997). Enhancing art teacher education with new technologies: Research possibilities and practice. *Art Education*, 50(5), 14-19.

Gavin, T. (1999). Going beyond limits: Integrating multimedia distribution systems into the curriculum. *Book Report*, 18(1), 37, 39-41.

Hartley, D. (2000). Aboard the e-Learning train. *Training and Development*, 54(7), 37-42.

Harwood, W. S. (1997). Effects of integrated video media on student achievement and attitudes in high school chemistry. *Journal of Research in Science Teaching*, 36(6), 617-631.

Hernecker, A. D. (1999). Instructional design for Web-based, post-secondary distance education. *Journal of Instruction Delivery Systems*, 13(2), 6-9.

Herron, C. (1999). The effectiveness of a video-based curriculum in teaching culture. *Modern Language Journal*, 83(4), 518-533.

Hooper, S. and Reiber, L. P. (1995). Teaching with technology. In Ornstein, A. (Ed.), *Teaching: Theory into Practice*. Boston: MA: Allyn & Bacon.

Jennings, M. (1999). Stakeholder theory: Let anyone who's interested run the business–No investment required. *Online Journal of Ethics*. Available on the World Wide Web at: http://www.stthom.edu/cbes/stakeholder.html.

Johnson, J. A. and Dupis, V. L. (1999). *Foundations of American Education*, (11th ed.). Boston, MA: Allyn and Bacon.

Kim, A. J. (2000). *Building Community on the Web*. Berkley, CA: Reach Press.

Larson, M. (2000). Cox sets ITV trial. *Mediaweek*, 10(24), 26.

Madden, N. (1999). Hong Kong telecom's ITV fights recession, apathy: Broadband service links to Microsoft's windows. *Advertising Age*, 70, 40.

May, W. (1994). The tie that binds: Reconstructing ourselves in institutional contexts. *Studies in Art Education*, 35(3), 136-148.

Parkay, F. W. (2000). Promoting group investigation in a graduate-level ITV classroom. *Technological Horizons in Education*, 27(9), 86-97.

Roberts, M. (2000). Back in the loop. *Techniques*, 75(5),14.

Rogers, P. L. (2000). Barriers to adopting emerging technologies in education. *Journal of Educational Computing Research*, (22)4, 455-472.

Simmons, B. (1999). Electronic field trip: Incorporating desktop conferencing in the elementary school classroom. (ERIC Document Reproduction Service No. ED 02-00587082).

Thiele, J. (1999). Effects of Web-based instruction on learning behaviors of undergraduate and graduate students. *Nursing and Health Care Perspectives*, 20(4), 199-203.

Thoms, K. J. (1999). Teaching via ITV: Taking instructional design to the next level. *Technologies Horizons in Education Journal*, 26(1), 9, 60-66.

Walsh, P. (1997). The Web and the unassailable voice. In Bearman, D. and Trant, J. (Eds.), *Museums and the Web*, 69-76. Pittsburgh, PA: Archives & Museum Informatics.

Chapter XII

United We Stand–Divided We Fall! Development of a Learning Community of Teachers on the Net

Sólveig Jakobsdóttir
Kennaraháskóli Íslands, Iceland

INTRODUCTION

In 1998, I became a program director of a Net-based distance education (DE) graduate level program at Iceland University of Education (Kennaraháskóli Íslands) focusing on information and communications technology (ICT) in education. The main goal of the program is to help people develop leadership skills in this area within the Icelandic educational system. However, many applicants for the program already are leaders or have been involved in innovative practices concerning use of educational technologies for a number of years as teachers at the preschool, elementary or secondary level. But a major problem for the last decade has been lack of connection and collaboration within the educational community to help spread the use of technology to enhance teaching and learning. With ever-increasing amounts of accessible materials and resources, it has become more and more important for people to cooperate and share what they have read and done in order to sail rather than sink in our new information-rich environment.

Objectives for this Chapter of the Section

In this paper I will describe how we have successfully created in our program, with the aid of different types of technologies, a strong educational community of teachers involved with ICT use. I will especially focus on how the first course of the program is organized where I can draw upon personal experience. Many of you are now in the process of creating or changing courses or programs to an on-line format. This article provides a good model to design such courses.

OVERVIEW

Kennaraháskóli Íslands (KHÍ) is the main teacher education institution in Iceland located in our capital city Reykjavík. KHÍ has about 1800 students, which is a 20% increase in students from last year. The increase is mainly due to the addition of distance learners who will, for the first time this fall, make up over half of the total number of students. The ratio of DE learners in the Department of Graduate Studies is much higher–93% of our approximately 250 graduates are DE learners. The ICT program in the Department of Graduate Studies was originally organized as a one year 15 credit program, but since the Fall 2000 students have been able to register for either 15 credits or a two year diploma program with 30 credits. Each credit is considered equal to one week or 40-50 hours of student work, so 15 credits per year is considered a half time load. To gain a Master's degree, students complete an additional 30 credits (core courses and a final project, usually a research-based thesis). The DE programs in our graduate departments are net-based with short face-to-face sessions on-site (usually close to the beginning and end of courses). The programs have been very popular among teachers within the country who can complete the programs and work from anywhere, given that they can come to campus once or twice per semester and have Internet access and a fairly new computer. Also, the half time study tempo adds to the popularity; students within our department work full time or close to full time with their studies. (Workaholism is very common in Iceland and teachers' salaries are also relatively low, so most teachers can ill afford to take much time from work. However, they usually are able to manage a half time study load).

In the following sections I will describe the students in the ICT program the focus and content of the program. I also describe how ideas and principles have been translated into practice and some of the effects those experiences appear to be having on the students.

Students

There have been four groups accepted into the program from 1998 with a total number of 103 students (see Table 1). The students (not counting the new group starting this fall) have come from 43 elementary and/or middle schools from different parts of the country (about 22% of the total number of schools at that level) and 9 upper secondary schools (grades 10-13), which similarly is about 24% of the total number of schools at that level in Iceland. Women have been in large majority (67-82% of students accepted into the program) from the start as is the case for the students in the Department of Graduate Studies and in the teaching profession in Iceland. The mean age of students has been about 40, but we have had a large age range (25-62). The vast majority of the students are (full time) teachers, most of them working with students at the primary or lower secondary level (see Table 1). Many have worked as "computer/information technology teachers" within their school, managing computer labs and assisting coworkers as well as teaching students. Some of the students have also been school administrators (principals, assistant principals or employees working in school district offices). Several of the students can be considered leaders in using computers and the Internet in Icelandic schools and have very valuable experience to share with others. The teachers who have taught the courses in the ICT program (including myself), on the other hand, have had little or no experience teaching in elementary or middle schools, which makes it especially important to tap into students' experiences to make the program more effective.

The technology background of the students has varied a lot, although everyone accepted into the program is required to have word processing skills and to know how to use email and some basic programs (graphics, spreadsheets). Many of our students come to our program with the idea that they simply need or want to strengthen their technology-related skills and think the main focus in the program will be on learning to use different types of computer programs (though the purpose and goals of the program are clearly stated in the curriculum guide for the University in print and on the Web). The private sector in Iceland offers such courses for exorbitant prices compared to the tuition rate at KHÍ, which is a state run institution. Some students are disappointed in the beginning to find that in the first course the emphasis is on educational application of computers and related theory. However, they learn to use many new tools in that course in the context of creating their portfolio, communicating with other students on Web conferences and the teacher or for project work. But as the course and program progresses, students realize how fast things are changing and that they need to get used to the idea to continue learning all

Table 1: Information on four different cohorts in ICT program

Cohorts	1998-9	1999-2000	2000-1(2)*	2001-2(3)*
No. of students starting program	17	36	25	25
% Women	82	64	67	80
Age (mean)	43	43	41	38
Age (range)	28-58	28-58	26-62	25-5
Employment backgr.				
Pre-school	6	6	8	
Elementary/	59	69	72	
middle	29	22	8	
Upper secondary		3	4	
Higher	6	3	12	
Other				
Prominent interest areas	Art ed. Danish Icelandic Soc. stud. Comp. skills Net-based learning	Staff development Math Science Soc. stud. Young children & computers Technology planning	Staff development Technology planning Art & media Science Special ed. Teaching methods	
% of students completing 15 cr. diploma	82	67		
% women of those that completed	79	75		

* *About two-thirds of both latter two cohorts registered for 30 credits and one-third of the groups for only 15.*

the time and how valuable it is to be able to get to know and rely on each other, as well as to focus on uses of technology versus the technology itself.

Interest areas of the students have varied (see Table 1) and a deliberate effort is made to bring together individuals that might want to work together on projects. On the whole, we have a mix of students with varied backgrounds, experiences, needs and interests, which enhances the program and the potential effects on teaching and learning within Iceland. They come from many schools and workplaces across the country and have a high potential to make a difference in the Icelandic educational system.

CONTENT AND ORGANIZATION

The students in the ICT program are exposed to a mix of theory and research, design and development, grounded in reflective practice. We currently offer nine courses, all related to computer or Internet in education, as a part of our 30-credit program (see the overview in Appendix A). In addition, students also have access to a variety of DE courses from other programs within our department (e.g., on research methods, educational psychology, instructional and curriculum design, and educational evaluation).

When starting work in Iceland in 1997 after obtaining my Ph.D. degree in educational technology from the University of Minnesota, I realized that it was not so much the knowledge I gained in the program that was valuable to me but some of the skills. I spent about two years (1994-96) writing my thesis about school computer culture. When I finally had time to look up from my thesis work the educational landscape had changed dramatically, with Web use and online teaching and learning exploding. Although the knowledge base I acquired during my Ph.D. program was valuable, the critical skills that enabled me to function in my new job as an assistant professor at KHÍ included a lack of fear to learn new things, and to be able to work well independently but also with others. And also to be able to work with information in a focused and critical way, avoid "drowning" in information, and be able to analyze, synthesize, evaluate, use, and present information. I learned little in my Ph.D. program about Internet use in education, and still I was expected to advise and teach others what to do with that type of technology! I could not go back to study more only to find the educational environment yet again changed after so many years of study! But the nice thing about the information revolution is that you do not have to rely so heavily on specific libraries anymore to be able to do academic teaching and research. One may simply access the information one needs from anywhere.

The skills mentioned above have been neglected in the past in the Icelandic school system. Now they are specifically promoted in an Icelandic educational policy (1996) and the new (1999) Icelandic curriculum for elementary and secondary schools. These skills are now recognized as necessary for people to function in today's information society. People have also started to realize that traditional teacher-centered methods do not work to promote such skills among students at any level and there is a deliberate trend towards a more learner-centered approach.

As a result, the main underlying educational philosophy of the ICT program at KHÍ is constructivism, which calls for a complex and flexible learning environment with authentic materials and tools, and students actively creating and developing as well as analyzing, working with and presenting information in collaboration with others so that different perspectives and views have to be taken into account. We use the ideas of Salomon and Perkins (1997) concerning the importance of social and cultural environment for learning where individuals are interacting with each other using various tools and artifacts. Salomon and Perkins present a continuum, with individuals on one end learning for themselves, through individuals learning on behalf of groups, to groups learning with knowledge distributed among participants.

In the next section I describe how the above ideas have been translated into practice in the first course of the program. The name of the course, which I teach, is Information Technology in Education and School Computer Culture (ITESCC).

METHODS AND MEDIA

Based on the principles and ideas outlined in the previous section and also based on experiences of myself and others (Creed, 1996; Zhu, 1998), the first course for new students (ITESCC) has been structured as shown in Table 2 below. The Table shows activities in relation to each idea and tools or vehicles that have been used to facilitate each type of activity. In the next sections I describe the theory-practice translation in more detail.

Educational Environment is Complex and Flexible

There are a number of authoring tools available specifically designed to create an online educational environment, for example WebCT, LearningSpace, and WCB (Web course in-a-box). These tools provide a certain structure with spaces to put goals and objectives, lessons or learning materials, tools, discussions, tests, and more. They can be described as "integrated" systems. I have instead chosen to use a "component" solution, that is, a web created by Frontpage with Access connection (to provide materials and information on the course and to gather information from the students online that can be automatically published on the web) in addition to a separate discussion web on Web board.

The advantages of using a component system include that they allow more flexibility for a person with good technical skills. Also, the look of the Web does not have to be standardized and text language can be in Icelandic only (many course authoring tools have standardized words in English; most can be translated at the administrative level but translations are expensive, particularly with the frequency of new versions and updates). In addition,

Table 2: First course (ICT in education and computer culture)–theory translated into practice

Theory	Activities	Tools/Software
Educational environment complex and flexible.	Course web with database connection, rich with information and materials related to the course; discussion web set up. Students required to add to course content.	Frontpage+Access: E.g., http://soljak.khi.is/umts00 Web board: http://Webboard.ismennt.is/~tolvupp00
Importance of communication and collaboration for learning.	Face-to-face communication: Theory: lectures and dicussion Technology: lab sessions Social: make different types of groups, get to know everyone well Attitude/emotional: emphasis on what to expect.	Facilities with good computer and Internet access very important; possibilities to offer affordable accommodation (for some sessions).
	Online and phone communication: Web conferences for "deep" discussions and information sharing where students, teachers and guests can participate from anywhere. Postlists for teacher-student communication/important announcements or instructions. Email for personal communications (one-to-one or one-to-few) between teacher and students or between students. Chat and paging for informal communication (student-student or teacher-student. Netmeetings for file sharing in pair work or for tutoring. Telephone conferences for decision making, small group work and Q&A sessions and/or discussion between students and teacher.	Web board with built-in chat and paging options. Any kind of email software (Outlook and Eudora are the most commonly used). Netmeeting (in the PC Office Package). Telephone.
Use authentic materials and tools.	Emphasis on project-based learning. Projects that students do usually relate to their own teaching or other kind of work (e.g., technology planning for their schools). Students are encouraged to apply for funding for their projects and/or publish their writing in the course. Students are also learning methods and how to use software and tools in the program that they can later use with their own students.	Various.
Students actively create and develop as well as analyze, work with and present information. Work can be distributed and shared.	Students actively gather information and present ideas on the closed Web board, in special databanks created by the instructor on the Web, or in their portfolio on the Web that they are required to set up. They also write papers and plans.	E.g., word processing, Web browsers, PowerPoint, Frontpage, or other authoring systems for the Web, Access, Web board.

student lists can be sorted by first name according to the Icelandic custom, and online data gathering is easy to provide with Frontpage. Also, Web board conferences still have had some advantages over conferences that have been provided in the integrated systems we have used, e.g., the option to see who is currently logged on and page those persons with short messages. On the other hand, it is hard to close Frontpage Webs (may provide access for certain groups only), and when discussions are intensive on Webboard students tend to forget to visit the course web. However, for myself the advantages have outweighed the disadvantages.

But regardless of the technological solution chosen, care must be taken to keep the course web less complicated, at least for student groups new to online learning. An alternative is to provide very good orientation/workshop in the beginning in face-to-face meetings, introduce everything that is on the course web and have students practice looking up information of different kinds. For the past two years, I have also had face-to-face meetings three weeks into the program and started people with simple online reading and preparing (e.g., introduction of themselves with jokes or indications of choices about the type of food to have in the upcoming face-to-face meetings). But those who still have trouble with the system during the face-to-face meetings may start earlier than others or stay later to get help with problems they have had with the programs.

We have also found that DE students tend to want clear structure, at least in the beginning, without which they would otherwise feel very uncertain and uncomfortable. A strong preference for structure has also been described by Jónasson (2000) among DE students at KHI in the undergraduate program.. To adjust for these needs, I have divided the first course (ITESCC) into 5 to 7 two to three week sessions, and many of them have a certain cycle: reading materials (1/2-1 week), discuss materials (1/2 -1 week), and wrap up main ideas (1/2-1 week).

In later semesters, students experience the use of different course delivery tools, which gives them a good comparison between systems. However, there are mixed feelings about changing later to new systems. Some students feel more insecure than if staying with one system only. But we think that trying different DE delivery tools firsthand is an important learning experience for students in educational technology.

Importance of Communication and Collaboration

Face-to-face sessions. Most courses in our graduate department are organized with one to three face-to-face sessions over a semester. In our program, the rule of thumb has been to have two face-to-face sessions (usually 2-3 days) for the 5 credit classes (one close to the beginning of the course and another one close to the end) and one for 2.5 credit classes. These sessions have proven critical to the success of our DE courses. Especially in the beginning, students need a chance to get to know each other well. We have found that students who have been unable to attend the first session have tended to do worse than other students and even drop out.

I sometimes refer to face-to-face sessions as our "aura sessions" because we get a chance to meet'. An important element is that everyone is located at the same place at the same time, which has been devoted to learning and to the group. In the face-to-face sessions, we provide live lectures and discussion experiences to work on concepts and theories that require the teacher to be more visible and have a stronger voice than in the online environment. In addition, workshops on technology use and information searching can be very useful, especially when there are groups where students do not have very strong technological skills.

The social elements are very important and help create a sense of a learning community. Students are divided into two types of groups– support or base groups and what I refer to as "alphabet groups" or short-term work groups. The support groups have had 2-4 members and have been single-sex groups. Based on the ideas of Johnson, Johnson and Holubec (1993), they have been organized as long term and with the purpose to provide support for the members. We also try to have these groups heterogeneous as recommended by Johnson, Johnson & Holubec (1993) except for gender.The reasons for having single-sex support groups include that intimate online or telephone conversations could antagonize spouses of students, and also it may be easier for the group members to understand each other's problems and seek help.

There have been incidents of students on the verge of giving up on the course where other members of their groups have helped prevent the student from quitting as well as there have been incidents where members of support groups have not felt comfortable providing such support. However, the support groups need to have some specified tasks in order to keep active and in communication.

The short-term work groups (4-6 members) have, on the other hand, had the task to moderate discussions in the online discussion periods, including summarizing main points at the end of each discussion period. The creation of more homogeneous and often more long-term interest groups that share more background and interests (e.g., in art education, Danish, or staff development) have also been facilitated on the Web conference before and after the first face-to-face session. These are groups that might choose to work together on a larger project. Based on experience, it has been too soon to create such groups formally in the first face-to-face session. Students are not ready to decide on what they want their final project to be and also do not get enough time to spend with members of the other types of groups.

We use ice breakers to help people to get to know each other during the former face-to-face session. For example, last year it worked very well to create a quiz based on students' online introduction sessions, where groups worked together to link student names to statements based on the intro-ductions. During the latter face-to-face session, student groups were required to come up with fun things to do during a social event in the evening. And I can assure the reader that line dancing cannot be enjoyed properly online in spite of the name. And a virtual piece of chocolate (that I have been "given" online) does not compare to real chocolate offered by students in face-to-face sessions.

For the last two years, we have had the latter session at University facilities in the countryside (about two hours from the city) where students have had access to low price accommodation. In spite of protests from many students prior to that session, maintaining they don't want to leave their families and spend the night away, everyone agrees after the event that they would not want to miss it. We have also experimented with getting students from earlier cohorts to meet with new students in face-to-face sessions to make presentations and to socialize. The older students have answered questions and told the new students what to expect, helping to prepare them emotionally for the course. In the DE program, it has been a problem how little new cohorts, have been able to interact with other cohorts unlike what happened in my own campus-based graduate program at the University of Minnesota. There it was extremely beneficial and a good learning experience to get to know and work with earlier and later student cohorts. Lasting friendships were formed at that time (e.g., with the editor of this book). We have plans to do more work in the future with peer mentors and mixing cohorts to create a less distinctly layered learning community than is currently the case.

To create a more positive attitude and less apprehension among new students, I have found it useful to present models of how teachers' use of technology can progress through different stages (Hooper and Rieber, 1995; Russell, 1995). And to follow Russell's (1995) recommendation of letting students know beforehand what kinds of frustrations and negative feelings they could expect in the beginning when coping with new technology.

Communicating at a distance. Clearly, it helps to have a good under-standing of different types of online communication and how they are best suited to enhance teaching and learning. I was lucky to come across Tom Creed's (1996) excellent classification some years ago. He recommended regular email as best suited for one-to-one or one-to-few type of communica-tion (usually personal with short information life span as well) and postlists [listservs] as best suited for one-to-many communication (e.g., announce-ments from teacher to students, usually more formal with short life span as well). On the other hand, Web conferences were suited for many-to-many types of communication and compared to face-to-face seminars/discussion groups with medium life span of information (perhaps a month). Information on "regular" Web pages, however, usually could have a much longer life span and could be used as one-to-many type of communication.

We have found Web conferences to be vastly superior to postlists for extensive discussion. On the Web board system, teachers can organize conferences as open or closed for groups, by time periods, or on special themes where individuals visit when convenient for them and submit contributions, whereas individuals would get all mail jammed into their mailbox any time they opened their mail when using postlists. During the past two years, we have had about 2,000 letters submitted to our Web board, from 25-36 students during the Fall semester, or about 16-17 letters per day!

The importance of these conferences is enormous for the success of the course. Students share thoughts and experiences there, visitors from outside (Icelandic or foreign) can be invited to participate in discussion, and students get a feeling of being part of learning community and acquire a voice in that community. Another advantage of Web conferences over postlist discussion is that letters can be deleted by a moderator. In the first cohort (1998) when we started with postlist discussion, there was some tendency for "flaming" to occur. On more than one occasion controversial letters might be sent out that initiated strong, negative responses and it took time and effort to lower the waves.

I recall only one instance in the Web conference where flaming occurred within a closed group. A student who was moderating the group's conference decided to delete all the offending letters after matters had apparently been solved and just continue with constructive work on the plan the group was working on. If those letters had been sent through a postlist, there would have been copies in everyone's mailbox, making it possible for students to reread the letter over and over and possibly continue reliving negative feelings and resentment instead of focusing on the tasks ahead.

Last but not least, students can acquire a "voice" in a professional community nationally and internationally. To encourage the latter to occur, we have experimented with having students participate in international discussion forums on the European Schoolnet (http://www.eun.org). There they have interacted with students from the United States and teachers and students from Icelandic and Norwegian schools about equity planning and ethics in relation to Internet use.

Care has to be taken to structure discussions and build incentives for discussion into the course. For the past two years, online discussion has counted for 25% of the grade and students have been required to submit a minimum number of contributions. A model that I derived from Zhu's (1998) description of online interaction has worked very well. I have a small group of students submit initiating comments and questions in relation to different themes and articles, then a larger group reacts to those comments and questions. Finally, the small group wraps up the discussion by submitting a summary of main points that can been published on the open course web. With 25-36 students I have divided the class in two (A and B) and each half into three smaller groups (A1, A2, and A3 and B1, B2, and B3). That way over a two week discussion period each half of the group has submitted about 80-120 contributions on one or two themes (there have been separate conferences for each half of the group). And the three groups within each half have taken turns over three two-week periods in moderating the conference (made initiating comments and summarized main points).

This communication model appears to facilitate deeper thinking and opportunity to relate what students read to their experiences that they have an opportunity to share. Comments often had references to thinking (translated from Icelandic):

- "It was enlightening to read your article and how you presented it. X's comments really made me think and I want to follow more how they do with Future Kids because that appears to be some kind of solution for everyone's problems today."
- "I think this article was very remarkable and in it they talk about something I have always wondered about, which is how deeply rooted it appears to be what controls how we teachers are."
- "Is it possible to link Taylor's opinion to the Icelandic reality – that development of information technology in the school system stands or falls with financial matters? Yes, I think that is how it is also here."

The first year I taught the ITESCC course I felt very guilty because I was unable to participate much in these discussion due to the high amount of contributions. When I submitted reactions, my contribution as a teacher was too invisible and came too late to be of much value because students had moved on to the next online session/activities. I felt I needed to be able to react in a more audible/visible way. A nice solution to that problem has been to use phone meetings. Service provided by a local phone company at a low cost allows us to call in to a specific number from Iceland or abroad and talk as a group. Small groups of students have also used phone meetings for group work and decision making where I have sometimes been invited for a part of the meeting. I have also started to use phone meetings in the beginning or during a course for personal communication with small groups, mapping their experiences and concerns and giving them a chance to ask questions and clarify the course organization. I have also used telephone meetings at the end of online discussion where I as the teacher have been able to react more strongly to students' ideas (such as in the reading circle class, see Appendix A).

We have also experimented with a program called Netmeeting that allows file sharing, which is very convenient when two people need to work together on a paper or project and/or one person needs to help another. Netmeeting also has a white board and chat as well as audio and video capabilities if microphones and Web cams are attached. Audio is important when collaborating with the program, but without a microphone a regular phone or GSM can be employed. We also have experienced some technical problems. It appears that some servers will not allow video and audio to come through when Netmeeting is used. Another limitation of Netmeeting is that currently it has only been available for PC computers. However, most Icelandic schools have PCs and last year all of our students had PCs or PC access.

Finally, chat was probably used a little by some students (the chat built into Web board), but for social occasions only. Anecdotal evidence indicates that the pager was more popular for informal communication. However, that may change when we start getting younger age groups into the program more familiar with that type of communication than has been the case with our current students.

Use Authentic Materials and Tools

The emphasis in the program is on project-based learning. Projects that students create usually relate to their own interests (see interest areas in Table 1), teaching, or other kind of work (such as technology planning for their schools). Students are encouraged to apply for funding for their projects or publish their writing in the course. Several students have had success in getting funding for their projects: to create web-based learning materials in life sciences for young children, to do a comparative study on distance education in different countries, to develop and carry out a project in an elementary or middle school involving use of technology, and to place teachers in cooperation with organizations and companies. Students are also learning methods and to use software and tools in the program that they can later use with their own students. Finally, students have been required to have field experiences where they have been able to relate what they have learned in the program to practice. Examples include working on policy for the Ministry of Education; developing digital materials at the National Centre for Learning Materials or for various software companies; or assisting KHÍ faculty in research and/or development projects.

Students are Active: Creating, Developing, Presenting, and Publishing

One of the most difficult task for me as a teacher at KHÍ has been to decide which resources and reading materials should be included in the courses I teach. It is very easy to "drown" in information. In the field of educational technology and distance education, there appear to be endless supplies of materials and it is only getting worse! I started thinking about all the time involved in information searching and "digestion" when I calculated that a group of 15 graduate students in the ITESCC course spent about 40-50 hours each on a project that required them to search for information on different topics related to computer use in education and present main ideas and findings. The total time involved was equivalent to about four whole months and still the students came up with material that was only the smallest tip of the iceberg! No one by himself, least of all a university professor, would have such time to spend if he/she wanted to make presentations on especially relevant topics for students. It should be obvious that groups can benefit enormously from cooperating in the finding and sharing of information.

Students in the first course in the ICT program get a workshop on strategies to search for information and they do projects that require them to choose topics of interest for them, search for relevant readings and submit references with annotated bibliographies into a "bank" (Frontpage web with Access database connection). They later present ideas for projects, often on PowerPoint presentations saved on the Web, read over each other's ideas and react to them both online and in a face-to-face session. A recent requirement in the program is that students create portfolios on the Web and there they are expected to publish their writing or other types of work. Some students have published writings in Icelandic journals and several have presented their work at an annual national conference on ICT use in education.

The Frontpage access "banks" (on http://soljak.khi.is/tolvuppbankar, in Icelandic) have worked very well for discussion of relevant concepts, evaluation of software, and even research (qualitative descriptions on children's Internet use). The main idea is that together we can accomplish a lot and hopefully experience feelings of empowerment instead of being overwhelmed. In the future, we also need to focus on uses of the materials collected in such banks. Students in later cohorts might be asked to evaluate or rate materials submitted into the banks to become more familiar with what was there and how it could be useful for them.

STUDENTS' REACTIONS—EVALUATION

Last Spring semester (2001) during discussion on Internet use in education, a couple of students found an interesting article by Levin, Levin, and Chandler (2001) for online discussion. (This actually illustrates very well the pluses of a learning community–the article had hardly been available for more than a couple of weeks.) The authors described an online Master's program on curriculum, technology and education reform (CTER) at the University of Illinois that appeared to be organized in a very similar fashion and based on similar pedagogy that we use in the Icelandic ICT program. The students in the Icelandic program were amazed by the similarities of the programs. In their paper, Levin, Levin, and Chandler described the great success of their program according to the following factors: dropout rate, student satisfaction, and student learning transferred into practice (the authors believed the last one was probably the most important).

Based on these useful and relevant measures, the Illinois program appears to be very good. Amazingly, the dropout rate in the CTER program is reported to be zero. As can be seen in Table 1, we have had considerably higher dropout in the Icelandic program, or 18% for the 1998 cohort and 33% for the 1999 cohort. However, those rates are still considerably lower than the rate of 40%, which according to Potashnik & Capper (1998) is the overall rate for distance education courses (range reported 19-90%). The rather high dropout rate for our 1999 cohort appears to be due to two main reasons: work-related (more prevalent for the males so far) and health or family-related (more prevalent for the females). It should be kept in mind that almost all students in the Icelandic program work full time or more with the program, and some people (not the least the men) work overtime or are even juggling more than one job.

According to our experience, it is also especially difficult for students to stay in the program when they are changing jobs. Many of the students dropping out express an apparently sincere wish to complete the program later, registering for the following year(s) and trying to take more courses. I therefore do not think that the dropout rate may be a very good measure of the quality of the Icelandic ICT program. In addition, tuition rates have been very low at KHÍ, which may make it easier for students to register later at a more convenient time. However, to avoid losing too many students we have worked on increasing student support in the area of technical assistance and to provide good instructions in the beginning of the program in face-to-face sessions and on the Web to make online work and life easier.

Another measure of our course and program quality is students' satisfaction. Based on results from our 1999 cohort, students displayed very positive attitudes during an evaluation meeting late in the Spring semester. Many students reported that they appreciated how ideas had been translated into projects and that they believed their thinking about relevant issues had become clearer, understanding increased, and ideas strengthened. They reported enjoying the readings and the online discussions. Several students said they had learned a lot, others that they had discovered how little they really knew. Several mentioned that in retrospect they had become pleasantly surprised how they had learned to become more searching and be more independent and free rather than to be fed all the time. Many students described very positive feelings towards the program: they said that it had been a very fun, enjoyable and/or exciting experience; they had great interest in the program; were happy with it; and some even described it as "an adventure." Many said that the learning had opened new doors for them or given them a new vision or changed their life. One student said she deeply regretted not having registered for the next year as well. Another student mentioned an increased feeling of security and confidence in using ICT in education.

About one third of the students talked about the learning materials and thought that the program linked well with other kinds of programs (e.g. educational administration) or their work. They thought students were exposed to interesting and useful materials and that the program pushed people to put ideas into action. Some mentioned that they had learned how to organize distance learning and that there was obviously a great need for a program of this sort.

About a quarter of the students specifically mentioned the value of the educational community and thought it was wonderful to get to know others; they reported they did not feel as isolated in their own schools and that it was really good to get advice from others. They were looking forward to be able to ask others in the group for help the following year.

On the other hand, students offered many useful suggestions for improving the program, including more emphasis in the beginning to introduce the work process and organization. The students suggested that we use more live interaction to decrease danger of isolation. Also, some students wanted the program to be stronger technologically (it should be noted, however, that the above comments came before the end of the program—students had not started a course on multimedia design and not completed the other course on Web-based design). Some students wanted more lectures, less openness and increased feedback.

Several changes have been made on the program based on students' reactions and access to new tools; for example, the addition of phone meetings, better preparation in the first face-to-face session, and collection and publishing of student work on database connected Web. On the whole, we are pleased with how the program has been developing, and we see many cases of students applying what they learn in practice in their field experiences or in their workplaces. One area we will have to work more with in the future is to offer more timely feedback to students and perhaps to include more peer evaluation than has currently been the case.

We seem to have been successful in creating a feeling of learning community, for which the use of the online communication has been vital. As an example, a student group from the 1999 cohort enrolled in a course outside the ICT program the following year, demanded that the teacher set up a discussion web on Web board, and helped her to set up and organize such a web. An interesting feature that students have found important in addition to the conferences is Web board's pager option, which prevented students from feeling lonely: they could see someone else logged on and page that person to say hello.

Another effect that the DE experience appears to have had on the participating students is that they may be less interested in "live" or campus-based programs. As an example, last spring two students who had been in the ITESCC course and a coworker of one of them accidentally signed up for a campus-based course that they thought was a DE course. When they found out it was campus-based they all dropped out immediately, even those living in Reykjavík where the campus is located. Since they wanted the flexibility of the online course, they felt the time schedule for the lectures was not convenient. When the third student from a school in a rural area was offered to attend the lectures via the university's new video conferencing facilities, she was flabbergasted and reacted by exclaiming: "Do you know I would have to drive for almost half an hour to get to the next village with video conferencing facilities? There is no way I will do that–besides, the time is not very convenient!"

CONCLUSION

Based on recent studies (Jakobsdóttir, 1999; Jakobsdóttir, Gudmundsdóttir, & Eyfjörd, 1998), and more recent but informal reports from teachers in the ICT program, so far there has been limited use of computers and the Internet in Icelandic schools. However, new national curriculum (Ministry of Education Science and Culture, 1999) aims at building students' skills of communicating and working with information with the aid of new technologies. These skills are clearly needed in today's society. With our developing ICT program at KHÍ, we are creating learning communities of teachers across the country that can share what they are doing within the group and with others to strengthen each other's practices. They are also developing leadership skills and many of them have been and will be active in the areas of research and design in the future.

However, at KHÍ, we want to avoid "inbreeding." Most of our current faculty have their graduate degrees from other countries, and we consider such diversity as strengthening our educational system. However, we have now started to graduate our own Master's students. But to help widen our students' horizons we are now exploring international collaboration with American and European teacher education programs in the area of ICT. With new technologies, collaborating partners, and new student cohorts, our program will hopefully continue to develop to meet the needs of individuals, schools, and the society.

FINAL THOUGHTS FOR FURTHER CONSIDERATION

Universities can build on their old values and practices by introducing new technologies to enhance students' learning experiences and provide quality education. Authors have used phrases like "new wine in old bottles" (Collis, 1998) or a "brick and click" model (Rogers, 2001) to provide online learning opportunities. Rogers has also described current educational trends as very market driven where students who want certain competencies and skills shop for courses they think will help them develop those skills. One negative aspect of that trend may be that students may not realize the importance of connectedness and how they can benefit by becoming a part of a group that works together towards common goals. As educators, we need to be aware of how we can use old and new technologies and methods to create strong learning communities. Our evolving model in the ICT program at KHÍ and in other places appears to be a good one to create such communities. But more evaluation and research is needed to examine the effects of such a program on individuals and how our practices can be further improved.

REFERENCES

Collis, B. (1998). New wine and old bottles? Tele-learning, telematics and the University of Twente. In Verdejo, F. and Davies, G. (Eds.), *The Virtual Campus: Trends For Higher Education and Training*, 3-17. London: Chapman & Hall.

Creed, T. (1996). *Extending the classroom walls electronically*. Available on the World Wide Web at: http://www.users.csbsju.edu/~tcreed/techno3.html. Accessed July 31, 2001.

Hooper, S. and Rieber, L. P. (1995). Teaching with technology. In Ornstein, A. C. (Ed.), *Teaching: Theory into Practice*, 154-170. Boston, MA: Allyn and Bacon.

Jakobsdóttir, S. (1999). Tölvumenning íslenskra skóla: kynja- og aldursmunur nemenda í tölvutengdri færni, vidhorfum og notkun. *Uppeldi og Menntun*, 8, 119-140.

Jakobsdóttir, S., Gudmundsdóttir, G. and Eyfjörd, J. (1998). *Símakönnun Ísmennt, Summer 1997*. Conference Poster at the KHÍ Research Centre Conference. Available on the World Wide Web at: http://www.khi.is/~soljak/matsumar97/.

Johnson, D. W., Johnson, R. and Holubec, E. (1993). *Circles of Learning* (4th ed.). Edina, MN: Interaction Book Company.

Jónasson, J. (2000). *Evaluation of the distance education (Ed.) program at The Icelandic University College of Education*. Unpublished Draft of M.Ed. thesis. University of Strathclyde, Glasgow.

Levin, S. R., Levin, J. L. and Chandler, M. (2001). *Social and organizational factors in creating and maintaining effective online learning environments*. Available on the World Wide Web at: http://lrs.ed.uiuc.edu/jim-levin/LevinAERA.htm 14.7.2001.

Ministry of Education Science and Culture. (1996). *Education and the Making of New Society*. Available on the World Wide Web at: http://brunnur.stjr.is/interpro/mrn/mrneng.nsf/pages/information. Accessed June 15, 2001.

Ministry of Education Science and Culture. (1999). *Aðalnámskrár*. Available on the World Wide Web at: http://brunnur.stjr.is/mrn/mrn.nsf/pages/upplysingar-utgefid-Adalnamskra-forsida. Accessed June 15, 2001.

Potashnik, M. and Capper, J. (1998). Distance education: Growth and diversity. *Finance & Development*, March. Available on the World Wide Web at: http://www.worldbank.org/fandd/english/0398/articles/0110398.htm. Accessed July 31, 2001.

Rogers, P. L. (2001). *e-Learning: The forced evolution of higher education*. Keynote presentation at the conference UT2001, March 9. Available on the World Wide Web at: http://mennt.is/ut2001/fyrirlestrar/patricia_rogers.pdf. Accessed July 31, 2001.

Russell, A. L. (1995). Stages in learning new technology: Naive adult email users. *Computers & Education*, 25, 173-178.

Salomon, G. and Perkins, D. N. (1997). *Individual and Social Aspects of Learning*. Available on the World Wide Web at: http://construct.haifa.ac.il/~gsalomon/indsoc.html. Accessed July 31, 2001.

Zhu, E. (1998). Learning and mentoring: Electronic discussion in a distance learning course. In Bonk, C. J. and King, K. S. (Eds.), *Electronic Collaborators: Learner-Centered Technologies For Literacy, Apprenticeship and Discourse*, 233-259. Mahwah, NJ: Lawrence Erlbaum Associates.

APPENDIX A

Appendix A: ICT in Education: An overview of courses in a 15 to 30-credit diploma program at Iceland University of Education.

Courses	Goals/Iformation
IT in Education and School Computer Culture	Participants will acquire holistic view of the use of computers and information technologies in education. They will get an overview of development of school computer culture and understand effects of computer use on learning and teaching. *Fall semester, 5 credits*
Innovation Planning for Development and Research	Participants will learn how to plan for ICT related development and/or research projects and get an overview of possibilities of funding for such projects. Students can plan their diploma project and apply for funding for the project. *Fall semester, 2.5 credits*
Reading Circle	Participants critically select, read and discuss materials related to ICT and computers in education and current topics in professional journals and in the media with the aim to become more active participants in the democratic information society. Participation in the course can help students to prepare for the final project. *Fall-spring semester, 2.5 credits*
Net-Based Teaching and Learning	Students will (be able to): Design, develop, and set up educational webs; Design and develop educational Web-based materials in various formats; Design educational Web-based environments and educational processes where materials, work space, evaluation, communications, and group work is all in one package; Know research and projects about the Internet in education and can link new technology with theories about teaching and learning; Organize various kinds of uses of the Internet in education; Advise administrators and teachers about uses of the Internet in education. *Spring semester, 5 credits*
Multimedia Design-- 5 credits	Students get an overview of the advantages of interactive multimedia for learning and teaching and educational application of such media, understand multimedia design processes, learn how to apply various authoring tools and get experience in creating educational multimedia materials. *Spring semester, 5 credits*
Software and multimedia: Theory, Analysis, Design	Students will know various types of educational software and be able to analyze and evaluate such materials and potential uses in home and school in the context of media development, culture and society. *Summer session, 2.5 credits*
Distance Education	Students will know the history and development of distance teaching and learning and will acquire experience in organizing distance learning. *Summer session, 2.5 credits*
Field studies	Practicum at an institute/organization of choice in ICT and education-related materials design & development, policy & planning, or research. *Any semester/session, 2.5 credits*
Final Project/Diploma Project	Research and/or development. *Spring semester to summer session. 2.5-5 credits*

Chapter XIII

What To Do With a C.O.W. in the Classroom

Cynthia L. Krey, Christopher Stormer and Janet Winsand
The College of St. Catherine, USA

The Computers on Wheels project began at the College of St. Catherine as a collaborative venture between the Dean of Education and the McGlynn Computer and Technology Center. We in Computing Services were interested in finding out how a wireless network (LAN) could function in a classroom building. Faculty members in the Education Department were interested in experimenting with the use of laptop computers in teaching and learning. At the same time, we made the decision to set up similar equipment in the library for checkout from the Circulation Desk to use within the building to do a variety of research related tasks such as word processing, printing, and Internet access.

OBJECTIVES FOR THIS CHAPTER OF THE SECTION

The purpose of this chapter of the section is to: (1) describe the preparation involved in setting up the Computer On Wheels project; (2) outline the initial uses of the technology at the College of St. Catherine; and (3) suggest possible instructional strategies for using wireless LANs in the classroom.

PREPARATION

Faculty Study Group

The Dean of Education and the Assistant Director of Instructional Technology created a faculty study group (FSG) with funds from Computing Services. The Director of the McGlynn Computer and Technology Center provided 24 laptops and a locked cart to house the computers and the network as well as provided a monthly lunch for a group of 15 faculty members in Mendel Hall. This building is home to the Education Department as well as the departments of Math and Sciences, Occupational Therapy, and Psychology. The FSG was made up primarily of Education faculty members with representatives from Math and Psychology. The group began meeting in September 2000. Our goal, as a group, was to explore how the laptops and the wireless network could be used in the classroom. Additionally, we were interested in integrating the electronic whiteboard, video data projector, digital camera, and other devices into our instruction.

Classroom Renovation

At the same time our FSG was getting started, the Vice President and Academic Dean provided funding to be used for classroom renovation and technology. We were able to upgrade three classrooms in Mendel Hall and three rooms in another classroom building. The Education Department also received a grant for technology in teacher training. These funds were used to purchase flexible furniture, electrical wiring, wireless LAN components, electronic whiteboards, and video data projectors. We also purchased a printer, a digital camera, two document cameras, and a flatbed scanner for use in the classroom.

Faculty Mentor Program

To help support classroom technology usage, we began a faculty mentor program in February 2001. We hired a faculty member in each classroom building to consult with and assist other faculty members using technology in their classes. With funding from the Director of the McGlynn Computer and Technology Center, we were able to fund one course release for each faculty mentor. We paired each mentor with a staff member in Computing Services. We asked the mentors to work ten hours a week on the project, keep a log of their activities, attend special faculty mentor training sessions organized by the Computing Services staff, and offer a weekly brown bag lunch for faculty in their buildings.

Background. We had considered wireless networking in 1997 when we were planning a computer lab in the art building. Because that building is made of poured concrete and difficult to wire, we hoped to save time and expense by going wireless; however, at that time, we did not feel the technology was sufficiently stable to use. When we began the C.O.W. project, we had no internal expertise with wireless networking and only two years of experience with laptop computing.

We had conducted several pilot programs with individual departments requiring leased laptops by student majors. Although the student and faculty response to leased laptops was very favorable, the college made the decision not to require all students to lease laptops or to charge a technology fee and provide students with laptops. However, all full time, ranked faculty members are currently provided with laptops, and some 400 students do lease laptops voluntarily. The Education Department decided to require leased laptops of their major beginning Fall 2001.

The cart (informally dubbed the C.O.W.). We purchased Datavision/ Prologix's MobileSchool wireless network cart, which features:

- Storage space for up to 32 laptops
- Lucent Technologies WaveLAN Wireless networking components (including two WavePOINT Access Points and PCMCIA cards for the laptops providing 11 Mbps with ranges up to 1500 feet)
- Plug and play solution. Simply plug in to power the cart and connect to the wired campus Ethernet
- Laptops recharge in the cart when not in use
- Locks securely

Figure 1: Laptop leasing offices with students

Originally, we imagined moving the cart from room to room in the building. We discovered, however, that the cart itself was far too heavy to move easily, and happily it wasn't necessary because the range from the cart was much further than we thought it would be.

We decided to purchase one additional WavePOINT Access Point and remove the two Access Points from the cart. By installing them in the ceiling on the second floor of the building, we were able to provide network access to the basement and all four floors of classrooms.

Hardware. Laptops. Twenty-four IBM 380/133mHz laptops with 32Mb RAM.

Software. All laptops were loaded with the standard set of campus software including MS Windows NT, MS Office 97, and Netscape.

PERFORMANCE

We tested the cart and the range of the network in both the library and in Mendel Hall. We discovered that the books in the library soaked up the microwaves extremely quickly. In some cases, the range was reduced to less than 50 feet. At the first meeting of the FSG, we asked faculty members to pair up with each other and take a laptop to test the range in the building. We sent them on a scavenger hunt, which asked them to complete a variety of tasks that would require the network and that they might use in the classroom with their students. Based on the information we gathered from this activity, we made

Figure 2: MobileSchool wireless network cart

Figure 3: Laptops stored in MobileSchool wireless network cart

the decision to add one Access Point in the middle of the building and move the other two Access Points from the cart to each end of the building. We also took one of the Access Points to several other buildings to test the range for future network expansion. We are particularly interested in providing network access to buildings that are difficult to wire. Based on our findings, we will probably purchase several Access Points for other buildings once we complete this initial project.

Speed was somewhat disappointing for users, in that many of them have newer, faster computers on their desk, and we are using older models for this project. Once an application loads, performance is not an issue except with Lotus Notes, which takes up a huge amount of RAM.

Initial Uses

The day after we introduced the laptops and the wireless network, we had Education Department faculty members using a single laptop and a video data projector to present information in their classes. In the library, we found administrators and faculty members wanting to use the laptops (which we intended for student checkout) in meetings and classes. Some students also inquired about purchasing a wireless PCMCIA card to put in their own purchased laptop to connect to our campus Ethernet.

Several weeks after our first FSG meeting, one of the Education faculty members decided to use the C.O.W. to teach an inservice for teachers from a local school. He designed his instruction to take advantage of the network. By placing a file on the network for the participants to access, he did not have to load the file on each machine. He created an interactive presentation that required participants to type in notes and answer questions online. They were able to save the file locally and print a copy to share with colleagues. The faculty member used a separate file that included the answers to teach the workshop. Other than not anticipating the range of abilities of participants to use NT, the inservice went very well. The faculty member offered the inservice to another group a few weeks later and made some refinements to his instructional strategy. He was extremely pleased with the experience. Informal evaluation of the workshop suggests the participants were also satisfied.

IMPLEMENTATION

Project Goals

From the very beginning, we saw this project as a way to experiment with and train staff and faculty to use wireless and other technology in their classes. Other goals for the project were to:

- Expose preservice teachers and local elementary and secondary school teachers to a variety of instructional technologies, including wireless LANs
- Research ways in which we can use technology to enhance teaching and learning in our classes and in the classes our student teachers teach
- Gather ideas and examples for using this new technology in the classroom and make them available to the campus community on our Web site

We are fortunate that we were able to create a faculty mentor program and renovate several classrooms at the same time we experimented with the wireless network and used laptops in the classroom. As our FSG members expand their use of technology in the classroom, we will be in a better position to meet their needs because we will have already invested in some of the hardware and software required to implement their ideas.

Methodology. The Dean of Education and the Director of the McGlynn Computer and Technology Center met to discuss the possibility of using a wireless network and laptop computers with Education Department faculty. Once it was determined that there was interest and budget money available to support the project, the Assistant Director of Instructional Technology and the Dean of Education met to plan the FSG meetings.

Our Networking Group and the Director of the McGlynn Computer and Technology Center handled the choice and purchase of the wireless network equipment. The Instructional Technology group did the setup and configuration of the network. Our laptop leasing staff and an instructional designer took care of the setup and configuration of the laptops. And our Instructional Technology staff provided consulting and support to the FSG throughout the project.

The cart arrived in early September. The network was setup and is maintained by the Instructional Technology staff. It took several days to load and test the software. We started with ten laptops in the cart and tested it in the library. Computing Services staff used the PCMCIA cards in their laptops for several days to test multiple users and applications. The Assistant Director used the wireless network to make a presentation at a conference on campus, and the Educational Technology Advisory Committee used the laptops at one of their first meetings in September. There were a few problems that related to the setup of the laptops but not to the network itself. We refined the "image" used to ghost the laptops and have not experienced any problems since then.

The carts were moved to their planned locations in mid-September. At our first FSG meeting, we focused on using the laptops connected to a video data projector, an electronic whiteboard, and a slave printer. An art education faculty member showed a presentation she developed for one of her methods courses. In October, we asked faculty members to tell us how they used technology in their classes since our last meeting. In November, a faculty member walked us through how he used this new technology in a teacher in-service. We also reviewed the directory structure of Windows NT since many Education Department faculty members were more familiar with Macintosh computers. In December, we reviewed connecting the instructor's laptop to a video data projector, to an electronic whiteboard, and using the network. The FSG did not meet during January term. In the spring, we will continue to explore uses for laptops in our two newly renovated classrooms.

SUMMARY OF INITIAL FINDINGS

Baseline Data

Given our initial experiences, we found the wireless network and laptops were reliable and performed sufficiently well in the classroom setting to recommend their use in other buildings and disciplines. The FSG was essential in supporting faculty use of new technology in the classroom. It gave faculty members a chance to ask questions and experiment with colleagues before going "live" with their ideas.

Project expansion. Based on our experiences so far, we plan to use wireless networks and laptop computers in Whitby Hall and the Music building. Whitby Hall is similar to Mendel Hall as a classroom building but the construction is early 1900s wood flooring covered by carpet with lathe and plaster walls. It will be interesting to test the range of the network and compare it to Mendel Hall. The Music building is difficult to wire. We have already tested the range of the network and are excited to consider wireless networking here. We will combine what we have learned in the Library about checking out computers to students for use in the building with what we have learned in Mendel Hall about using laptops in the classroom for instruction. We hope to complete these two buildings over the summer of 2001.

Technology issues. We are looking for ways to add to the bandwidth of the wireless network. Speed is so far the only complaint we have had from faculty and students using the technology. Software licensing became an issue when faculty and students requested discipline-specific software be installed on the laptops for in-class use. This required us to purchase additional licenses for programs we typically have installed only in our public labs.

Operational issues. The carts provide an easy method for charging laptop batteries. However, we felt the need to wire our classrooms with electricity so students and faculty would not be dependent on batteries, particularly when laptops are used in back-to-back classes for more than a few hours at a time. Keeping track of the laptops in the library was not an issue because they and the network cards were barcoded and would set off the alarms if someone attempted to leave the building with them. Having the laptops locked in the cart provided one measure of security. However, in the classroom buildings, faculty were responsible for handing out the laptops and making sure they got them back at the end of the class, including the cards and power cords. As more faculty choose this option, we will need to find ways to make the process as simple and secure as possible.

Support issues. We have already discovered that assistance using this new technology in the classroom is crucial. Currently, we provide:

- Documentation and training for faculty and departments interested in using new classroom technologies
- Advertising and application ideas
- Installation of software and setup of laptops and network components
- Repair of hardware and software
- In-class support, hands-on help (Instructional Technology staff, faculty mentor, or departmental colleagues)

INSTRUCTIONAL STRATEGIES

We spent some time recently brainstorming and researching how classroom technology can facilitate student learning. We have not had a chance yet to implement them all, but we will continue to revisit this list over time. Some of our ideas for using wireless networking and laptops in the classroom include the following activities:

- Students research a topic, develop a presentation, add multimedia, and practice their presentation before giving it to the class. They also post their findings as a new topic for a class discussion online. An incidental effect of this type of exercise could be that students choose topics that are more easily pursued electronically than in print. Collaborative learning is often stimulating and results in more complex projects than possible by single individuals. Multimedia offers a variety of presentation modes that engage us with information in unique ways.
- In an English class, for example, students regularly contribute video and audio recordings of their own poetry as well as others. A small group works on a project studying major productions in popular culture to test a hypothesis about the poetry, film and music of the times. Students used a specialized graphics package to create concept maps and flow diagrams and create Web pages. The class then builds a mini Web site around course content.
- Students also research cultures using the Internet (e.g., French, Spanish, Hebrew) and create multimedia guides based on their research and post them to the Web or press them to a CD-ROM. Students and faculty note that access to huge amounts of historical data has altered who and what the subjects of study are in Humanities Research. To track learning gains, instructors create online forms (e.g., questionnaires, surveys, etc.) for students to complete and submit via the Web. Faculty use Web images, sound, movie clips, data and simulations to enrich their courses and create "situated learning" experiences for students.

- Students already use asynchronous technologies (e.g., email, conferencing, news groups) for general communication and real time, synchronous technology (e.g., chat rooms, NetMeeting, TalkNation). A portion of the student's class participation can be tied to use of these technologies if each student has access to the necessary technology. These conversations, which often take place outside class, offer an opportunity for peer-to-peer learning that is difficult to replicate in the classroom.

- Students, working in small groups, decide on critical issues around a topic and post the issues in the form of questions for online discussion. Students are asked to reflect on how their own writing, thinking, and collaborating are interrelated. Students and faculty cultivate richer, more inclusive classroom discussions when they consider opportunities for cross-cultural and international collaborations.

- Students in Accounting and Finance classes visit Web pages of companies in the news in preparation for in-class discussion activities. The instructor draws attention to key passages of the materials under discussion from a variety of sources (e.g., CD, online postings, email, Web sites, etc.). In this way, materials from outside of class may be brought into the classroom and made relevant. This technique also gives credit to students as contributors of content and offers an opportunity to clarify difficult concepts.

- Instructors invite guest experts to join their class and look for ways to create local as well as worldwide teams.

- Students revise and write papers in many disciplines. The use of specialized software and shared files via email or a shared space on the LAN can model the revision process in writing and research. Students have the opportunity to participate in peer editing activities. They are also able to take their laptops to a variety of settings to conduct research and work on assignments (e.g., the library, the parking lot to collect data on rocket launches, a neighbor's room, etc.). As a result, the process of revising and writing changes with the use of laptops and wireless network connections.

- Students use email for prewriting exercises, brainstorming with one another and with faculty as they develop their topics. They exchange drafts via email, annotating and commenting on the work as it develops.

- In an Economics class, the instructor assigns topics; students look for relevant articles (Dow Jones News Index, etc.), draft essays and submit via email. Instructor, TA, and classmates post questions and comments. Students revise and turn in final essays. Students learn Boolean logic and apply it to Internet search engines.

- Course textbooks are often provided on a CD. The content is fully searchable and can be copied and pasted into other applications. This presents opportunities to discuss issues of copyright and plagiarism. Students can be assigned topics or chapters to study individually or in small groups. Tutorials and 3D models can also be studied without having to take the class to a computer lab.
- Students and instructors use links to existing resources on the Internet. Instructors and students assess the validity and credibility of sites and sources. Instructor and students use a laptop and/or an electronic whiteboard to capture possible solutions to problems in the brainstorming session. The file is saved and shared via the wireless network during the class for review outside of class. Students download assignment sheets; homework submitted electronically.
- Faculty use PowerPoint for drill-and-practice exercises in a language class. They add audio and use the Real Player Plug-in for PowerPoint so students can access the materials via the Web.
- Student teachers develop portfolios of their work as tools for reflection and to evaluate the skills and knowledge they acquired while student teaching.
- In Music, students use MIDI software to play and create active musical staves.
- Students participate in a hypothetical archaeology dig via software simulation and the Internet. A team of three works in each sector. One student focuses on dating and chronology, another on cultural influences and patterns, and a third on reconstructing the human ecology and economy. Periodically, all seven teams meet to discuss the overall picture of the site. The students use specialized software to excavate, describe, record and interpret hundreds of artifacts.
- Students conduct experiments using simulated instruments connected to laptops.
- Students conduct hands-on lab experiments using special software and peripheral sensors and probes.
- Students use models to predict climate change and to track bond and home mortgage lending rates.
- In Biology and Sociology, students use demographic software to explore the interaction of population variables.
- Students use special document cameras connected to their laptops that enhance and project images from microscopes to study the processes of mitosis, meiosis, and genetic recombination (see also San Diego State's Electron Microscope Facility: http://glef.org).

- Students contribute important information to their communities by participating in global research projects such as wildlife migration and water quality of rivers (see also http://www.learner.org/jnorth and http://www.igc.apc.org/green).
- Students participate in faculty research expeditions, exchanging Q and A's, digital images, and real time chat (CUSeeMe technology) (see also, Dr. Robert Ballard's JASON Project at http://www.jasonproject.org).
- Students studying plant biology prepare slides and digitized images at key development stages to include in their final reports/presentations.
- Faculty videotape subjects with language disorders to create case studies on CD-ROM to distribute to students to use in small group in-class activities.
- Electronic "case books" are used in Business Administration courses. Students read the cases, work in groups, and solve real world business problems. Instructors restructure the class period to include 20 minutes of lecture with PowerPoint slides (used to increase student eye contact), students write a one minute essay giving feedback about what they learned, the class discusses the one minute essays, and students describe a useful computer tip they found that week.

CONCLUSIONS

There are many opportunities for us to use classroom technology to enhance teaching and learning. Our experiences so far have been very positive. We will undoubtedly consider using wireless networking and laptops in other classroom buildings. In addition, we have used this technology for open registration days where faculty advisors must connect to the network to assist new students registering for classes.

Our institution places an emphasis on interactive, collaborative education. We believe wireless networks and laptop computers are well suited for small group and peer-to-peer learning. They provide a tremendous amount of flexibility. Faculty members who are trained and ready to use this technology in their classes will generate opportunities for teaching and learning that we expect will be cross-disciplinary. Students may brainstorm a biology project, create a spreadsheet to gather data, refine their calculations in math, document the project with a digital camera in art, and write about their experiences in English. Another group may study how the Internet changes scholarship in theater: a team of journalists cover the event, a team of educators create lesson plans and instructional resources for the event, while the team from the theater department focuses on the production itself.

There is a shift in the teaching/learning paradigm from instructor-led "information transfer" to a noisier, more informal experience with students working in groups around a single laptop. Issues such as copyright, bandwidth, and when to use what technology become questions not just for faculty members but also for students.

It has been said, "Teaching isn't interesting unless it results in learning." Neither is classroom technology. The question for us shouldn't be "how are we going to use all of this stuff?" but rather "can we use technology in ways that make sense?" Contrary to popular option, students do not expect to use technology 100% of the time. However, they do expect technology to be readily available and teachers to be comfortable using it when appropriate. We hope this project gets us closer to that end.

QUESTIONS FOR FURTHER CONSIDERATION

Now that we have tested the technology and are satisfied that it works, some questions that still need to be addressed include:

1. Are there discipline-specific issues that need to be considered when using a wireless network, laptops, and other classroom technology?
2. Are there health or occupational hazards associated with long-term use of this technology that should be addressed?
3. Given the ideas presented here, do I personally want to use this technology in my teaching? If so, in what ways?
4. How can we assess the impact of this technology on actual student learning?

REFERENCES

Brown, J. (2001). Where have all the computers gone? *Technology Review*, 104(1), 86-87.

Bork, A. (2000). Learning technology. *EDUCAUSE Review*, 35(1), 74-81.

Burderi, R. (2001). Computing goes everywhere. *Technology Review*, 104(1), 53-59.

Edmonds, G. S., Branch, R. C. and Mukherjee, P. (1994). A conceptual framework for comparing instructional design models. *Educational Research and Technology*, 42(2), 55-72.

Fuchs, I. H. (2000). Multimedia is coming…Get ready! *EDUCAUSE Review*, 35(3), 58-59.

Hawley, M. (2001). Khmer kids link to the future. *Technology Review*, 104(1), 28-29.

Levine, L. E., Mazmanian, V., Miller, P. and Pinkhan, R. (2000). Calculus, technology and coordination. *T.H.E. Journal*, 28(5), 19-23.

McCannon, M. and Morse, G. E. (1999). Using multimedia visual aids in presentations. *TechTrends*, 43(6), 29-31.

Paterson, W. A. (1999). Distance learning: Up close and personal. *TechTrends*, *43*(6), 20-25.

Quick, R. and Lieb, T. (2000). The Heartfield project. *T.H.E. Journal*, 28(5), 41-45.

Rickman, J. and Grudzinski, M. (2000). Student expectations of information technology use in the classroom. *Educause Quarterly*, 23(1), 24-30.

Sanford, S. (2000). Round rock partners up to go wireless. *CONVERGE*, 12(3), 28-30.

Sanford, S. (2000). The e-Volution of ThinkPad U education at UMC. *CONVERGE*, 12(3), 67-70.

Wilson, B. G., Jonassen, D. H. and Cole, P. (1993). Cognitive approaches to instructional design. In Piskurich, G. M. (Ed.), *The ASTD Handbook of Instructional Technology*, 21(1-22). New York: McGraw-Hill.

Afterword

The interesting thing about publishing most books that deal with teaching and technology is the problem of the short shelf life. Teachers need the information *right now*, but it takes some time to get that information out to the audience (though I must say here that Idea Group Publishing is committed to rapid turnaround and timely production, which is why you have this book in your hands today). Our *right now* information becomes very quickly *left behind* old practices as technologies change. However, because this book is not tied to any particular technology, we know it will be useful to teachers well into the next decade: Sound instructional design based on research, experience, and best practices do not go out of fashion or change versions every year. No crashes, no temporary patches, and no viruses. I think you will find yourself referring to many of these articles for some time to come.

I write this afterword from the comfort of a hotel room, late at night. I have been attending distance learning conferences for the last ten days and am now in Madison, Wisconsin at a major conference on distance learning. At our dinner table this evening were people from (in alphabetical order) Barbados, Brazil, Canada, Columbia, Iceland, India, Sweden, and the United States. We shared a meal, laughter, ideas, and music. We shared a love for teaching and learning and our unique perspectives on technology-enhanced learning. (We also shared a long evening of music, dancing, and singing with a talented musician, but that is another story.)

The people at that table, and indeed all of the participants at this and similar conferences around the world, recognize the importance of sound instructional design as being an essential ingredient for successful learning in any technology-enhanced classroom, whether it is online or campus-based. As I write this, conference attendees are at various stages of designing quality online learning materials. We heard from instructional designers, seasoned teacher-designers, and policy-making administrators. Everyone delivered a similar message: It is *NOT* the technology that matters, it is how we use it to effectively enhance and facilitate learning.

Quality e-learning is, as has been discussed in this book, a matter of sound design, which includes careful market analysis (needs assessment), thorough understanding of the goals (task analysis), clear understanding of the audience, client, or learner (learner analysis), the right technologies and teaching methods (media and methods), and so on. No matter how we think about e-learning and designing for these new environments, we must pay careful attention to the design principles necessary to create successful learning environments. My contention is, and will likely always be, that good teaching requires good instructional design, whether that means a formal use of design models or an intuitive practice of the design process. But, as many people found when they began using desktop publishing and graphics software to design and develop their own newsletters or newspapers, there are few natural or intuitive designers. We have the power to create these works, but we might lack the skills to make the products "sing," i.e., to be effective and relevant to the audience. The authors in this book are not only effective songwriters; they represent the maestros who are designing effective instruction for technology-enhanced learning.

I think you will agree that the authors have provided a good set of guidelines and suggestions for your own entry into designing for technology-enhanced learning. If an author in this book has been of particular help to you or if you have questions, please see the About the Authors section for contact information.

About the Authors

Patricia L. Rogers, PhD, is a Professor at Bemidji State University in the department of Professional Education, with doctoral preparation in both Art Education and Instructional Systems and Technology. She is on several state level committees and is a consultant for the Minnesota State Colleges and Universities' Office of Instructional Technology where she recently served as the interim system director. Dr. Rogers is a Getty Fellow (Dissertation Fellowship from the Getty Center for Arts Education) and a Fulbright Scholar (2000-2001) working on designing distance learning programs. She consults internationally on e-learning, is the author of several articles on instructional technology, and regularly presents at technology and art education conferences. She was the keynote speaker at UT 2001, a technology and education conference held in Reykjavik, Iceland. Dr. Rogers is the editor of this book and may be reached at plr@bemidjistate.edu.

***

Anne-Marie Armstrong, PhD, is an Instructional Design Consultant for Lucent Technologies, a global telecommunications corporation. She has extensive experience in designing training in defense industry, military, and manufacturing settings. She not only contributes to the development and evaluation of training but also participates in human-machine interface design and is a Certified Professional Logistician. She can be reached at Room 344, One Main Street, Cambridge, Massachusetts, 617-395-2133, email aa20@lucent.com.

Mary C. Baily is an Assistant Professor for Bemidji State University. Ms. Bailey began her teaching career in 1971 in Bronx, N.Y. Since that time she has managed to teach every grade level from K-12 and also several years at the college level. The educational settings have also given Mary a diversity of experience, ranging from a two room schoolhouse in the mountains of California to the inner city urban classroom. She has seen it all and brings that experience with a strong theory-to-practice connection into the classroom.

She was recently an Assistant Principal in the Redlands District, California, a year round school boasting 1,000 students. Mary holds an M.A., with additional certification for administration and teaching ESL, and is working on her doctorate.

Zane L. Berge is currently Director of Training Systems, Instructional Systems Development Graduate Program at the University of Maryland System, UMBC Campus. His scholarship in the field of computer-mediated communication and distance education includes numerous articles, chapters, workshops, and presentations. Notably are Berge's books, co-edited with Collins. First, in 1995, was a three volume set, *Computer-Mediated Communication and the Online Classroom*, that encompasses higher and distance education. Following that was a four volume set of books, *Wired Together: Computer-Mediated Communication in the K-12 Classroom*. More recently, he and Schreiber edited *Distance Training* (1998). Dr. Berge's newest book is *Sustaining Distance Training* (Jossey-Bass, 2001). He consults nationally in distance education and can be contacted at zberge@eModerators.com.

Barbara Rogers Bridges, PhD, is an Associate Professor and Director of the Bemidji/Metropolitan Urban Teacher Education Collaborative–a teacher licensure partnership program located on four Metropolitan State University campuses: (http://bsued.bemidji.msus.edu/Metro/index.html) for Bemidji State University. Dr. Bridges is currently developing the first blended technologies teacher licensure program in the state. Barbara Rogers Bridges holds a doctorate in Curriculum and Instruction from the University of Minnesota, where she taught and supervised student teachers. Dr. Bridges was named 1998 Minnesota Art Higher Educator of the Year by the Art Educators of Minnesota. She has published articles in a variety of journals and an eight-poster Mexican Arts timeline for Crizmac, Inc. Dr. Bridges also acts as the Coordinator for ArtsNet Minnesota. In this project, Dr. Bridges coordinated and wrote curriculum for this interdisciplinary Web site. ArtsNet Minnesota is a constituency-based curriculum site and virtual community that continues to grow. This site received a First Place Global Award from the Museums and the Web Conference in 1999. She can be contacted at http://www.artsnetmn.org.

Tracy Chao holds a Masters degree in Educational Technology from Concordia University in Montreal, Canada. She works as an instructional designer in the Faculty of Arts' Technologies for Learning Centre at the University of

Alberta. Her main responsibility is to promote the appropriate use of technology in teaching. Through one-on-one consultation Tracy has led many instructors through a pedagogically-driven process of technological integration. She sees herself as a "guide on the side," working closely with instructors to adopt change in a positive and beneficial way. This collaboration has made possible a distributed learning environment where students' learning is better supported both inside and outside the classroom.

Sara Dexter, PhD, is a Research Associate at the Center for Applied Research and Educational Improvement (CAREI) at the University of Minnesota, where she conducts research on the integration and implementation of educational technology in K-12 schools. She has taught preservice and inservice teacher education courses on educational technology in the College of Education and Human Development.

J. Ana Donaldson, EdD, has been providing instruction to inservice teachers and preservice teachers in the area of technology integration for many years. She has worked as an educational consultant providing workshops to instructors on how to integrate technology into an engaged learning environment. Dr. Donaldson received her doctorate in Instructional Technology from Northern Illinois University and is employed as an Assistant Professor at the University of Northern Iowa. Besides her years of classroom experience in creating Web-supported learning environments, she is a published author, international presenter, and award-winning multimedia developer.

Gay Fawcett, PhD, is the Executive Director of the Research Center for Educational Technology at Kent State University in Kent, Ohio. Dr. Fawcett has taught kindergarten through university level and has published over 65 articles and book chapters. You may reach him at hfawcett@kent.edu.

Sally Gibson, MA, is an adjunct professor of Art for Bemidji State University. Ms. Gibson has a Master's degree in Elementary Education and a B.S. in Art Education. Ms. Gibson is a 25-year teaching veteran and has served as a Master Teacher for the University of Minnesota's student teaching program and as a New Teacher Mentor since 1994. Ms. Gibson has illustrated three textbooks for the learning impaired, has served as a reviewer for State Arts Board Grants, was National Coordinator for the Arts-to-Arts Exhibit, served on the Moundsview Technology Committee, taught computer technology, and received the Minnesota's Teacher of Excellence Award and the New Brighton "Best Teacher of the Year" Award. Ms. Gibson brings a unique perspective on art in the elementary school and offers her well-equipped classroom for preservice education students to enjoy a real "field experience."

Michael Hiatt is an adjunct professor in Music at Bemidji State University. Mr. Hiatt serves as the Director of the Professional Development Institute (PDI) and Music Education Coordinator at the Perpich Center for Arts Education located in Golden Valley, Minnesota. Mr. Hiatt served as music educator in Minnesota for 20 years, the last 16 years at Anoka High School where he was the Director of Bands and department chair. Michael Hiatt, a native of Fergus Falls, Minnesota, holds a Bachelor of Music degree from Concordia College in Moorhead, MN and has also received a Masters in Music Education from the University of Minnesota–Minneapolis. As Director of PDI, Mr. Hiatt is responsible for overseeing an educational outreach program committed to strengthening education in the arts through successful statewide initiatives and innovative programs that place learning and teaching in the arts at the heart of education. As Music Education Coordinator at the Center, he is responsible for professional, technical, and research support in music education for teachers, administrators, artists, and school districts throughout the state of Minnesota. Mike is also responsible for administering the pARTner School program, which is a group of eleven schools throughout the state that are working at model arts education and quality professional development. Michael is an active member of MENC, MMEA, MBDA, ASBDA, ACDA, ASCD, and MASCD.

Diane L. Judd, PhD, has 18 years of teaching experience in elementary education. Since 1996, she has taught educational technology to preservice teachers. Dr. Judd designed and developed the educational technology course at Valdosta State University, integrating and applying technology into the Early Childhood and Elementary Curricula, which focus on the integration in technology for early childhood and elementary preservice teachers. During the past four years, Dr. Judd has presented inservice workshops to elementary teachers on ways to integrate technology into their curriculum. Diane Judd is a reviewer for MERLOT, Multimedia Educational Resource for Learning and Online Teaching, a resource designed for faculty and students in higher education (http://www.merlot.org/Home.po). Dr. Judd is an Assistant Professor and teaches Educational Technology in the Department of Early Childhood and Reading Education at Valdosta State University, Valdosta, Georgia 31698; Phone 229-333-5630; Fax 229-333-7176; Email djudd@valdosta.edu.

Margarete Juliana currently coordinates and conducts research in the Ameritech Classroom at Kent State University, Kent, Ohio. Ms. Juliana also participates in other RCET research and evaluation projects. She is a doctoral candidate in Curriculum and Instruction at Kent State University.

Nancy Nelson Knupfer, PhD, earned her doctorate in Educational Technology at the University of Wisconsin–Madison and has enjoyed a full career as an educator, researcher, media producer, and author. She brings a rich background of experience as professor of Educational Technology, classroom teacher at all levels of K-12 education, and instructional designer for military, corporate and government settings. Dr. Knupfer's unique experiences include starting a high school in a remote Alaskan village, founding an interactive children's museum, and extensive travel and international consulting that has cultivated her interest in multicultural groups and quality education. Dr. Knupfer's numerous presentations and publications have led to an international reputation for her work in instructional design of electronic interactive learning materials for local and distance education and socially responsible use of technology for educational change and equity. Dr. Knupfer has served on the Board of Directors of several professional organizations and as President of the International Visual Literacy Association. She currently lives in East Lansing, Michigan where she is an author, Editor of the Journal of Visual Literacy, and President of Digital Horizons, a company that designs Web sites and provides training about responsible use of emerging technologies for quality communication and education.

Cynthia L. Krey, PhD, is the Assistant Director of Instructional Technology at The College of St. Catherine, 2004 Randolph Avenue, St. Paul, MN 55105; Email clkrey@stkate.edu; Phone 651-690-8642. She also serves on the steering committee for the annual Classrooms of the Future Conference held by the Associated Colleges of the Twin Cities. Dr. Krey is studying poetry via distance learning (www.writers.com) and received a Denny Prize Honorable Mention for The Practice of Poetry: A Study of Poetic Form in March 2001.

Lin Y. Muilenburg, an instructional design consultant, has developed and evaluated training programs for various clients including international labor unions, major corporations and universities. She teaches graduate courses in instructional design and adult learning at the University of Maryland–Baltimore County and is a core faculty member of the International Masonry Institute. Ms. Muilenburg is currently pursuing a PhD in Instructional Design and Development at the University of South Alabama.

Som Naidu, PhD, is an Associate Professor and Head of Research and Evaluation Services in the Department of Teaching, Learning and Research Support (Information Division) at The University of Melbourne, VIC, AUSTRALIA, 3010; Phone +61-03-8344-7575; Fax: +61-03-8344-4341; email Som Naidu <s.naidu@unimelb.edu.au>. Dr. Naidu is Executive Editor of Distance Education: An International Journal (http://www.usq.edu.au/dec/decjourn/demain.htm), founding Co-Editor-in-Chief of e-JIST (http://www.usq.edu.au/electpub/e-jist/homepage.htm), and serves on the Editorial Advisory Board of the Indian Journal of Open Learning (IJOL), and The Global E-Journal of Open and Flexible Learning (GEJOFL). He also serves on the editorial review board of Educational Technology & Society.

Christpher Stormer, MA, is an instructional designer at The College of St. Catherine, 2004 Randolph Avenue, St. Paul, MN USA 55105; email cestormer@stkate.edu; Phone 651-690-8788. Mr. Stomer recently co-wrote (with Ms. Janet Winsand) a paper entitled "Making Traditional Classrooms Hot: Adding the Online Element" for a virtual conference sponsored by The Collaboration for the Advancement of College Teaching and Learning (www.collab.org).

Bruce Stovel, PhD, is a faculty member of the Department of English at the University of Alberta. He has a B.A. from Concordia University in Montreal, an M.A. from the University of Cambridge, and a PhD from Harvard University. He has published articles on many British and Canadian novelists, and particularly several on Jane Austen's novels. He also has a keen interest in blues music; he is the host of a weekly blues radio show and has written for several blues magazines. He has now taught two courses at the University of Alberta on blues lyrics as lyric poetry; one of these courses is described in this book and the second is a graduate seminar taught in 2000-2001.

Deborah Timmerman is an adjunct professor of Physical Education/Creative Movement for Bemidji State University. Ms. Timmerman teaches physical education in River Falls, Wisconsin in a public school setting. She has taught at the Junior High level for four years, coached high school varsity, AAU, middle school and community sports for 24 years, and taught at the elementary level for 24 years. Her undergraduate work was done at the University of Wisconsin–River Falls. Her postgraduate work was done at the University of Minnesota, The College of St. Catherine's and the University of Wisconsin–River Falls. Her Master's degree is from Hamline University. The academics and physical education have a strong connection. Ms. Timmerman connects academic concepts to movement to make each discipline a more meaningful learning experience. In addition to this aspect of curriculum, Ms. Timmerman stresses fitness, cooperative activities, sports skills and creative expression. In addition to her work in the public school setting, Ms. Timmerman has worked extensively with the University of Wisconsin–River Falls. She has had student teachers and preservice teachers in her classroom for field service experiences since 1972. She has also taught PE Activities for the Elementary School Teacher, Perceptual Motor Development and Sports Skills and Curriculum. Her work with public school students and the university preservice student has allowed her to develop curriculum that is developmentally appropriate for the child to receive and the adult to deliver.

Lorna Uden, PhD, is a senior lecturer in the School of Computing at Staffordshire University, Stafford, UK. Phone +44-1785 353276; Fax: +44-1785 323497; email L.uden@staffs.ac.uk. Dr. Uden's research interests include Courseware Engineering, Web Engineering, Human-Computer Interaction (HCI), Multimedia, Hypermedia, GroupWare, CSCL, e-learning, Object-Oriented Technology, Problem-Based Learning and Activity Theory. She has designed a courseware engineering methodology for designing technology learning and has published widely both in journals and at conferences.

Janet Winsand is an Academic Computer Consultant on the Minneapolis campus of The College of St. Catherine, 601 25th Ave. South, Minneapolis, MN 55454; email jmwinsand@stkate.edu; Phone 651-690-7710. Ms. Winsand's Master's degree is in Media Technology. She recently co-wrote (with Mr. Christopher Stormer) a paper entitled "Making Traditional Classrooms Hot: Adding the Online Element" for a virtual conference sponsored by The Collaboration for the Advancement of College Teaching and Learning (www.collab.org). She also teaches computer skills in the Sage Scholar program at The College of St. Catherine.

Index